Crisis

Crisis

Sylvia Walby

polity

The right of Sylvia Walby to be identified as Author of this Work has been asserted in accordance with the UK Copyright, Designs and Patents Act 1988.

First published in 2015 by Polity Press

Polity Press
65 Bridge Street
Cambridge CB2 1UR, UK

Polity Press
350 Main Street
Malden, MA 02148, USA

ISBN-13: 978-0-7456-4760-9
ISBN-13: 978-0-7456-4761-6 (pb)

A catalogue record for this book is available from the British Library.

Library of Congress Cataloging-in-Publication Data

Walby, Sylvia.
  Crisis / Sylvia Walby.
      pages cm
  Includes bibliographical references and index.
  ISBN 978-0-7456-4760-9 (hardback : alk. paper) -- ISBN 978-0-7456-4761-6
(pbk. : alk. paper) 1. Financial crises. 2. Financial crises--Political aspects.
I. Title.
  HB3722.W344 2015
  338.5'42--dc23
  2015012753

Typeset in 10.5 on 12 pt Plantin by
Servis Filmsetting Ltd, Stockport, Cheshire
Printed and bound in the UK by CPI Group (UK) Ltd, Croydon, CR0 4YY

For further information on Polity, visit our website:
politybooks.com

Contents

Acknowledgements

I would like to thank the many who have debated these ideas with me in recent years, including colleagues in the Department of Sociology at Lancaster University, the International Sociological Association and its Research Committee 02 on Economy and Society, the European Sociological Association, the Women's Budget Group, Agnes Hubert, Scarlet Harris, Jude Towers, Liz Kelly, and in particular those who made very helpful comments on the manuscript: Jo Armstrong, Sue Durbin, Aaron Pitluck, John Urry and Mieke Verloo.

Abbreviations

CDO	collateralized debt obligation
EDF	Excessive Deficit Procedure
FSA	Financial Services Authority
GDP	gross domestic product
GVA	gross value added
IMF	International Monetary Fund
NGO	non-governmental organization
OECD	Organisation for Economic Co-operation and Development
ONS	Office for National Statistics
SNP	Scottish National Party
TTIP	Transatlantic Trade and Investment Partnership
UKIP	United Kingdom Independence Party
VAT	value-added tax
WTO	World Trade Organization

1
Introduction

What crisis? Is 'austerity' the result of excessive spending on welfare? Or were the financial crisis and the decline in living standards it produced the result of the failure to regulate finance in the interests of the 99 per cent?

These rival interpretations of 'the crisis' drive different intellectual and political agendas. 'Austerity' focuses attention on the reduction in welfare spending and on the structural adjustments to the economy through which it is achieved. 'Financial crisis' focuses attention on the deepening of democracy so that the regulation of finance in the interests of the whole society becomes possible once again. At the heart of the debate is whether 'markets' are the most 'efficient' mechanism to govern the economy and distribute its benefits, or whether regulation by democratic states is necessary to ensure markets are not distorted by powerful interests.

Most people, including economists and other social scientists, did not see the crisis coming. The theoretical tools to foresee the crisis did exist but had been so marginalized that few knew of them. This book excavates those theories and reworks them in the light of evidence and theory generated during the current crisis. It offers a renewal of the theory of society to analyse not only the current crisis but also future ones.

The crisis has cascaded through society: first, a crisis in finance; next, a crisis in the real economy of production and employment; then a fiscal crisis over government budget deficits; and a political crisis, which is on the edge of becoming a democratic crisis. Some small instabilities, such as 'bubbles' and 'business cycles', can be regarded as 'normal', in the sense of being frequently repeated and with few consequences for the wider social system. Other crises are not so contained, and lead to large changes, catastrophe and societal transformation or collapse. The current crisis is not yet over, and continues to cascade through political systems.

The effects of the crisis are borne unevenly, exacerbating class and other inequalities. The crisis is gendered, in both its causes and its consequences. After the first wave of the recession when men lost their jobs, women have borne the brunt of austerity, and are central to alternative visions of the future. These issues concern democracy, not only in the sense of voting occasionally, but also in the depth of application of democratic principles to the governance of the economy. The failure in the governance of finance is gendered: the exclusion of women from economic and financial decision-making is part of the cause of the crisis. The potential routes out of the crisis into economic growth are also gendered strategies.

For some, crises, as when banks crash and the economic order is challenged, are firmly established objects for investigation (Calhoun and Derlugian 2011a, 2011b, 2011c). For others, crises can be socially constructed out of minor events to serve political projects (Hay 1996); or, at least, can be manipulated (Klein 2007) as suggested by the notorious phrase 'never let a crisis go to waste' (Mirowski 2013). How the crisis is 'narrated' (Ricoeur 1984) matters; positioning causation within the temporal sequencing of events that are identified as significant, the emplotment of agents and victims, has implications for the definition of the crisis event itself. However, the way social science 'narrates' the crisis is not merely a 'story'; it depends upon the sifting of evidence and the development and testing of theories.

While the current focus of the crisis is often considered to be 'austerity', the argument here is that the crisis in many countries in Europe and North America had several interlinked phases, which jointly constitute 'the crisis': first, the banking, credit and financial crisis between 2007 and 2009 caused by the deregulation of finance, in which banks went bankrupt and the supply of credit to the economy ceased, and where the financial system and banks were rescued by the government and large bailout funds; second, a deep economic recession and contraction of economic output caused by the financial collapse and ensuing credit crunch, followed by a long period of near-zero growth, then a recovery in output but not in wages or living standards; third, attempts to reduce government budget deficits by cutting public expenditure under pressure from financial markets, international financial institutions and domestic political forces; and fourth, a political crisis that might become a democratic crisis, as governments and traditional political parties fall and the European

Union faces either fragmentation or restructuring. The cascading crisis starting in finance intersects with other crises that follow different trajectories, particularly those concerning the environment and energy, creating a 'perfect storm' (Beck 2009; Urry 2011).

Financial Crisis: Democratic Failure

The financial crisis was a result of a failure in the governance of finance, as many official inquiries have established (G20 2008; de Larosière 2009; Stiglitz 2009). For example, the G20 (2009) declared that 'major failures in the financial sector and in financial regulation and supervision were fundamental causes of the crisis'. There had once been legislation and policies to regulate finance, which had been put in place after the lessons of the Great Crash of 1929 had been learned. These policies, inspired by Keynes and negotiated at Bretton Woods in 1944, were intended to stabilize finance and regulate capital in the wider public interest. But they were removed during the 1980s as part of the deregulatory project to free up markets.

The justification for the deregulation of finance was that this was good for the economy as a whole. The development of finance and financialization had been seen as a route to economic growth. The financial services industry was supposed to deliver capital to those places in the economy where its use would be optimal; instead, it delivered a catastrophic crash. With hindsight, the head of the Financial Services Authority (FSA), which was supposed to regulate finance in the interests of the public, declared that much of this financial activity was 'socially useless' (Turner 2009). Yet financial derivatives have been allowed to grow to many times the size of the real economy: the value of financial derivatives was \$693 trillion in 2013 (Bank of International Settlements 2013), nearly ten times the \$73 trillion value of the world gross domestic product (GDP) (World Bank 2014).

Those who argued that finance was intrinsically destabilizing to an economy and needed careful regulation to minimize these risks had been marginalized in social science and ignored by governmental policy makers. Minsky (2008 [1986]), building on Keynes (1936), had argued that finance was inherently pro-cyclical; exacerbating rather than mitigating booms and slumps in the economy. During the early stages of a cycle he found enthusiasm for investment and the ability to pay returns to such investment from profits. During the middle stages the ability to pay returns becomes dependent on funds from further investment. As prices fall in the latter stages it becomes impossible to pay returns and bankruptcy ensues with spiralling downward effects. Finance is intrinsically destabilizing of the real economy unless it is robustly and effectively regulated by government and central banks.

So why did central bankers and regulatory authorities such as the FSA allow finance to expand in a way that was dangerous to the economy and useless to the public? It has been argued it was due to complacency among the elite (Engelen et al. 2011) or a failure by many central bankers to understand the complexities of financial systems that require a macro-prudential approach (Haldane and May 2011). Alternative views are that this is a more deep-rooted failure of the capitalist system driven by the exhaustion of the regime of capital accumulation (Aglietta 2000a [1976]; Arrighi 2007) or was a result of excessive commercialization undermining the conditions of its own existence until civil society intervenes to restore balance (Polanyi 1957).

Is the failure to regulate finance prudently, gendered? There are few women involved in financial decision-making (van Staveren 2002; Schuberth and Young 2011). Finance is a high-risk masculine monoculture (McDowell 1997). There are few women on the boards running finance companies (Singh and Vinnicombe 2004) or on governmental finance committees. The male monoculture could be reduced by including women through measures such as gender quotas on corporate boards, thereby reducing uncritical high-risk group-think practices (Armstrong and Walby 2012; Terjesen et al. 2009). If the problem is more deeply rooted, involving the separation of finance from the democratic processes where the interests of a wider public are more likely to be represented, more fundamental action is required. According to the Economics Nobel Prize winner and head of a UN Commission investigating the crisis, Stiglitz (2010), all those who were exposed to the risks that finance creates are entitled to a voice in the running of finance.

Economic Crisis: Recession

The Great Crash in finance caused the Great Recession in the economy. Financialization has had devastating effects on the economy and society, creating a deep and widespread recession, with sharp drops in GDP and increases in unemployment and poverty. According to the Bank of England's director of financial stability,

Haldane (2010), the crisis reduced world output in 2009 by approximately 6.5 per cent ($4 trillion) and by around 10 per cent in the UK (£140 billion). If these losses persist, then the loss in output rises to between $60 trillion and $200 trillion for the world economy and between £1.8 trillion and £7.4 trillion for the UK (equivalent to between one and five times annual GDP) (Haldane 2010: 3). A narrower interpretation of the costs includes only the fiscal costs of the wealth transfer from government to the banks during the bailout. This measure results in a lower but nonetheless significant figure of approximately 1 per cent of GDP; which is around $100 billion for the US and £20 billion for the UK. However, as Haldane notes, including only direct fiscal costs underestimates the scale of the damage to the wider economy from the crisis.

More important than the loss of money is the damage caused by the crisis to human well-being through lost jobs, homelessness, food and fuel poverty, and increases in domestic violence.

The economic recession has been uneven among the countries of Europe and North America; with uneven effects on classes, genders and ethnic and national groups.

The route out of recession is contested. The notion that deregulating markets is the most efficient way to run the economy persists despite the role of this approach in causing the financial crash. However, it is possible to increase the democratic depth of governance and to use the state to steer investment into areas of economic growth from which all can benefit, such as low-carbon energy sources, education for a knowledge-based economy, and a social infrastructure to support full employment by enabling the combination of work and care.

Fiscal Crisis: Austerity

Public expenditure on state-funded services was reduced in the aftermath of the financial crisis in many countries in Europe and North America. The costs of the crisis have been unevenly distributed by class and gender in the recession and in the policies that address the loss to government budgets. For example, in the 2010 UK budget, the House of Commons Library (2010) reported that 72 per cent (£5.8 billion) of the £8.1 billion net personal tax increases/benefit cuts would be borne by women and 28 per cent (£2.2 billion) by men.

There is a question as to whether this was inevitable. Pierson (1998, 2001b) argues that many developed countries have entered an era of 'permanent austerity' which is an outcome of a long-running fiscal crisis of the state (O'Connor 1973); that public expenditure on the welfare of the poor, the sick, the frail, children and pensions for the elderly has been creating a structural government budget deficit which needs addressing. However, Taylor-Gooby (2013a) argues that this view is mistaken; that the resources required to support welfare are not so large and could be afforded. A robust welfare state is still an available option for democracies if the rich pay their taxes (Sayer 2014).

Indeed, public expenditure may be considered as 'social investment' rather than 'welfare' (Morel et al. 2012) and as a contribution to economic growth rather than a drain on the economy. This approach recognizes, for example, that nurseries enable mothers to be employed as well as providing early education. In the social investment perspective, justice and economic growth go together and are not in opposition. The route to economic growth out of the economic and fiscal crisis is contested: the neoliberal strategy cuts state expenditure and regulation; the social investment strategy invests in human capacity.

These issues of tax and welfare are gendered. The conventional view is that the combination of rising unemployment and cuts in state services drive women back to the home to engage in care-work that had, in better times, been performed collectively. But the recession and cuts in public expenditure have not driven women back to the home. Women have rather experienced the intensification of their employment and a rise in unemployment rather than withdrawing from economic activity. A more nuanced approach to theorizing changes in gender relations is required than that of a simple oscillation between work and home. It is important to distinguish between the neoliberal and social democratic forms that can be taken by the public gender regime (Walby 2009).

Political Crisis

Why hasn't the neoliberal economic model that led to the crash been swept away? The model remains a powerful force in economic policy despite the evidence of its role in causing the crash. Crouch (2011) describes this situation as 'the strange non-death of neoliberalism', which, in turn, raises the question as to why neoliberalism as a political project has been so resilient (Schmidt and Thatcher 2013). During the ascendancy of the neoliberal project, public services were removed from direct democratic control; waves of privatization and deregulation eroded the scale and scope of the democratic state. Democracy thus became more 'shallow'.

The crisis has cascaded into politics. Governments fell in many European countries and many traditional political parties lost support. New political projects have emerged in civil society, with some leading to the creation of political parties to the left and to the right of the mainstream parties. A high level of unemployment can demobilize and reduce engagement in democratic institutions even though it increases discontent (Korpi 2002). Will the crisis cascade from a political crisis to a democratic crisis, with political mechanisms no longer able to channel disagreements, thereby leading to violent conflict (Arendt 1970, 1973 [1953])? Will political conflict spill over into violence as state legitimacy declines and policing tactics harden (della Porta 1995, 2013)? Does the use of coercion and the erosion of consent to the existing social order mark a distinct phase of the crisis (Gramsci 1971)? Is the crisis a sufficiently existential threat to society to enable authorities to invoke a state of exception to democratic political processes in order to maintain 'security' (Agamben 2005; Buzan et al. 1998)? If normal politics cannot channel conflict, then democracy itself is in crisis.

The most important polity for the regulation of the economy in Europe is that of the European Union. Within the EU, the Member State level of governance has significantly less powers over the regulation of the economy than does the European Union level. Hence, the potential power to regulate financial matters lies at the European Union level.

Would it have made a difference if it had been Lehman Sisters rather than Lehman Brothers? How important is the gendering of decision-making? There is gender imbalance in financial and economic decision-making institutions as well as in centralized political institutions in states. Would it make a difference if the EU were to insist on gender quotas on boards of directors? Or is the gendering of decision-making more subtle and indirect than a focus on gender composition suggests? Would a wider focus on the various dimensions of gendered political institutions, including changes in gendered priorities, be more appropriate?

Finance is intrinsically destabilizing of the economy. The financial and economic crisis was the consequence of a failure of democracy; the failure of democratic forces to regulate finance in the wider public interest. This is not inevitable. But the democratic forces to pursue such a regulatory project are weak.

Alternative Approaches to Economy and Society

Underpinning different approaches to the crisis and the route to economic growth are alternative visions and theories of economy and society. In particular, they differ as to whether markets are more efficient if left alone or if democratically regulated.

On the one hand, there is the 'efficient markets' thesis, popularly associated with neoliberalism. Efficient markets are supposed to deliver the best of all possible economic outcomes; neutrally balancing disparate sources of supply and demand. The resources of capital and labour are allocated to the locations best able to use them profitably and removed from those locations that were failing to do so. In the 'efficient markets' thesis, the deregulation of financial markets is supposed to lead to economic growth and well-being; the economy is believed to function best if left alone by government. However, the Great Crash of 2007/8 challenged this thesis. The economists who had been promoting the deregulation of financial and economic markets in the cause of growth had not foreseen the crash. What was wrong with their theories of finance and the economy? Looked at in more depth, the theorists of neoliberalism, such as Hayek (1945, 2001 [1944]) and Friedman (2002 [1962]), appear more complex, indeed contradictory, in relation to the role of the state, which appears to be needed to support markets after all (Peck 2010; Gane 2014a, 2014b).

On the other hand, there is the thesis that the economy works best when it is effectively embedded in a wider set of social institutions and regulated to avoid distortions due to power and corruption, often associated with social democracy. Markets are a type of social institution that do not exist in a pure and isolated form but are always shaped by the social relations in which they are inextricably entwined. These include gendered social relations, for example, in labour and in political representation. There has long been criticism of the 'efficient markets' thesis; that markets need regulation to prevent their distortion by the powerful and the corrupt. Democratic interventions to regulate markets and their associated institutions and to coordinate collectively and reflexively their economic and social institutions produce better outcomes than unregulated and uncoordinated markets. In this perspective, economic growth and social justice are treated not as alternatives in a trade-off but as necessary for each other. Theorists of social democracy, such as Polanyi (1957) and Crosland (1956), offer quite varied accounts as to how this is to be achieved (Berman 2006).

A simple reading of these alternative approaches would fit them into a binary distinction between ideal types of neoliberalism ('efficient markets') and social democracy ('democratic regulation'). But the distinctions that appear clear in theory can become hazy and complicated in practice (Hanké et al. 2007; Hanké 2009). Rounds of restructuring over long periods of time produce hybrid institutions that demand additional distinctions between sub-types for their analysis. For example, distinctions between gender regimes do not always neatly map onto distinctions between types of class relations, requiring further theoretical categories (Walby 2009). Neoliberalism takes different forms in different times and locations (Ong 2006; Bruff 2014). It is necessary to investigate the intricacy of actual developments and social practices.

One of the mistakes of conventional analysis of economy and society has been to treat institutions as if they were separate from one another. For example, central bankers considered it possible to evaluate financial risk by examining the books of each firm separately, rather than considering the effects of their interconnections within a single financial system. This error contributed to the financial crash since regulators had not sufficiently analysed the implications of the failure of one finance company for another. The perturbations in the economic system, which had been assumed to return automatically to equilibrium, escalated through positive feedback mechanisms into a gigantic crash. Future analysis needs to consider systems, not only institutions; it needs to understand their complex dynamics, with positive feedback effects, rather than assuming a return to equilibrium. Social science needs 'complexity' theory to analyse social systems.

The analysis needs to investigate: how finance should be regulated so that it does not destabilize the economy; who bore the brunt of the recession, in which job loss and income loss were unevenly distributed; and the way deficits in government budgets are addressed. There are further questions concerning the restoration of economic growth and the meaning of 'fairness' in the context of financial and economic crisis, including class, gender, ethnic and national inequalities.

Since the nature of the crisis is disputed, so are the responses and 'solutions'. Initially, the crisis meant the collapse in banking and finance; but recent debates have focused on the austerity response to the government budget deficit; while others offer a more systemic approach. Different constructions of the nature and cause of the crisis have implications for the policies put forward to address it: from banking reform to public expenditure cuts to the rejection of neoliberalism.

Economic growth policy is emerging as the new centre of contestation over post-crash economic policy (Hay 2013). Economic growth is thought to offer a route out of unemployment and to the recuperation of living standards. The old growth model depended on financialization, which led to the Crisis. The orthodox perspective, which assumes a trade-off between economic growth and social justice, has been destabilized during the financial crisis, opening the way to alternative possible approaches to the governance of the economy. Deregulating financial markets has been shown to be a very risky approach to economic growth. There has been an emergence of 'macro-prudentialism', of greater caution, in the regulation of finance among some central bankers (Haldane 2010). However, the orthodoxy has not disappeared; indeed it is experiencing a revival (Crouch 2011).

Social justice is sometimes positioned as if it were an alternative goal to that of economic growth; as if there were a 'trade-off' between justice and growth. But social justice is necessary to a successful economic growth project, since social inclusion is required for the mobilization of all human resources and the effective distribution of its proceeds. This means that social investment by the state in human resources is necessary for an effective economy and society. The route to economic growth is made more complicated when gender divisions are taken into account, since this brings into focus the issue of care for the very young and very old and how women, who often spend a few years but no longer a lifetime in domestic care-work, can engage effectively in the market economy. The ways in which such gendered differences can be accommodated within an economic growth strategy are central to the argument here.

Alternative beliefs as to how economy and society function should be subjected to appraisal by social science, rather than being treated as if they were fundamental values. The analysis of the crisis is used in this book as a source of evidence to test these rival theories.

Gender

The crisis is centred on gender relations as much as it is on class relations. The attempts to cut public expenditure under the guise of reducing the budget deficit are gendered in that they affect women more than men, since women are more often carers. Both neoliberalism and social democracy are gendered projects.

Conventional analysis of gender in the economy has often made a simple distinction between production (paid work) and reproduction (unpaid care-work in the home). Within this perspective, the crisis was expected to push women from production to reproduction. But this did not happen in the UK and many other countries. Although the rise in unemployment was disproportionately among women and the cuts in public services disproportionately affected women as both workers and carers, this did not lead to an increase in women staying at home. Women stayed economically active.

However, there were major changes in gender relations during the crisis; indeed many aspects of the financial crisis, ensuing recession and emergent economic growth strategies have been gendered. Their analysis requires a model of gender relations that is more complex than one based on a dichotomy between production and reproduction (or between market and home). Variations in the form of gender regime need to include more distinctions than that between public (market) and domestic (home).

The gender regime can vary not only as to whether it takes a more domestic or more public form, but also in whether the public form takes a more neoliberal or more social democratic form. The socialization of domestic labour can be achieved through the use of market mechanisms (e.g. buying childcare from a child minder) or through the use of state-provided services (e.g. childcare provided by a state-funded and state-run nursery). These changes parallel and intersect with wider changes in the economy, such as the intensification of work during the crisis.

The crisis has led to a change in the form of the public gender regime, from a more social democratic to a more neoliberal form. This is bound up with the intensification of work for women, especially mothers. Women have not left the labour market, but are typically working harder for less real pay.

What are the implications of these changes for politics and democracy? Traditionally, support for state-funded and state-provided services has been part of the social democratic project. The social democratic project has historically drawn its strongest support from trade-unionized manual workers in manufacturing. There is now a re-gendering of the constituencies supporting the social democratic project. Gender relations are cause as well as consequence of the crisis.

Society

In order to understand the way the crisis has cascaded from one institution to another it is necessary to have a concept and theory of society. Analysing social institutions in isolation from each other, as traditionally happens in divided social science disciplines, hinders the understanding of the crisis. The crisis has cascaded through finance, the economy, the welfare state and politics. It is important to be able to analyse the intersections and connections between these institutions at the level of society. This understanding requires the concept of society as a social system. It demands sociological inquiry at a macro level, not only at the meso and micro levels.

The Book

The book offers a critique and revision of the social science needed to understand the crisis and to prevent such an event occurring again. It produces a reworked concept and theory of society, drawing on complexity theory, in order to achieve this. It is a call to revitalize the traditional goal of sociology to study all of society, not only small parts of it.

The book provides an analysis of the financial and economic crisis starting in 2007 in Europe and North America. While empirical examples are most frequently drawn from the UK situated in this wider context, the argument has much wider resonance. The financial and economic crisis cannot be comprehended using the tools of mainstream economics alone since its origin lies in the social system as a whole, including polity and civil society. Contestations over gender relations are core to the causes and consequences of the crisis. The crisis started in finance and has cascaded into a recession in the real economy, fiscal crisis in state budgets followed by austerity, and an emerging crisis in democracy.

Chapter 2 develops the concept and theory of 'crisis'. It situates the crisis, starting with finance in 2007, within a broader field comprising a variety of forms of crisis, from accidents to disasters. Crises can be small or large, 'normal' or 'catastrophic', business as usual or tipping points to societal transformation. Complexity science is drawn upon to develop the conceptualization of crisis and produce a unified field of analysis.

Chapter 3 argues for the theorization of finance within the discipline of sociology as well as other social sciences. Building on a review of the concept and theory of finance, including that in the work of Keynes and Minsky, it offers a revised theorization of the relationship of finance to economy and society. It shows how finance destabilizes the economy unless it is regulated and governed appropriately.

Chapter 4 analyses the crisis in the real economy, the uneven distribution of losses of output and employment in the recessions generated by the financial crisis. In the UK by 2015, there has not been recuperation in productivity and in living standards to pre-crisis levels.

Chapter 5 considers whether or not the deficit in state budgets, sometimes considered to constitute a fiscal crisis of the state, meant austerity was inevitable. The use of gender budgeting techniques shows the gender imbalance in the methods used to narrow the deficit. It will be shown that tax is a feminist issue. The chapter addresses the contested conceptualization of public expenditure as either 'welfare' or 'social investment'; with implications for economic growth strategy.

Chapter 6 analyses the resulting political crisis: governments fell; old political parties decayed while new ones emerged to their right and left. The potential competences of the EU have emerged as pivotal to the selection of alternative pathways leading either to renewal and deeper union of its financial, fiscal and political institutions or to the fragmentation of the European project.

Chapter 7 pulls together the threads on gender relations which are woven through the fabric of the book. All phases of the crisis have been gendered, but in different ways. Here the implications of the diverse changes in gendered institutions for changes in the overall gender regime in society are assessed. Since 2010, the trajectory of the gender regime has taken a more neoliberal form. This turn follows several decades of slow incremental change in a more social democratic direction.

Chapter 8 concludes with the implications of the analysis for social science and public policy. It offers a revised vocabulary of concepts to theorize the crisis, drawing on complexity science to re-invigorate sociological theory. It provides a new model of sustainable gendered economic growth and social justice to lead the way out of the crisis. It demonstrates the importance of a theory of society as a social system in order to understand contemporary social change.

2

Theorizing Crisis

Introduction

How should 'the crisis' be conceptualized and theorized? Can someone or something be blamed for causing it? While the focus of the book is a particular crisis and its cascade through finance, the economy, the fiscal, austerity, politics and democracy to the wider social system, there are broader questions to be asked about the relationship between crisis and society. These concern the nature of crisis in general and how this is addressed in social theory.

A crisis is defined here as an event that has the potential to cause a large detrimental change to the social system and in which there is lack of proportionality between cause and consequence. Crises are both 'real', in the sense of actual changes in social processes, and socially constructed, in the sense that different interpretations of the crisis have implications for its outcome. The interpretation of a crisis may under- or over-state its magnitude and impact, as well as attribute blame as to its cause.

Several fields of social science deploy concepts that overlap with that of crisis including risk, catastrophe, disaster and revolution. These fields are traditionally separated from each other, but there are insights and analytic tools that could be usefully exchanged if there were a shared conceptual vocabulary. The development of such a vocabulary is attempted here by drawing on complexity science, which has created a sophisticated range of concepts for issues relevant to the analysis of 'crisis' and systems. These concepts enable the development of a new typology of forms of crisis containing a limited number of the most typical trajectories taken by crises. This typology is offered as a contribution both to the development of the general field of 'crisis', which is currently scattered across the social sciences, and to the specific analysis of the crisis that started in deregulated finance in 2007.

Real or Socially Constructed?

Is the crisis 'real' or is it 'socially constructed' (Jessop 2013)? It is real in that there have been rapid changes in finance and the economy detrimental to human well-being; and it is socially constructed in that the meaning of these events and changes is malleable and contested. The relative balance between treating the crisis as 'real' and as a 'social construction' varies in analyses. This chapter reviews these analyses, starting with those that consider a crisis in the economy to be real, followed by those which emphasize its social construction, and lastly proposing a way to reach a synthesis. These various approaches to the crisis share the assumption that there is a relationship between power and knowledge; in particular, that power shapes knowledge. However, the approaches understand this relationship in diverse ways using a range of concepts including: hegemony (Gramsci); discourse (Foucault); and narrative (Ricoeur).

In the approach informed by Gramsci (1971), there is a 'real' crisis, produced by the contradictions in the economic aspects of social relations, the meaning of which is subject to contestation. The crisis cracks the hegemonic interpretation of the world, thereby offering an opportunity for the reassessment of dominant social meanings and the rise of counter-hegemonic forces. The common-sense understanding of the world is broken to allow the potential emergence of new blocs with their own interpretations of the world. Gramsci's concept of 'hegemony' offers a way of conceptualizing how and why populations in democracies can support political positions that appear to be out of alignment with their material interests. Political parties in democracies depend upon gaining the consent of the people through elections to win governmental power. The concept of 'interests' assumes a person's interests can be read off from their social location in a simple and direct manner. This assumption is a mistake because political preferences are only indirectly related to an individual's material position or perception of their 'identity'. The links are mediated by many processes and institutions, from private ownership of the press, through the channelling of the economics profession, to the engagement of informal associations. Hegemony over beliefs and practices is essential to establishing power in a democracy. In order to become the ruling group or party, it is necessary to establish the ascendancy of the project, which is a cohesive set of ideas and practices that provide an account as to how the world works and how it can be improved.

Hegemony may be achieved by coercion as well as consent; but once won may be maintained through consent centred on ideas. Crisis is a time when consensus is fractured. During this period, the modality of power used by dominant groups to retain control may shift away from consensus towards coercion. The use of coercion, repression and violence increases the visibility of the relations of dominance in a society, thereby increasing the potential for systemic change. The concept of hegemony enables analysis to go beyond the reductionism of treating ideas as if they are mere reflections of material interests, while not abandoning concepts of power and inequality. Contestation over ideas is treated as having serious implications for political and economic action (Burawoy 2003).

A related approach treats the crisis as real but seeks explanation of the unexpected resilience or 'strange non-death' of the neoliberal project (Crouch 2011). In the first elections after the financial and economic crisis, in 2010, many countries in Europe, including the UK, elected governments further to the right, not further to the left, of the one that had been in power during the financial crash. Crouch had anticipated that the neoliberal model of light regulation would be blamed for the financial crisis and would be replaced by a more interventionist social democratic government at the first electoral possibility. Crouch and others (e.g. Mirowski 2013) have investigated the institutional base of the neoliberal project in seeking to explain the lack of political change. Crouch suggests that this base can be found in the power of corporations. Mirowski finds this base in the institutionalization of neoliberalism in the economics profession and other knowledge-producing institutions. In this approach, the crisis is treated as 'real' and the analysis of the struggle over its meaning is approached through an investigation of institutions ranging from corporations to think tanks, the economics profession and universities.

In a different approach, the analytic distinction between a crisis that is a real event in the economy and a crisis that is constituted in discourse is eroded, if not erased. There are nuances here between a position in which the crisis does not exist outside of its representation and another in which there is a struggle over the meaning of already existing (ontologically real) events. Hay (1996), drawing on Foucault, Hall and Ricoeur, argues that crises are constituted through meaning. For Hay, the ability to define a set of circumstances as constituting a crisis creates a political opportunity for more substantial change than would otherwise happen. In his analysis of an earlier UK 'crisis' in the 1980s, the so-called 'winter of discontent', Hay (1996: 255) argues:

> Crisis, then, is not some objective condition or property of a system defining the contours for subsequent ideological contestation. Rather, it is subjectively perceived and hence brought into existence through narrative and discourse. State power (the ability to impose a new trajectory upon the structure of the state) resides not only in the ability to *respond* to crises, but to *identify, define and constitute* crisis in the first place. (Hay's emphasis)

The middle sentence in this passage may appear to suggest that there is no crisis outside of one that is identified, defined and constituted by narrative and discourse. However, this is qualified and contextualized by Hay in the third sentence through the reference to state power and its role within this discursive process of identification, definition and constitution. The processes might be discursive but that does not mean that the state is absent from them. Hay draws on Ricoeur's concept of 'narrative' as well as Foucault's concept of 'discourse'. The concept of 'narrative' goes beyond the concept of 'discourse' for the purposes of analysing the crisis by offering a method to examine processes over time that can distinguish between actors, plots and morality. This more dynamic analysis helps to make visible the significance of temporality and the sequencing of actions in the relations between actors during the construction of meaning.

This approach is paralleled in the work by Agamben (2005) on the state of exception and by Buzan et al. (1998) on the process of securitization. Their work concerns the way that 'crisis' can be used to side-step the democratic processes of more normal times. For Agamben, a state of exception, or the ability to declare a state of emergency, allows the executive branch of the state to take actions without the need to follow the usual democratic procedures. The power to define a situation as in need of the use of emergency powers is an extraordinary power. Similarly, Buzan et al. analyse how the power to declare that something constitutes a threat to security is an extraordinary power. If something is considered to be a threat to the existence of the state or society, then the state is legitimated to use levels of coercion and force that would otherwise not be acceptable. To produce the authority to declare a situation to be a crisis is to acquire the legitimacy to bypass the democratic processes that would normally regulate the use of such power.

In this approach, the declaration of crisis, of a state of emergency, is a move in a power game. The discursive ability to constitute events as if they were a crisis potentially reduces democratic capacity by increasing the power of the executive branch of the state. In this body of work, the analysis of the social and political construction of a set of events as if it were a crisis is central to the analysis of crisis.

Synthesizing these strands of argumentation, it is argued here that the financial and economic crisis is real and serious, but control by the neoliberal project over the dominant narrative of the crisis has led to its misrepresentation as one centred on fiscal rather than financial matters. There is a real crisis, but the meaning of the crisis is contested. In particular, the site of the crisis is disputed. The analysis in this book shows that the crisis originated in the failure to regulate finance but that the main focus of political debate has become the fiscal crisis and 'austerity'. Thus the critical focus on the weaknesses of the neoliberal project of deregulation has been replaced by a focus on state expenditure and an attempt to blame the social democratic project for promoting such spending. In many European countries, the hegemonic narrative of the crisis has centred the location of the blame for the crisis on 'excessive' state spending, exacerbated by the role of the Euro, in creating a government budget deficit, which was considered to justify the introduction of austerity. The development of this narrative has entailed a shift in the perceived origins of the crisis away from the excessive deregulation of finance towards excessive state spending on welfare.

The focus of the hegemonic narrative on the crisis became austerity in many European countries, with the blame for austerity divided variably between excessive state social expenditure and EU institutions. Several counter-hegemonic narratives are emerging, rooted in projects in civil society and becoming institutionalized in a range of new political parties. Projects on the left identify neoliberal capitalism as the cause of the problem while those on the right blame immigration and the EU. The crisis is treated as if it were 'real', in the sense of existing in the economy prior to the discursive and narrative contestation of its meaning; but the outcome of the struggle to establish its dominant meaning has significant implications for politics, the state and the ensuing shape of the economy.

Causes Not Proportionate to Their Consequences

The concept of crisis challenges the conventional approach to change. Conventional ways of thinking about change usually assume that the cause of a change is proportionate to its effect. The bigger the event causing the change, the bigger the ensuing change is likely to be. This is the general assumption of 'linear reality' that has traditionally been found in sociology and other social sciences (Abbott 2001). However, most analyses of crisis contest this assumption. Central to the meaning of the concept of crisis is the notion that something potentially having large, long-term consequences is the result of something small happening in a short period of time.

Conventional accounts of change are usually gradualist. Changes are seen as the outcome of the steady accumulation of many events, as proportionate to the accumulation of causes, of the addition together of the relevant factors. For example, this assumption underlies most 'modernization' theory, from Lipset (1959) to Inglehart (1997). A further example of this approach is found in Braudel's (1966 [1949]) distinction between three different timescales of change. First is the short timescale of conjunctures, of events and episodes, where the actions of individuals can only make a small difference. Second is the medium timescale of social structural change, of civilizations and empires, of long-term secular trends in economy and demography, which are beyond the reach of individual action. Third is the longue durée, the glacial rate of change of deeper environmental and technological conditions. For Braudel, events sit within the first, short timescale of the conjuncture. The outcome of the event depends on the longer and deeper context of social structure and environment. According to Braudel (1966 [1949]: 1244), 'All events against the prevailing tide of history – which is not always obvious – are doomed to failure.' In this approach, events are usually of minor significance compared with the processes involved in social structure and the longue durée. Only if an event is in alignment with these larger changes can it be expected to have much effect.

Traditional theories of change sometimes include a moment of social disruption which is labelled as a crisis and has an outcome proportionate to the underlying changes. In this approach, the term 'crisis' merely refers to the moment at which changes, driven by underlying tensions in social development, come to fruition. This is not a theory of crisis in the sense of the one being developed here; merely an account of proportionate changes occurring at a moment of social disruption labelled as a crisis. For example, Arrighi (2007) argues that the crisis in capital accumulation in the West may lead to a change in the hegemon, in which the US is replaced possibly by China. Such a change in the regime of accumulation and associated hegemon is considered to be usually preceded by financialization and marked by war. For Aglietta (2000a [1976]) and Arrighi (1994, 2007), the crisis is a consequence of the exhaustion of a regime of capital accumulation, when profits are no longer being generated by a particular combination of forces and relations of production. At this point, the search for profits by the owners of capital shifts from productive industry to finance. Financialization is an alternative route to profit and heralds a potential shift in the regime of accumulation led by a new capitalist hegemon. Financialization is an indicator, not a cause, of the crisis in the regime of accumulation. The current crisis is indicative of a shift away from the US to a new hegemon, probably that of China. Previous historical transitions in hegemons have been identified as those from the Dutch to Britain to the US (Chase-Dunn et al. 2000), with each marked by warfare involving the declining and rising hegemons (Bornschier and Chase-Dunn 1999). In this analysis, the driver of change is changes in the mode of production, situated within a set of social structures that facilitate or limit the profitability of capital. Crisis is the moment of change that is driven by these large underlying forces.

By contrast, most of the theories of crisis discussed in what follows are focused on small events that can potentially lead to very big change. The key issue is to identify the circumstances under which a small event can cause large changes. This usually involves a concern for the nature of the underlying systems, rather than only of the precipitating event. If the underlying system is unstable, or the interaction between systems can produce instability in these systems, then a small event can lead to a large change. Crisis concerns events that potentially have disproportionate impact. The change is non-linear rather than linear. Crisis concerns a temporal period that is short relative to those that precede and follow. It is a moment when small causes appear to have large consequences. They have this effect because they sit on the tipping point or pivot of potential changes in systems. Such analyses of crises in general share an interest in three things: the short period, or event, of crisis; the large underlying systems (especially those that are social or socio-technical) whose dynamics are changed by this crisis event; and the contrast between those systems before and after the crisis.

Approaches to Crisis

In order to develop a new vocabulary to understand 'crisis', a range of concepts in parallel and overlapping topics and fields are reviewed.

These accounts are provided to show the potential scope of the field of crisis and to build a repertoire of relevant concepts. This development of a shared set of concepts, informed by complexity science, could facilitate more effective transfer of knowledge between these fields. The approaches to crisis discussed here include a range of substantively different types of crisis, including financial and economic crises, but additionally encompassing environmental, demographic and political crises. They use a range of diverse concepts that partially overlap with that of crisis, from catastrophe to revolution. The concepts and topics include: risk, especially in relation to the possibility of environmental catastrophe (Beck 1992, 2009); normal accidents in high-technology systems that can become catastrophes (Perrow 1999 [1984], 2011 [2007]); 'natural' disasters that have varied impacts on people (Yodmani 2001); political revolts that might become revolutions (Skocpol 1979; Goldstone 1991); business cycles and bubbles (Perez 2002, 2009); financial instability (Minsky 2008 [1986]); descent into and recuperation from over-commercialization (Polanyi 1957) ; and crisis as opportunity for economic renewal (Schumpeter 1954; Haas 1958) .

Risks/catastrophes

Risks are unavoidable in modern society, according to Beck (1992), but they can be managed so as to mitigate their effects. 'Second' or 'late' modernity intrinsically generates risks as a consequence of its institutional and technological development. The central contradiction of second modernity is that social, economic and technological progress produces risks. While risk is endemic, it can be managed and mitigated so that the outcome becomes catastrophic in only some circumstances. Risk inequalities are more general than inequalities generated through class divisions. The classic example of a routine risk that became catastrophic is the development of nuclear power that produced the Chernobyl nuclear reactor meltdown. Global financial risk and terrorist threats are new forms of risk in world society, taking their place alongside the environmental risks that were the focus of Beck's early analysis (Beck 2009: 199). The financial crisis is harmful; it is disruptive of economies and damaging to human well-being. Potentially these risks of modernity are catastrophic; but it is possible that the risks could be managed and mitigated. Beck does not routinely use the term 'crisis', instead dividing this concept into two, so that 'risk' signifies routine potentially harmful events, and 'catastrophe' what happens when the 'risk' materializes into a large-scale harm. Indeed, in response to Curran (2013), Beck (2013) claims that the concept of risk subsumes that of crisis, since it includes both the anticipated and the actual risk and the relationship between them. However, the parallels with the more general concept of crisis are clear. Small events can generate large harms in the context of unstable systems.

Normal accidents/catastrophes

According to Perrow (1999 [1984]), 'accidents' are 'normal' in most systems, occurring as a routine result of unwitting mistakes. Whether such accidents are minor and insignificant or lead to a catastrophe with dramatic consequences depends upon the inter-relationships between the systems in which they occur. The more closely the systems are interconnected or 'tightly coupled', then the more likely it is that an accident in one system will cascade into other systems and have a large effect. A small perturbation (change or accident) in one system can lead to large changes in systems that are tightly coupled; but this same small perturbation may have few consequences if systems are more loosely coupled (connected). Changing the nature of the system can reduce the scale of harm that results from accidents. There are several ways this change can be achieved. One approach, derived from Perrow's work, is to locate high-risk technical systems at a large distance from centres of populations, so reducing the potential impact of accidents. Another is to reduce the interactive complexity of the system, thereby loosening the coupling between systems. These attempts to mitigate the harms of normal accidents aim to reduce the likelihood of the effects of the accident cascading into adjacent and linked systems.

However, not all problems with systems are the result of 'normal accidents'. Perrow (2011 [2007]) argues the financial crisis was not a 'normal accident'. Rather, those responsible for the changes that made finance so vulnerable to crisis were aware of the likely outcome but nevertheless proceeded because it was in their interest to do so. Perrow refers to this conduct as 'malfeasance'.

Disasters

The analysis of disaster has significant parallels with the study of crisis. A key finding of the field is that the same level of external shock, such as an earthquake, has quite different human consequences depending upon the social vulnerabilities of the population affected. The field of disaster studies includes a range of competing approaches, including focus on an external threat, the vulnerability of the community, and entrance into a state of uncertainty (Gilbert 1998). There are important attempts to move beyond a view of disasters as extreme events to analysing their most important aspects as consequences of wider social structural processes (Yodmani 2001). The varied and complex vulnerabilities of the population at risk are more important in determining the scale of the effects of the disaster than the 'natural' event that is conventionally regarded as the focus of the disaster. There is a tension in the understanding of the political dimensions of disaster between treating 'disaster' as if it were a politically constructed object and treating it as if it were an already existing object that has political implications (Guggenheim 2014). This tension is similar to that found in the earlier discussions of political crises.

Revolts/revolutions

Revolts and revolutions are the focus of adjacent literature in sociology and political science on political and societal crises. Revolts are small crises that are crushed or absorbed; revolutions are large crises that lead to change in the form of the social system. This literature on political and societal crisis addresses: the nature of the structural tensions and imbalances that underlie revolution – for example, the contradictory development of the forces and relations of production (Marx and Engels 2012 [1848]); industrial revolution and structural strain (e.g. Smelser 1959); the significance of the balance of different class forces for the development of dictatorship or democracy (Moore 1966); the role of the state in revolutions (Skocpol 1979); the significance of divisions in the security apparatus of police and army for revolts (Kandil 2012); the significance of the depth of institutionalization of democratic procedures in civil society (Rueschemeyer et al.1992); and multi-faceted, multi-factoral explanations linking financial/fiscal crisis of the state, divisions among elites, the mobilizing of popular groups, and changing ecologies for revolt and revolution (Goldstone 1991). Here 'crisis' is understood as being the moment of change, rather than the driver of the change, which lies in a multi-faceted wider social system. In these sociological analyses of revolution, a wide range of social institutions are seen as relevant to the origin, nature and effect of the revolution; including not only those that found in the economy and the polity, but also in civil society. These analyses offer a conceptual vocabulary to distinguish between the short-term events of the crisis, the moment of revolution, and the longer-term, deeper, slower changes in social structures which generate the conditions that allow revolution.

Business cycles, bubbles and financial instability

The regular business cycles and bubbles in asset prices within the economy may be considered as minor crises that are absorbed without changing the overall system. The business cycle is constituted by regular variations in the rate of economic activity which entail the boom and slump in output and employment. Bubbles can emerge as the prices of assets (e.g. property, tulip bulbs and shares) rise; only to crash suddenly as an event pricks the bubble (Perez 2002, 2009). Small crises are normal and routine. They are harmful to those caught up in them, but not of wider significance. A return to the previous state of the economy is usual. For Marx (1959 [1894]), such minor economic instability was a routine and intrinsic feature of capitalist economies. For Keynes (1936) and Minsky (2008 [1986]), as for Marx, the capitalist economy is inherently unstable as a consequence of the role of finance capital. Minsky's account of finance shows how the phases of the investment cycle intrinsically generate instability in the 'real' economy (see the next chapter for a fuller discussion). However, writing after the development of democracy, Keynes and Minsky, unlike Marx, considered that such instability could be moderated by the state through actions to regulate finance.

Recuperation from crisis

Not all accounts of crisis suggest it ends in catastrophe. Polanyi (1957) argued that there was the possibility of a double movement in which the initial move towards the damaging commercialization of land, labour and money, which in its extreme form threatens human survival, is met by a movement from within civil society to re-embed the economy in society. This double movement, towards commercialization and back through civil society to a better balance of economy and society, contains the notion of an effective negative feedback loop through which society is restored to equilibrium.

Crisis as renewal

Crisis can be understood as a route to renewal that is positive for, not only detrimental to, human well-being. This understanding underpins the work by Schumpeter (1954) on economic crisis and by Haas (1958) and Hallstein (1973 [1969]) on the development of the European Union.

For Schumpeter (1954), economic crisis is a moment for 'creative destruction' in which old parts of the economy are destroyed, thereby allowing the emergence of new forms. The closure of older, less productive industries in times of economic recession has the beneficial consequence of freeing up resources for newer and potentially more productive industries in the upswing in the economy expected to follow recession.

For Haas (1958), political and economic crises were the mechanisms that would drive forward the deepening institutionalization of a new Europe, to support ever closer union, through 'spillover'. Finding a solution to the problem of militarist nationalism and the pursuit of ethnic, national and religious purity that had led Europe to fascism, genocide and world war required, argued Haas, the cessation of the project in which each national group in Europe sought purity in a state of its own. This required the ending of the traditional project of the nation-state, which had led to so much death and destruction in Europe. This was a bold vision, which was too controversial to win immediate political support. The political support was to be built step by step, using economic instability to drive the building of the institutions that would lead to ever deeper union. In a strategy to prevent Europe ever again descending into war and holocaust, the new European leaders deliberately created unstable economic institutions at the centre of Europe which, at each crisis, would need stabilization through the development of political institutions (Hallstein 1973 [1969]). At each economic crisis, the political institutions would be deepened in order to stabilize the economy. The successive waves of crisis would create an integrated Europe that could not go to war with itself (Ball 1973 [1969]; Walby 1999). The goal of the renewal of Europe through political and economic crisis was peace; which, remarkably, has been achieved, at least within the borders of the EU.

Theorizing Social Change and Society Using Complexity Science

From this review, it can be seen that the core features of these approaches to apparently diverse phenomena significantly overlap with those concerning the concept of crisis. Each approach includes two elements: sudden change in an aspect of society, in what initially appear as events within a short timeframe; and slower changes in larger-scale social or socio-technical systems. These approaches to crisis therefore contain, either explicitly or implicitly, a theory of social change and of society alongside the distinction between small events and larger systems. Each theory entails an underlying set of assumptions about the concept of society even when this is not foregrounded for analysis.

The range of concepts used in these analyses is very wide; so wide that writers often do not engage with or learn from each other even when addressing things with significant similarities. In developing a theory of crisis, it is useful to build a common conceptual vocabulary that enables the various studies and theories to contribute to the cumulative scientific development of this field. The field of crisis could contain all the substantively focused fields identified in this chapter, including the financial, economic, environmental and political. The theories encompass a spectrum of social changes from small changes with little consequence for society to cataclysmic events that change forever its social order or lead to its destruction.

Concepts developed within complexity science offer a route towards the development of a shared conceptual vocabulary to analyse crisis more effectively. They offer a way to address the tension that exists between macro-level analysis and the nuance and detail of situated actions. Complexity science is especially powerful in analysing non-linear change and the relationship between small events and larger systems (Walby 2007a, 2009).

Complexity science developed earlier and faster in the natural sciences (Capra 1997; Waldrop 1992) than the social sciences. This was partly due to the incorporation of simple equilibrium concepts of systems in the early founding texts of sociology, such as those by Durkheim and Parsons, which have been strongly criticized. These criticisms of simple equilibrium conceptualizations of systems tended to lead to rejection of the concept of system altogether rather than to its revision and gradual improvement. This was part of the turn against the 'metanarrative' (Lyotard 1978); away from modernism, and towards postmodern and poststructuralist perspectives in social science. This turn was further fed by the concern to analyse multiple forms of social inequality and difference rather than reducing these to a central dynamic of class (Barrett and Phillips 1992). However, there are now substantial advances in the social sciences that utilize the developments in thinking about systems and complexity that draw on the developments in other sciences.

Despite this relatively late interest in complexity concepts, there are now several approaches to complexity theory in social science

(Luhmann 1995; Byrne 1998; Cilliers 1998; Urry 2003, 2005; Walby 2007a, 2009; Castellani and Hafferty 2009). Some concepts developed in the natural sciences have become assimilated into social theory, such as the concept of path dependency (Pierson 2000); others are less familiar and under-utilized, as in the case of multiple equilibria (Esping-Andersen 2009), or remain sites of controversy, such as 'system' (Luhmann 1995).

A set of concepts derived from complexity theory that are relevant to the analysis of the crisis is explored here. These concepts are organized into six clusters using the adjacent concepts already discussed. These clusters include: when the system changes (crisis, tipping point, critical turning point); what a system is; not assuming equilibrium; dynamics that reinforce or change system (negative and positive feedback loops); understanding stability (multiple and punctuated equilibria); path dependency; and relations between systems.

Concepts for when the system changes
(crisis, tipping point, critical turning point)

A crisis is a potential 'tipping point' or 'critical turning point' in a system. It is a point at which there is potential for change in the wider system. There is a lack of proportion between cause and consequence. While there is the potential for change, it is not necessary that this potential is realized for it to be termed 'crisis'. However, the terms 'tipping point' and 'critical turning point' are only used when there is actual change. The more popular term is that of 'tipping point' (Gladwell 2000). There is a range of substantively oriented concepts in the social sciences which encompass this meaning, including those of disaster, catastrophe and revolution, as already discussed. The natural sciences have a range of overlapping concepts including bifurcation (when a system divides), saltation or crystallization (when a potential major change moves a system from a fluid to stable form), and 'phase transition' in physics (Capra 1997).

What a system is

A system is self-reproducing, repetitive and self-organizing (Maturana and Varela 1980). Generic terms in the social sciences for this concept of system include social system and socio-technical system, while more specialized terms include society, capitalism, regime, gender regime, institution, field, domain and social formation.

A key distinction in complexity science is between a system and its environment, such that a system takes all other systems as its environment (Bertalanffy 1968). This conceptual innovation was adopted and used by Luhmann (1995). It allows social science to move beyond the notion that a system is made up of its parts (Parsons 1951), that a society is a whole made up of parts, a notion which has proved to be problematic because of its rigidity. The distinction allows analysis of the relationship between systems to be more nimble and fluid. It allows for systems to be non-nested, non-congruent and only partially overlapping, even while interacting and having effects on each other. Using this distinction enables social science to go beyond the over-simplistic notion that a society is a nation-state (Giddens 1990) by facilitating theoretical recognition that there are more nations than states and allowing for the theorization of the EU with its multiple, non-nested systems (Walby 2003, 2009).

Not assuming equilibrium

Systems are not always stable. Complexity science allows the rejection of the assumption that systems always return to equilibrium; return is possible but is not necessary or inevitable. Systems may return to equilibrium or they may move far from equilibrium. This approach facilitates an analysis of crisis, as it contains the possibility that either there may be a temporary destabilization with a later return to equilibrium or the system may move further from equilibrium.

Dynamics that reinforce or change system (negative and positive feedback loops)

Feedback loops may be negative or positive. Systems return to equilibrium when there are negative feedback loops whereas positive feedback loops drive the system away from equilibrium (Arthur 1994). A system may absorb a change, shock or perturbation because negative feedback loops return it to equilibrium. Alternatively, the change may set off a positive feedback loop driving the system away from equilibrium. Equilibrium depends on the existence of negative feedback loops. Whether negative or positive feedback loops predominate is an empirical question.

Feedback loops give rise to non-linear changes. In particular, positive feedback loops give rise to non-linear changes that escalate change away from equilibrium. When the system is balanced on the edge of change, a small intervention can tip the system into a large change. This is non-linear change.

Minsky (2008 [1986]) identified such positive feedback loops in the operation of finance. These loops underpin his analysis of the intrinsic instability of finance and its tendency to destabilize economies, to move the system away from equilibrium. In contrast, a 'bubble' is an example of an instability which is met by a negative feedback loop to return the system to equilibrium. The concept of positive feedback loops and non-linear change has become especially important in the analysis of the socio-technical systems producing climate change (Urry 2011).

Understanding stability (multiple and punctuated equilibria)

There may be more than one point at which a system is in equilibrium as a result of competing pressures. There may be multiple equilibria. This phenomenon can be conceptualized using complexity theory, and it stands in opposition to the notion that the application of universal laws can produce only one point of equilibrium. Thus, differences in forms of society may be the consequence of the emergence of different stable points of equilibrium rather than constituting differences in their 'stage of development'.

Using this approach allows for the possibility that capitalism can take more than one form, as in the 'varieties of capitalism' proposed by Hall and Soskice (2001). These varieties of capitalism can co-exist in time; different forms of capitalism are not limited to variations over time. The approach underlies thinking about multiple welfare state regimes (Esping-Andersen 1990). The concept of 'multiple equilibria' is used explicitly by Esping-Andersen (2009) in his work on the variation in forms of families in different parts of Europe. It also underpins the conceptualization of multiple varieties of gender regimes (Walby 2009).

Change may be absent; or it may take a gradual or sudden form. The concept of 'punctuated equilibria' was developed to encompass such variation in stability and change (Eldredge 1985). There may be long periods of stability, or equilibrium, which are 'punctuated' by short periods of rapid change. It is important not to assume that complexity theory is only applicable to non-linear change; it is compatible with an assumption of periods both of stability and of rapid change.

Path dependency

Path dependency refers to the different trajectories of development that are possible because there are multiple potential points of equilibrium for a system. The path of development of a system may bifurcate during a crisis, forming divergent path dependent trajectories.

In social systems, these paths of development are 'locked in' through their sedimentation in institutions (North 1990). The distinctiveness of the paths may erode or increase over time. The concept of path dependency has become more widely assimilated into social science than some other concepts of complexity science (Mahoney 2000; Pierson 2000). An example is the path dependency of socio-technical systems of mobility through motor cars and the difficulty of changing this system (Urry 2013).

Relations between systems

The analysis of the relations between systems replaces the analysis of the internal relations between the parts of a system in the old concept of system used by, for example, Durkheim and Parsons. The nature of the relations between systems is varied. Three concepts are particularly useful: mutual adaptation of complex adaptive systems; coupling of systems; and fitness landscapes.

Complex systems that interact change each other. This is known as the mutual adaptation of complex adaptive systems. The notion of one-way impact is rejected and replaced by the notion that both the interacting systems are likely to change, and that temporality and sequencing are important aspects of this process (Luhmann 1995). The interaction of the systems has effects that neither are merely additive nor change the essential nature of the systems. The systems shape rather than mutually constitute each other (Walby et al. 2012a).

Systems may be linked in ways that are close or loose. Perrow (1999 [1984]) distinguishes between the tight and loose coupling of systems. When the coupling is tight the effects of changes in one system are more likely to affect, and to affect more quickly and more strongly, the systems to which it is connected. The tighter the coupling, the more likely it is that a change (e.g. an accident) in one will 'cascade' into changes in the adjacent system. The concept of modularity is similar. If systems are 'modular' then they are relatively separate from each other. Hence increasing the modularity of a system increases its 'resilience'; so changes in one module are less likely to lead to changes in others. For Haldane and May (2011), increasing the modularity of the financial system would reduce the likelihood of systemic risk, in which the failure of one bank would lead to the failure of other banks and then to the entire banking system.

The concept of 'fitness landscape' is introduced by Kauffman (1993) to address the uneven nature of the 'landscape' or terrain on which systems interact and compete. Changes in the nature of the landscape may benefit one system but at the same time disadvantage other systems. The fitness of the landscape can differently affect the success or otherwise of the varied systems within it; some entities may flourish while others will not.

Typology of Relationship Between Crisis and Outcome

Crises are events that may have huge potential consequences. The possibility of systemic breakdown lurks within all accounts of crisis, even though breakdown may not occur. The uncertainty regarding the outcome of a crisis is part of the definition of crisis. There are systematic differences in the relationship between a crisis and its outcome. There is a simple contrast between one type of crisis that leads to a breakdown in the system and another type that has little long-term effect. In between are further possibilities: a crisis might drive forward changes that are compatible with a system, or it may cause changes in the nature of the system. The forms of relationship between the crisis event and the outcome for the system can thus be divided into four. These four types of relationship can be conceptualized using complexity science in order to assist the learning from one substantive field of analysis of crisis to another. The first is when a crisis leads to system breakdown, which has been variously called catastrophe, disaster, the end of civilization and apocalypse. The second is when a crisis is followed by a return to pre-crisis conditions, variously called bubble, business cycle and double movement. The third is when crisis leads to renewal of the system within its trajectory of development – for example, creative destruction and spillover. The fourth is when the crisis leads to a change in the type of system with a new path-dependent trajectory different from the pre-crisis path.

System breakdown

The possibility of the breakdown of the system is ever present in analyses of crisis. It is this possibility that drives the analysis and the urgency of the search for preventative measures. The terms used to refer to system breakdown vary across the substantive fields of social science. They include catastrophe, disaster, meltdown, apocalypse, end of civilization and existential threat to the existence of a society or

state. Analyses of large-scale history find that civilizations end as well
as start (Chase-Dunn and Hall 1997; Diamond 2005). Environmental
analysts point to the possibility that burning fossil fuels is changing
the earth's atmosphere to such an extent that it will become uninhab-
itable for human beings (Urry 2011). The risks generated by modern
industry have potentially catastrophic effects (Beck 1992). The financial crisis, ensuing economic depression and rise of fascism produced
genocide and world war during the mid-twentieth century. The possibility of the breakdown of the economic and social system is real.

Self-correcting system

By contrast, many small crises do not become large ones or lead
to system breakdown. In many instances, small instabilities lead to
negative feedback loops which result in the self-correction of the
system and restoration of the previous equilibrium. This can be seen
in temporary bubbles in asset prices where the damage is confined
to a small group of investors (Perez 2002). The thesis of 'efficient
markets' entails a belief that there are automatic stabilizers in markets
which return markets to equilibrium through the mechanisms of self-
balancing supply and demand. In other theses markets only return
to equilibrium with appropriate regulation. For Keynes (1936)
and Minsky (2008 [1986]), state regulation is a necessary part of
the processes that generate a return to equilibrium in the economic
and social system. The absence of such regulation would mean the
system moving far from equilibrium. Similarly, Engelen et al. (2011)
conclude that the 2007 crisis in the UK was a result of 'elite complacence', in that while finance could have been regulated there was
a failure to do so. The notion that systems ultimately self-correct
and return to equilibrium can be applied not only to specific economic markets but also to the wider social system. Polanyi (1957)
offers an account of the problems of excessive commoditization. He
argues that civil society is likely to rise up in actions to achieve the
re-embedding of the economy in society. In this account, the equilibrium which has been temporarily disturbed through treating money,
land and labour as commodities can be restored by civil society successfully acting to prevent catastrophe.

Renewal of the system

Crises can drive the system forward to something different though
still recognizably the same. For Schumpeter (1954), crises in the

capitalist economy are occasions for renewal – they are 'creative destruction'. The downturn of the economic crises is the time when old, poorly performing industries are destroyed to open up the field for the emergence of new industries. This is a time of restructuring in which old industries are replaced by new industries with more sophisticated technologies and better forms of internal organization. Thus the post-crisis economy is likely to be more effective than the pre-crisis economy. The crisis has an effect on the wider economic structure, meaning there is no simple return to the earlier situation. For Haas (1958), political and economic crisis was the mechanism that would drive Europe forward to the ever closer union that was needed to prevent it from destroying itself through war. Crisis for Haas was a necessary part of the process of the repeated readjustment of political institutions to produce this change.

Transition to a new type of system

Crisis could be a tipping point or critical turning point to a new type of system. The concept of revolution grasps this notion. There is a short period in which actions have particular importance in creating changes that forever recast the nature of the system. The classic accounts are of the French Revolution and the Marxist account of the prospect of a socialist revolution. Accounts of revolution include the significance of events in a short space of time and also of the underlying systems that have become unstable (Goldstone 1991). Other accounts of critical turning points use the language of 'historic compromise' and 'settlement' rather than revolution, but nonetheless contain the large historical scale. An example is found in the historic compromise reached by capital and labour which led to the development of social democracy in Sweden in the 1930s (Korpi 1983). Hence in those years, the trajectory of northern Europe was social democratic while that of central and southern Europe was fascist. There was speculation in Europe in the early twenty-first century as to whether the financial crisis would be a critical turning point away from neoliberalism to social democracy (Crouch 2011). This was possible but did not occur.

Conclusions

Social crises are both real and socially constructed. There are real crises, the meaning of which is constructed through discourse and narrative during which power confronts knowledge. The struggle to become hegemonic is conducted through discourse and narrative and is fuelled by variations in a multiplicity of forms of power. In times of crisis the range of meanings under consideration opens up, only to narrow again as social relations take new forms of institutionalization.

Crises share general features that are common across many domains. Developing a shared vocabulary by drawing on developments in complexity science, especially as it pertains to systems, is productive of the transfer of insight and analysis between different domains.

A crisis is a moment when there is the possibility of large-scale change consequent upon a small event in a narrow window of time. The lack of proportionality between cause and consequence is inherent to the definition of crisis.

Crises differ in their consequences. There are four main types: the crisis leads to system breakdown; after the crisis there is a return to pre-crisis conditions; the crisis drives the renewal of the system along its existing path of development; or the crisis leads to a new type of system.

System breakdown, meaning catastrophe or disaster, is the threat that lurks behind the concept of crisis. The nature and severity of such a potential breakdown are debated in different domains. Environmentalists fear the end of conditions suitable for human habitation on the planet. The European nightmare is that a financial crisis will once again lead to economic recession and depression which will generate fascism, genocide and war.

A return to pre-crisis conditions after a period of instability is an alternative vision. In this scenario, the crisis is momentary and does not lead to serious long-term damage. After recession and austerity there might be renewed economic growth. The neoliberal model was resilient to change by the crisis, despite expectations that it would be replaced by social democracy.

Crisis can lead to renewal of the system. The temporary destabilization of systems leads to their reconfiguration in a more effective manner. The European dream is that economic and political crisis can drive forward political integration to prevent war and genocide from ever happening again in Europe, by reducing the significance of political nationalism.

Crisis can lead to a change in the type of the system. It might provoke a break in the existing trajectory of development and the creation of a new, path-dependent trajectory of development. The result might be a different model of capitalism or gender regime.

3

Financial Crisis

Introduction

Finance caused the crisis. More precisely, the failure of the state to regulate finance caused the crisis. Finance is intrinsically unstable; but this can be mitigated. The reduction in democratic control over finance led to the financial crisis.

Following the Great Crash of 1929, finance had been regulated so as to reduce its propensity to cause instability and crises in the real economy. The removal of this regulation was part of a wider project of deregulation increasingly institutionalized in governmental programmes since the 1980s. In order to explain the financial crisis, it is necessary to examine not only finance itself but also this wider set of institutions in society with which finance intersects.

The chapter starts with accounts of financial crises, focused on 1929 and 2007, of finance and of financialization in order to inform the subsequent theoretical analysis. Next it addresses the conceptualization and theorization of finance and its relations with society. There are four competing frameworks, drawing on Hayek, Marx, Keynes and Polanyi. These frameworks explicitly or implicitly address five issues: the conceptualization of finance as an object or social relationship; the relationship between finance and the economy; the relationship between finance and the state; the relationship between finance and society; and the nature of the social system as a whole. A new approach to the analysis of finance and society is developed that draws on the critical discussion of these four frameworks in relation to these five issues. The gendering of finance is introduced, since this significantly shapes the practices involved. Finally, the chapter discusses the nature and potential of democratic regulation to mitigate the extent to which finance generates crises. This discussion of the potential of democratic regulation continues throughout the book and is concluded in chapter 6 on political and democratic crisis.

Financial Crisis, Finance and Financialization
Financial crisis

Financial crisis can be the start of a series of crises that is cascading from finance to the real economy, to a fiscal crisis focused on government budget deficits, to political crises and potentially to democratic and systemic crises. Here, the financial crisis is separated as a distinct phase in this cascade.

Financial crises are one among several forms of instability that are generated by finance. These forms of instability include business cycles and bubbles as well as larger-scale crises. Smaller forms of instability have been analysed as 'business cycles'. In a 'credit crunch' banks cease to perform their usual function of lending money. In a 'bubble' asset prices rise and fall, which benefits those who invest during the upswing (the insiders) and disadvantages others (often outsiders) (Perez 2002).

Crises are moments of sudden redistribution of value as finance is restructured; the losses being borne unevenly. Financial crises often lead to recessions in the 'real' economy and to unemployment. This instability of capitalism is conceptualized by Schumpeter (1954) as 'creative destruction' through which old industries are destroyed when new, more productive forms are developed. Crises can be critical turning points to a different kind of society. Rather than the crisis being followed by a return to business as usual (Crouch 2011), it may be more profound (Robinson and Barrera 2012); indeed crises often provide opportunities for restructuring social and economic institutions (Klein 2007). Financial crisis has been seen as a sign of the exhaustion of a regime of capital accumulation, heralding a shift in the capitalist hegemon (Arrighi 1994), or even the end of capitalism (Hilferding 1981 [1910]; Harvey 2011).

Crash of 1929 The Great Crash of 1929 is the reference point against which the current crisis has often been compared. This collapse in banking and financial institutions followed the bursting of a large bubble in asset prices (Galbraith 1975 [1954]). The Great Crash was followed by the Great Depression of the 1930s. Europe then fractured to follow two very different paths of development.

In central and southern Europe, centred on Germany, the recession precipitated the emergence of fascism, extreme nationalism, holocaust and war. Only by war was the fascist path of central and southern Europe defeated. In northern Europe, including Sweden, by contrast, the 1930s was the moment of class compromise between capital and labour and the establishment of social democracy in governmental programmes which, over time, became consolidated in a social democratic social formation, albeit subject to some erosion of its distinctiveness in recent years.

The institutionalization of some aspects of the social democratic project in governmental programmes was the eventual outcome of the response to this crisis: the restructuring of the international financial architecture at the Bretton Woods conference in 1944; Roosevelt's New Deal in the late 1930s US; in Europe, the achievement of full adult suffrage for women, and the creation of the welfare state. These new programmes included the regulation of finance by states in an attempt to contain the power of finance and its propensity to generate instability. In the US, retail and casino banking were separated and banks were prevented from growing in size by restrictions concerning state boundaries. States asserted their power to regulate flows of capital across their borders. Thirty 'golden years' of economic growth and stability followed; until the regulations on finance were removed from the 1980s onwards (Stiglitz 2006; Krugman 2008).

Europe and North America tend to treat the Great Crash of 1929 as the most important reference point for the current major crisis. However, there have been regional financial crises elsewhere in the world with effects on an equivalent scale for the countries concerned. There have been many regional financial crises in both Latin America, leading to the default by government on its debts in Argentina, and East Asia during the 1990s (Stiglitz 2002).

The conclusion to draw here is that even a major financial crisis is not so exceptional. Everyone should expect to witness at least one in a lifetime. There is a common refrain during the build-up to a crisis that 'this time is different' (Reinhart and Rogoff 2009); yet the odds are that it is not.

Crash of 2007/8 What happened during the events of the Great Crash of 2007/8? The focus here is on banks and financial institutions, with the late arrival of the state onto the scene. The over-extension of banking and finance became visible in the US during the crisis in 'subprime' housing finance in 2006. Defaults on unaffordable mortgages led not only to a downward spiral in housing prices, but to failures in a wider set of financial institutions that had become involved in housing finance through new ways of selling debt and risk. While precipitated by the rise in interest rates and in oil prices (Cortright 2008), the fall in house prices had devastating consequences because of the new vulnerability of the financial system to systemic failure, resulting from new financial products and reduced regulation of organizational practices.

In Europe, a sign of what was then called a 'credit crunch' was in August 2007, when the French bank BNP Paribas stopped investors taking money out of two of its funds. In the UK, the first publicly visible sign of the financial crisis was in September 2007, when a run on Northern Rock, a housing bank (formerly a 'building society' and not long demutualized), involved people queuing around the block to withdraw their money because they thought the bank was going to collapse and their funds would be lost. It was the first run on a British bank for 150 years.

In the UK, in an effort to quell the panic, the government stepped in with funds that effectively nationalized the bank in autumn 2007. In the US, bank after major bank announced losses that threatened their survival – Citigroup October 2007, Merrill Lynch October 2007, Bear Stearns March 2008, Fannie Mae and Freddie Mac September 2008 – and they were variously taken over or bailed out by the government.

In the US on 15 September 2008, Lehman Brothers announced their potential bankruptcy; but this time no bank or government came to their rescue. The collapse of Lehman Brothers turned a crisis into a catastrophe. Default on its debts triggered the collapse of other financial institutions which, in turn, triggered the collapse of still more in a domino effect. The effect was magnified into a systemic failure as the banks stopped lending to each other, not knowing which would be the next to fail.

The US Treasury proposed to rescue the failing financial institutions with $700bn of taxpayers' money. But on 29 September 2008 the plan, which lacked detail on what would happen to these funds, was rejected by the US House of Representatives (Senate). In response, the Dow Jones, which indicates the price of shares on the Wall Street stock exchange, dropped by 7 per cent – its largest one-day fall. On 3 October 2008, the US Senate agreed the transfer of federal funds to financial institutions.

In quick succession other governments agreed to bailouts of their banks. The UK government increased its guarantee to private investors against bank default to £50,000 on 3 October; the German government provided £38.7 billion to save one of Germany's biggest banks, Hypo Real Estate, on 6 October; and the Icelandic government provided the funds to take control of the country's second largest bank, Landsbanki (which owned Icesave in the UK), on 7 October 2008. Over the next few months, governments provided substantial funds to save the financial institutions in their countries from collapse.

In the EU, 13 per cent of EU GDP (€1.6 trillion) was provided by national authorities to banks between October 2008 and 31 December 2011 to address the financial crisis; largely for liquidity support and measures to support bank solvency. The UK accounted for a larger proportion of these funds (19 per cent) than any other single EU Member State (European Commission 2012b). Public finances across the EU deteriorated by 20 per cent of GDP as a result of these contributions and the reduced economic activity resulting from the financial crisis (European Commission 2013d: 2).

The financial crisis caused a recession in the 'real' economy. While the financial crisis originated in the US, UK and linked northern economies, the effects on the real economy rippled around the world. Companies went bankrupt as banks refused to extend loans and debts during the 'credit crunch'. The value of 'assets' such as property and shares fell, which reduced the ability of companies, households and individuals to borrow. The process of de-leveraging, as banks reduced the proportion of loans assured by their capital, led to even tighter conditions on credit.

In order to understand the cause of the financial crisis, it is necessary to consider in more depth the theorization of the relationship between finance and society, starting with consideration of the concept of finance.

What is finance?

The definition of finance is contested. One issue concerns whether finance, or money, is an object or a set of social relations. A second concerns the range of activities included within finance which itself is linked to the conceptualization of financialization and financial crisis. The more narrowly finance is defined, the less significant it appears to be for society; the more widely it is defined, the more important.

Is finance, or money, an object or a social relationship? The conventional understanding of money is as a thing, object or commodity; an alternative approach treats money as a social relationship. The traditional approach to finance considers that financial activities distribute capital to places where it can be used most effectively (Krippner 2011). This is the application of 'efficient markets' theory to finance (Friedman 2002 [1962]). Banks take deposits from savers and make loans as investments in firms. The banks lend more than they receive and the ratio of bank capital to loans constitutes the leverage which contributes to their profits. In conventional theory, finance companies redistribute risk through insurance to those places where it can be borne with greatest resilience.

The alternative approach to the nature of money is to understand it as a social relationship rather than as a thing. In this view, money is a promise to pay (as, for example, is stated on bank notes); a claim rather than an object. Money connects the present to the future through such a claim (Keynes 1936; Mellor 2010; Minsky 2008 [1986]). When money is understood as a social relationship, then the assumption of efficient markets is rejected and replaced by one that acknowledges an ecology of unstable institutionalized competition. Ingham (2001, 2004) develops this theme, locating the social relations of money/finance at the centre of the power struggles in modern capitalism. The key social relations are between those who produce money, institutions such as banks and ministries of finance, and those who produce commodities, goods, capital and labour. There is a tension between the producers of money and the producers of goods as each manoeuvres for advantage in the possession of value. At stake is not only the distribution of value, but also the stability of the financial system, which is vulnerable during this contest.

> Agents attempt to monetize their market power either by bidding up prices in money of account or by the expansion of value through borrowing and the creation of money.... This trade off and tension between the expansion of value through the elasticity of supply of credit-money ... and the breakdown of monetary stability is arguably the central dynamic of the modern capitalist system. (Ingham 2001: 318–19)

The conceptualization of money as a social relationship enables a more effective analysis of the relations between finance and society than the conceptualization of money as an object; it includes relevant institutions and dynamics while the latter draws on misleading abstracted fictions of perfect markets.

From one angle, finance is a sector of the economy, generating employment, GDP and taxes. Within the UK Standard Industrial Classification system, the finance industry, Section K (SIC 64–66), is made up of monetary intermediation (banks), holding companies, trusts and funds, credit, insurance and pensions (earlier classifications had previously included real estate) (ONS 2007). Its profits are dispersed as dividends, salaries and bonuses. From another angle, finance is a form of capital, a social relationship centred on profit-taking and capital accumulation (Krippner 2005; Arrighi 1994).

The range of activities that are included within the concept of finance has been expanding, encompassing both new techniques and new organizational practices. Financial activities potentially include: trade and speculation in currency, assets and risk, including 'futures'; tax avoidance and evasion entangled with financial instruments; corporate financialization; and the financialization of the personal and social life risks of everyday life. There are new forms of organization including 'shadow banking' that is 'offshore' and thereby outside the traditionally regulated institutions. The processes of financialization and financial crisis link finance and society. 'Financialization' refers to the increased significance of finance in the economy and society in both scale and depth. 'Financial crises' are forms of instability generated by finance that have wider consequences for economy and society, such as recession.

Finance involves the manipulation and flow of money and the risks associated with it. Finance is linked to the economy, but is distinctive, since it concerns money rather than the production, circulation and consumption of objects. These flows of money can be for investment and for speculation, involving social relations of credit and debt; there are also flows of money from individuals and corporations to states in the form of taxation. Some form of finance is common in advanced economies, but its extent and nature are very varied. The range and scale of the financial products traded increased in the period before the 2007 crash, with new developments in derivatives, futures markets, CDOs, credit default swaps and securitization in attempts to price and sell 'risk' (Epstein 2005; Krippner 2011; Krugman 2008; MacKenzie 2006). Finance grew larger than the productive part of the economy in some countries before the crash; in the UK, 'debt' rose to around five times the size of GDP in 2007 (Turner 2009: 18). These new technical and related organizational developments are outlined in what follows.

Banks and other forms of financial institutions found new ways to increase profits. Banking is historically based on the practice of lending out more money than has been taken in deposits, since not all people want their money back at the same time. This difference between sums deposited and lent, the capital ratio, enables the bank to gain 'leverage'. Banks make significant profits from this leverage, not only from the gap in interest rates between those paid to depositors and those charged to borrowers. Banks and new finance companies developed new financial instruments to increase the capital ratio, in ways that were not limited by banking regulations. By making its (deposited) capital 'work harder', at a higher 'leverage', the banks increased their profits. The growth of new institutional forms outside of banking regulations is known as 'shadow banking' and 'offshoring'. There was a significant increase in financial transactions that were 'off balance sheet' in this way from the mid-1980s onwards, with most growth from the late 1990s (Akerlof and Romer 1994; Epstein 2005; Krippner 2005; Krugman 2008; MacKenzie 2006; Urry 2014).

Finance involves exchange and trading using financial instruments, the more complex forms of which are known as financial derivatives. The trading of 'risk' that involves complex calculations as to what might happen in the future has been developed using new forms of financial derivatives. This involves practices of securitization, collateralized debt obligations and credit default swaps. An old-fashioned example of a trade in risk might be that of a farmer who sells their total harvest in advance to a merchant, whatever the quality of the produce at the actual date of transfer of the commodity from farmer to merchant. The advantage to the farmer is that they will get a fixed price for the harvest, even if there are storms on harvest day that reduce the crop. This is risky for the merchant, who may get a better or worse commodity than anticipated. In exchange for accepting this risk, the merchant may expect to get a better price from the farmer. Thus the farmer has 'sold' the 'risk' to the merchant for a price. A more sophisticated example is when a trader buys an option to purchase a commodity on a certain day at a certain price. On the day concerned, the trader may make a profit or a loss, according to whether the price has risen or fallen in the meanwhile. This market in 'options' is again a market in 'risk'. A more convoluted example is that of 'short selling', when a trader pays a fee to the owner of shares to 'borrow' them; then sells them on and buys them back again before returning them to their owner. The profit or loss depends on the calculation of the risk of the prices of the shares going up or down during the period in which they are borrowed, and it is this 'risk' that is being traded for a fee (Cooper 2008; Ferguson 2008; Fleckenstein with Sheehan 2008; Haseler 2008; Krugman 2008; Morris 2008; Shiller 2008).

The increasing financialization of housing is an important example of the development of these new financial instruments. Early building societies and housing banks in the UK and US simply took in deposits and lent out loans for house purchase. There was some risk in this process, in that not all borrowers would be able to keep paying back their loans, for instance due to disintegration of the household finances through divorce or unemployment, and would default on their loans. The new financial instruments, developed first in the US, bundled up these risks to sell on to others, thereby ostensibly spreading the risk. They did so by collecting together many mortgages that had an income stream from mortgage repayments together with a specific risk of default, then dividing them into tranches of mortgages that had different levels of risk attached, and selling these at different prices, according to their level of risk. The bottom 'junior' level had the highest level of risk and produced the most short-term profit on the sale of the risk; the highest 'senior' level had the lowest risk and the least profit on the sale of risk. There was a further level, 'super-senior' that bore any remaining risk. This was often retained by the originating financial institution, since there was little risk to sell and thereby little profit to make by selling it on. This process of bundling up loans that had income streams and risks, re-dividing them and selling them on, is known as 'securitization'. While the example here is of housing loans, it was a process that was applied to many other forms of loans, from car purchase to corporate debt. These were also referred to as collateralized debt obligations (CDOs), which used the creation of a special-purpose company or vehicle, with assets and liabilities, with which to transfer risk between financial institutions. A related device was that of 'credit default swaps'. In this case different institutions that had complementary needs and attributes would have a specific arrangement made that involved pricing and selling risk. These were tailor-made for these institutions so in the first instance were not traded on the open market, although later on they could be sold on. These were not held on the books of banks and finance houses, though these institutions took significant fees for arranging them. These financial derivatives were part of the growth of the 'shadow banking system' (Picone 2002; Cooper 2008; Ferguson 2008; Fleckenstein with Sheehan 2008; Haseler 2008; Krugman 2008; Morris 2008; Shiller 2008).

In 2007, while the total assets of the top five US banks were around $6 trillion, those of the five major 'investment' banks were around $4 trillion and the hedge funds' just under $2 trillion (Krugman 2008). The new financial derivatives included synthetic securitizations or CDOs and credit default swaps. From the 1990s until the crash of 2007–9, there was a rapid increase in the scale of this market. In 1990 the size of the CDO market was estimated at \$2.2bn, rising to \$250bn in 2002, of which 75 per cent was estimated to be the new synthetic CDOs (Tavakoli 2003), rising by a further \$600bn in 2007 (Treanor 2008). By 2007 the combined size of asset-backed commercial paper conduits in structured investment vehicles, auction-rate preferred securities, tender option bonds and variable rate demand notes in the US was around \$2.2 trillion (Krugman 2008). Perez (2009: 798), using data from the International Swaps and Derivatives Association, found that \$382 trillion was outstanding in interest rate and currency derivatives in 2007, which is seven times the size of the world GDP of \$54 trillion in that year, noting that there were in addition \$72 trillion in credit default swaps or equity swaps. It is the extraordinary scale and interconnectedness of these new forms of financial instruments that are key to the current fragility of the financial system, since they have systemic effects, but are not governed with this systemic level in mind.

The most important part of the changes that facilitated the development of these new forms of financial instruments was contributed by the political process of deregulation. The relative absence of regulations on the financial sector was part of the neoliberal orthodoxy (Greenspan 2008). There was a belief in market fundamentalism and that economic systems were self-equilibrating (Soros 2008). The financial institutions and financial elites developed both secrecy about their developments (even senior bank executives did not fully understand the new derivatives and the risks they carried) and effective lobbying practices (Tett 2009). Controls over capital and banks that had been created after the crash of 1929 were dismantled, especially during the rise of neoliberalism in the mid-1980s in the US and UK, while new forms of financial instruments developed outside of even the remaining regulations (Krugman 2008).

Tax is not conventionally regarded as part of finance. However, it should be, since the development of complex financial arrangements to avoid, evade or dodge tax is a significant part of contemporary financial activity. This activity involves the use of tax havens (secrecy jurisdictions) as well as the movement of funds between different tax regimes to take advantage of lower rates of taxation. Finance companies advise clients, including rich individuals and large firms, on how best to avoid taxation through complex routing of financial transactions across state borders so as to take advantage of differences between tax regimes, known as 'tax arbitrage'. Tax avoidance is legal and evasion is not, though the location of the boundary is often disputed. Finance companies not only search for loopholes in the law to provide tax-dodging services to rich clients but also lobby governments to ensure that such legal opportunities exist (Palan et al. 2010; Shaxson 2011).

The sums of money lost to the public by the failure to collect the taxes democratically mandated by government are significant. Even according to the UK HM Revenue and Customs' own estimate, 'the tax gap stood at £35 billion (7.9% of all the tax due) in 2009–10'. However, according to the UK Public Accounts Select Committee, 'other estimates suggest the figure is much greater', since the estimate of HM Revenue and Customs does not include the funds lost to the Exchequer through aggressive tax-avoidance schemes (House of Commons Public Accounts Committee 2012b). Tax dodging is gendered, since more taxes are paid by men than women while women are disproportionately beneficiaries of public expenditure (Browne 2011; De Henau and Santos 2011) (see chapter 5 on austerity for further discussion). The development of tax-dodging devices by finance companies challenges the democratic will expressed in state policy and increases social inequalities.

Finance capital is often considered to be different from the industrial capital fixed in buildings and machines. However, this analytic distinction has become blurred in practice as finance has penetrated and increasingly dominated industrial capital. The rise of 'shareholder value' has increased the extent to which competition between firms to make profits occurs on finance and capital markets rather than in more productive activities (Lazonick and O'Sullivan 2000). This increases the incentive to financialize assets and to drive down the position of suppliers and workers (Baud and Durand 2012). Aglietta (2000b: 148) argues that 'Shareholder value helps to legitimize the predominance of shareholders over other stakeholders, and the predominance of a capital market view of the firm over an industrial one.' This new finance-led approach to company ownership shifts the focus to realizing value through buying, restructuring and selling companies rather than through long-term investment and incremental improvement of a specific company (Clark 2009). These processes increase the proportion of profits derived from financial rather than industrial activities while blurring the boundary between industrial and financial capital (Krippner 2011). The extension of the priorities of finance in mixed assemblages of financial and fixed capital can be at the expense of the quality of the service provided by the firm. For example, movement of funds following financial priorities contributed to the bankruptcy of the Southern Cross care-home company. The bankruptcy led to vulnerable elderly residents losing their homes in residential care centres, to the detriment of their well-being, and then required emergency support from the state (House of Commons Public Accounts Committee 2012a).

The process of financialization has extended beyond the conventional arenas of banks, finance houses and commercial companies. The sphere of finance is extended by the financialization of everyday life (Martin 2002). Individual (consumer or household) investment products claim to redistribute money across the life-course from times when most income is most earned to those when it is least earned and most needed. This includes mortgages to access housing (Montgomerie and Young 2010), pensions to access income in old age (Blackburn 2002), credit cards and other forms of consumer debt (Lawson 2009; Lapavitsas 2011). When the definition of finance is extended to include individual consumer products then many more individuals are seen to be incorporated into the web of financial interests.

These 'consumer' financial products are uneven in their gender, ethnic and class effects. For example, women typically have access to loans under worse conditions than men. These conditions mean women are more vulnerable to acquiring debts which they have difficulty in repaying. During the build-up of the subprime housing crisis in the US, the loans with the most onerous conditions, such as highest rates of interest, were disproportionately sold to women and minority ethnic groups. Consequently, people in these categories disproportionately lost their homes when the Great Crash happened and the mortgages on their homes were foreclosed (Fishbein and Woodall 2006).

Financialization has grown in scale and importance for the dynamics of both economy and society. Financialization is more than marketization. Financialization involves intrinsically risky speculative investment in assets. The range of things that are treated as assets has been significantly increased beyond the traditional ones of shares and commercial property to mortgages on homes, pensions and student debts. The range of people engaged in these risky activities has significantly increased beyond specialist financiers to most businesses and to the majority of citizens. The range of activities in which finance companies are involved has extended beyond investment to include tax dodging through moving finance via the proliferation of legal identities behind companies and across state borders. The implications of finance for other economic and social institutions and practices have become increasingly significant.

Developing the Framework to Analyse Finance and Society

The most significant differences in the frameworks of analysis of finance are those between orthodox economic and heterodox frameworks. There is a further division in approaches within the heterodox framework between those that draw on Marx, on Keynes and Minsky, and on Polanyi. As noted earlier, the frameworks differ along five major dimensions: whether finance is conceptualized as an object or a social relationship; whether finance is seen as neutral in its effects on the economy; whether the state can effectively regulate finance; whether civil society and other aspects of society are significant; and whether the social system of which finance is part is assumed to return to equilibrium (Walby 2013a).

The orthodox framework draws on the heritage of Adam Smith (1986 [1776]), Hayek (2001 [1944]) and Friedman (2002 [1962]). Money is conceptualized as an object rather than as a social relationship. Finance (as money and investment) is either invisible or treated as neutral, with the implication that it is not important in shaping the economy. Money is treated as if it can and should be transparent, as if it has no impact on the rest of the economy, or society; the functioning of finance reflects the rest of the economy. Money is a superficial cover or veil over the processes that really matter and should be ignored in order to understand the economy properly. The important processes in the economy are the production of goods and their exchange. For example, Friedman, despite being known as a 'monetarist', thought money should be treated as passive in the economy: 'the central characteristic of the market technique of achieving coordination is fully displayed in the simple exchange economy that contains neither enterprises nor money' (Friedman 2002 [1962]: 14).

The notion that finance has no independently significant effects on the economy further rests on the thesis that the price mechanism and markets are efficient and effective, leading to the exchange of goods at their value. It is assumed that markets in finance neutrally distribute capital in a rational and efficient way to where it is most productive and profitable. Markets are considered self-equilibrating. Indeed, for Friedman, since finance flows through free markets, which are self-regulating, there is no need or good purpose served by state intervention: political freedom is considered to follow economic freedom.

The development of the neoliberal thinking (Hayek 1945, 1948, 2001 [1944]; Friedman 2002 [1962]) that today dominates orthodox financial and economic governance is, however, internally riddled with intellectual as well as practical contradictions. Hayek (1945) celebrated the price mechanism as a 'marvel' in that it communicated information effectively even in the absence of perfect knowledge. However, Hayek (1948: 110) also noted that the state was necessary in order to enforce the legal framework that made competition possible. The neoliberals (such as Hayek and Friedman), in contrast to the earlier laissez-faire liberals of the nineteenth century (such as Mill), understood that the market needed the state in order to function (Peck 2010; Jones 2012). This results in an intellectually incoherent position on the state: the state is both not necessary for the functioning of the economy (since the price mechanism and markets perform the essential coordination) and at the same time necessary for markets (in order to secure the legal framework that is necessary for the institution of property). The neoliberal rhetoric focuses on freedom for markets from the state; their practice is to use the state to promote markets (Gane 2014a, 2014b).

The models of analysis used within the orthodox framework today are usually abstract, highly mathematized, and based on the assumption that economic systems return to equilibrium. Sophisticated statistical models were developed using evidence from relatively short-run data sets and were then used to make predictions about future developments. These models underpinned the development of financial derivatives and other products that were sold in the expectation that they would distribute risk effectively. These financial products generated enormous profits in the short run; but the models were severely flawed for the longer term. One of the problems of the models was that that the data used to support them only included the proximate years when there had been stable growth and did not go back far enough in time to encompass previous periods of crisis. Another problem was that a focus on the risk for each individual firm was insufficient to grasp the implications of the risks for the financial system as a whole (MacKenzie 2006; Haldane and May 2011; Soros 2008). A further difficulty was the tendency towards 'herding' in markets, in which many traders follow leaders rather than using their individual judgement (Keynes 1936; Pitluck 2014).

Finance was missing from many mainstream social scientific accounts of the economy. An assumption of the neutrality of finance is more common than explicit argument for its lack of effect. The lack of significance of finance is implicit in the work of many sociological writers on capitalism and modern society (e.g. Giddens 1984), in which analysis of the economy is centred on employment, in articulation with the welfare state and, occasionally, domestic care-work.

In summary, the orthodox framework conceptualizes money as an object rather than a social relationship; treats finance as superficial and unimportant; considers that finance self-balances through markets without state intervention; assumes freedom in society is more likely when the state does not interfere; and assumes the economic system as a whole is self-regulating and equilibrating.

The different heterodox frameworks share a treatment of money as a social relationship (rather than as an object). This relationship is produced and embedded in social and economic institutions which exist in an ecology of institutions within a fitness landscape, or wider environment, riddled with power. These frameworks share the view that finance is intrinsically unstable. However, under certain circumstances, this instability may potentially be moderated by states and central banks. The ontology and analysis of the ecology of institutions vary between the different heterodox frameworks.

One such framework draws on Marx (1959 [1894]) to offer an analysis of finance within a theory of a capitalist system. Finance is a distinctive form of capital that seeks profit from investments and is thereby understood as a social relationship rather than as an object. For Marx, finance, or money capital, was one form of capital alongside industrial and commercial capital. Only industrial capital is productive of value and surplus value, since the value of commodities is determined by the amount of labour embedded in them. Changes in the mode (forces and relations) of production, in the regime of capital accumulation, drive wider changes in social formations. Capitalism is inherently unstable, with tendencies to produce more goods than the wages available to purchase them, producing regular crises of over-production of goods and services or under-consumption since workers do not have the money to buy them. These crises may escalate, getting larger and more significant and, in the long term, potentially lead to system failure. Instability in the economy is understood as an intrinsic feature of a capitalist system (Brenner 2006; Callinicos 2010; Foster and Magdoff 2009; Gamble 2009). This is a consequence of the difficulties in continuously maintaining capital accumulation. There are variations between writers within this framework as to the relationships between finance capital, industrial capital, the state and society.

The relations between finance and industrial capital have been debated. Hilferding (1981 [1910]) argued there is a tendency for finance capital to dominate industrial capital, as part of the process of development of monopoly capital and imperialist systems. For Bukharin (1972 [1915]) and Lenin (1934 [1917]), the development of financial capital was a stage of capitalism in which imperial rivalries threatened world war. Immiseration leads to political activity that leads towards revolutionary politics. The future they foresaw was a choice between barbarism and socialism. However, this moment could be endlessly deferred as a result of changes in production or in state repression.

A second heterodox approach is regulation theory, which draws on but develops the Marxist heritage, integrating the insights of Braudel (1992 [1979]) to locate the process of capital accumulation within a more complexly developed and nuanced theory of institutions in society (Aglietta 2000a [1976], 2008). Following Braudel, Aglietta distinguishes between the market paradigm, which concerns exchange between equals, and capitalism, which is a force of accumulation seeking monopoly to advance. Regulation theory situates finance as one of several institutions that make up a regime of capital accumulation. Variations in the form of state regulation of finance are sources of capitalism's historical variability. The central bank plays a particularly important role in (usually) ensuring financial stability. The relative importance of the regulation of finance varies; more recent writings (Aglietta 2000b; Boyer 2000) attach greater importance to finance as compared with the wage relation than the earlier work (Aglietta 2000a [1976]; Grahal and Teague 2000).

A related development is the work of Arrighi (1994), which draws on the insights of Braudel and world-systems theory (Wallerstein 2000) to go beyond Marx. Arrighi places more emphasis on the significance of states, especially hegemons, in the analysis of the relationships between finance capital, industrial capital and states. Financialization occurs when a regime of capital accumulation is exhausted; when no more profits are to be made using a particular combination of forces and relations of production, technology and social organization. For Arrighi, the next stage is not barbarism or socialism, but rather a new capitalist hegemon based upon a different regime of accumulation. In this account, financialization is a signal that the leadership of the global capitalist economy is about to change, with the exhaustion of the profitability of the old regime of accumulation.

In summary, the political economy framework conceptualizes finance as a social relationship rather than an object. The main driver of change is the regime of capital accumulation. Finance has implications for the economy and society and has varied relations with industrial capital, the state, war and society more broadly; there is no assumption of a system returning to equilibrium. The strength of the political economy framework derives from situating finance within the context of a wider social system, and its weakness from the extent to which forces other than capital, such as the state and civil society, are underestimated or neglected.

A third heterodox framework draws on Keynes and Minsky. It conceptualizes finance as a social relationship rather than an object. It treats finance as a component of the economy that is distinct from productive capital. Finance has destabilizing effects on the rest of the economy. These effects can be mitigated by the state. In this framework, money, or finance, has important effects on the economy. Keynes (1936) demonstrated the significance of money for the social and economic system in his general theory of employment, interest and money. Noting the significance of the balance between financial and industrial capital, Keynes argued that speculation had deleterious consequences for the economy if it became more important than productive capital:

> Speculators may do no harm as bubbles on a steady stream of enterprise. But the position is serious when enterprise becomes the bubble on a whirlpool of speculation. When the capital development of a country becomes a by-product of the activities of a casino, the job is likely to be ill-done. (Keynes 1936: 103)

Minsky (2008 [1986]) develops this argument, proposing that while finance is a necessary part of capitalism concerned with investment for profit it is intrinsically destabilizing rather than self-balancing. Minsky differentiates between three forms of investment and profit-taking: hedging, where income is sufficient to cover interest payments as well as profits; speculative, where income is only partly sufficient; and Ponzi, where there is little income and payments are only met by taking in new funds. The first practice appears consistent with stability, the second is less so, and the third not at all. In periods of relative tranquillity, investors take on greater amounts of risk which are decreasingly covered by their routine revenues and increasingly dependent upon the investment generating profits; that is, they move through the three models. A crisis occurs when this reaches a peak or tipping point. Investors then have to sell to meet their obligations but, since prices are falling, this creates a downward spiral. The degree of instability of the economy is a consequence of shifts in the balance between these three financial practices.

Finance entrepreneurs continually attempt to create new financial practices. They are constrained by the financial authorities of the state, such as central bankers and financial regulators, but during periods of relative tranquillity usually triumph (Minsky 2008 [1986]:

279). In simple commodity markets the self-interest of the producers and consumers might lead to market equilibrium; but this is not the case in relation to finance.

> In a world with capitalist finance it is simply not true that the pursuit by each unit of its own self-interest will lead an economy to equilibrium. The self-interest of bankers, levered investors, and investment producers can lead the economy to inflationary expansions and unemployment-creating contractions. Supply and demand analysis – in which market processes lead to an equilibrium – does not explain the behavior of a capitalist economy, for capitalist financial processes mean that the economy has endogenous destabilizing forces. Financial fragility, which is a prerequisite for financial instability, is, fundamentally, a result of internal market processes. (Minsky 2008 [1986]: 280)

Minsky draws on Keynes; but this is a different interpretation from that assimilated into mainstream neoclassical economics. Keynes understood the interconnectedness of socio-economic institutions and the mechanisms which mean that capitalism is not self-balancing. State intervention was needed to regulate the economy, to pump money into the economy to feed demand and prevent depression, to regulate flows of capital, and to develop the financial architecture to stabilize the international financial system. The assimilation of Keynes into mainstream economics was, however, partial and selective (Hutton 1986). Only those parts consistent with econometric modelling and its presumption that the system ultimately returns to equilibrium were included; the institutional architecture of finance that generates instability was left out of focus. So Keynes' work is simultaneously a major source of inspiration for the analysis of the relations between finance, economy and society and a hugely disputed intellectual heritage.

For Minsky, capitalism is an inherently unstable economic system when financial institutions develop to trade in capital assets. The larger the scale of capital assets, the more likely is the development of monopolistic practices. The larger the development of innovative financial practices, the greater is the potential for instability. Minsky considers that states can intervene and moderate this instability by Big Government and a Big Bank through, for example, counter-cyclical spending and dampening the development of financial practices. Minsky does not theorize the circumstances under which this might occur, since he does not embed his theory of finance within a comprehensive theory of society. Others who have discussed aspects of such circumstances include: Stiglitz (2002, 2006, 2010); Haldane

(2010); Haldane and May (2011); Krugman (2008); Ingham (2004); Soros (2008); and Heyes et al. (2012).

Stiglitz, former World Bank director and winner of the Nobel Prize for Economics, analysed nearly one hundred economic crises occurring in the preceding 25 years, including the regional financial crises in Latin America and South-East Asia and before the Great Crash of 2007/8 in Europe and North America. On the basis of his analysis, Stiglitz (2002: 99) declared: 'I believe that capital account liberalization was the single most important factor leading to the crisis.'

The macro-prudentialists at the Bank for International Settlements in Basel developed the analysis of the instability of finance in a manner consistent with Minsky. They have shown the way in which the focus of prudential regulation on the micro level of the firm is insufficient because the instability is emergent at the level of the financial system as a whole (Crockett 2000). Haldane, director of financial stability at the Bank of England, draws on insights from ecological applications of complexity theory to argue for revisions to the wider financial architecture. These revisions include the increased modularization of the system to contain the effects of problems in one part so they do not spread to the whole (Haldane 2010; Haldane and May 2011).

Keynes and Minsky inspired a school of analysis that treats finance as a social relationship, as a social system, and which demonstrates how it causes instability in the rest of the economy. Finance intrinsically generates instability rather than equilibrium in a capitalist economy; though this effect can be reduced by the state and central bank.

The fourth heterodox framework draws on Polanyi (1957) to place finance within a wider account of society. Polanyi addresses money as a social relationship rather than as an object. Changes in the social relations of money alter its relationship with economy and society. Polanyi's work includes an analysis of the state and civil society which serves to embed finance in a theory of society. He offers a wide-ranging historical sociological account of changes in commoditization, its effects on society, and the response of society to the effects of this commoditization.

Polanyi suggests that there is a tendency towards the commoditization of money (financialization), of land (environment, nature) and of labour (workers) in capitalism. However, money, land and labour are not really commodities, and treating them as such undermines their effective maintenance. This tendency to commoditization is inherently self-destructive because of the instabilities associated with the process. For example, labour needs continuous income in order not to starve to death, but economic recession might mean this income is not always available. Capitalism only survives because civil society acts to protect these 'fictitious commodities' from the full effects of commoditization. Society responds with support such as the provision of welfare. There is thus a 'double movement': on the one hand, the commoditization of money, land and labour leads towards their destruction; on the other hand, society responds so as to regulate markets in fictitious commodities in order to protect them. Capitalism would destroy itself unless restrained by 'society'. In this way, Polanyi adds civil society as well as the state to his theory of the relationship between economy and society.

Polanyi offers an account of financialization (the commoditization of money), crisis and social response within the same text. His book is a series of assertions and fragments of arguments that can be interpreted as weaving these elements into a theory of a social system. However, Polanyi's text is open to more than one reading. An alternative interpretation is that the text is too fragmented to constitute a social theory and is merely an account of contingent events in which, at a particular moment in history, forces in civil society responded to ensure state support for workers facing destitution as a consequence of capitalist development. If this latter reading is followed, then his work has few implications for social theory; however, it is not adopted here. Instead, Polanyi's text is interpreted as social theory which can challenge the tendencies to reductionism in traditional Marxism because it introduces the concept of civil society into a theory of economy and society (Burawoy 2003). In this way, Polanyi can be understood as providing a comprehensive social theory that integrates an account of the instability of the financial and economic system as well as responses to it into a theory of society.

However, a weakness of this interpretation derives from the assumption that the social system is self-equilibrating; that there is an automatic response by civil society when the processes of commodification of money, land and labour become too damaging. The instability of the financial system is assumed to be met by feedback to re-stabilize the system. This assumption of automatic response is unwarranted in the light of historical evidence (Burawoy 2010). Theories of social systems should not assume that they are self-equilibrating.

A New Approach to Finance and Society

As can be seen from this discussion, a model of the relations between finance and society needs to address five issues: the conceptualization of finance; whether finance is neutral or has significant effects on the economy; the relationship between finance and the state; the relationship between finance and society; and whether the social system of which finance is part is assumed to return to equilibrium or not. The four frameworks already discussed – orthodox, Marxist/political economy, Keynes/Minsky and Polanyi – differ in the way each of these issues is addressed. A new model of the relations between finance and society is constructed here. This model builds on the frameworks to put together the best answers to resolve each of the five issues.

Conceptualizing finance

Finance is better conceptualized as a social relationship, as a social system, than as an object. The orthodox framework treats finance as an object, but the other three address it as a social relationship. Treating finance as a social relationship means the inner dynamics of finance can be exposed for analysis. This is most effectively established in the work of Minsky, drawing on Keynes. Financialized relations have extended into an increasing number of economic practices, from everyday life to tax avoidance. It is useful to adopt a wider range of financial practices than did Minsky, who was writing several years ago, to grasp the significance of current processes of financialization for economy and society. The concept of financial crisis also needs to be conceptualized more broadly. It needs to go beyond banking crises to include economic recession and ensuing policies for economic restructuring so that it can adequately capture the effects of finance on society and multiple social inequalities.

Finance and the economy

Finance is best conceptualized as a distinctive part of the economy. The orthodox framework views finance as neutral in its effects on the economy as a consequence of treating money as an object and markets as inevitably efficient. The other three frameworks correctly treat the relationship between finance and the rest of the economy as dynamic. The political economy framework usually, though not always, treats industrial capital as dominant. Minsky offers a valuable way to understand the changing relations between financial and industrial capital as a consequence of shifts between three types of investment. The relations between financial and industrial capital are subject to tension and change rather than representing a fixed hierarchy.

Finance and the state

The relationship between finance and the state is best conceptualized as both important and contingent upon other forces. The state
is not irrelevant to the effective working of finance as suggested by
the orthodox framework. Instead, as Keynes and Minsky argue, the
state is central to whether finance has small or large destabilizing
effects on the rest of the economy. The political economy framework
tends to view capital as capturing the state for its own purposes, but
there is significant internal debate regarding the extent to which this
occurs in various circumstances. The 1944 Bretton Woods agreement shows that the regulation of finance is possible under some
circumstances.

Finance and society

The relationship between finance and society is best conceptualized as contingent on political forces. The significance of finance
for society depends upon the inter-relationship of all institutional
domains, including: economy; polity (including states); violence
(including war); and civil society. The orthodox framework assumes
finance has no effects on society unless there is interference by the
state. The Marxist/political economy and Keynes/Minsky frameworks assume there are indirect connections but leave them out
of focus. The significance of violence is rarely noted in theories of
finance, but is acknowledged to some extent in political economy
if there is consideration of state power over taxation and war. More
important, though, as Polanyi suggests, is the potential significance
of civil society as a site of democratic forces that might lead to state
regulation of finance.

Social system

Finance is part of a wider social system but this system is not self-
balancing. The assumption of an automatic return to equilibrium is a
problematic feature of both the orthodox and Polanyian frameworks.
Both assume economic and social systems are self-equilibrating in
that an external force perturbing the system will be met by a negative
feedback loop which returns the system to equilibrium. The newer
complexity approach to systems does not make this assumption of
necessary self-equilibration. Instead, internally or externally generated instabilities may lead to positive feedback loops which drive the

system further from equilibrium, and potentially lead to a tipping point with major systemic changes and new paths of development.

The Gendering of Finance

Finance is gendered in at least two aspects. The first is the gendered consequences of finance, financialization and financial crises. The second concerns the gendering of financial decision-making institutions in terms of their composition, projects and interests. Does gender inequality cause financial crisis as well as being a consequence of it? Would the financial crisis have been different if it had been Lehman Sisters rather than Lehman Brothers?

The gendered consequences of the crisis are broad and encompass the effects of the recession and economic restructuring. The consequences discussed in the current chapter are limited to those concerning finance; other gendered consequences are considered in later chapters. The gendered consequences of finance include the gendered consequences of the financialization of everyday life. There are few matters where women and men are openly and directly treated differently because they are women and men. However, the disproportionate numbers of women and men engaging in different kinds of activities leads to indirectly gendered effects. These effects include the disproportionate loss of wealth and increases in poverty and home-loss among women compared to men.

An example of the indirect gender effects of financialization during the financial crisis is found in the gender composition of those who lost their homes during the US subprime mortgage disaster. More onerous conditions, such as higher interest rates, were applied to those who were considered to have higher levels of risk due to, for example, low and erratic earned income. The latter tended to comprise women more than men and minority more than majority ethnic groups. When the bubble in house prices burst, as a consequence of increases in oil prices and general interest rates and the crisis in financial institutions, it was these groups who were disproportionately affected. They were more likely to become homeless as they were unable to meet the conditions of their loans, which led to foreclosure on their mortgages (Fishbein and Woodall 2006; Montgomerie and Young 2010).

This example shows that financialization of housing does not merely reflect already existing market inequalities in gendered income but actually exacerbates them. The financial cycle of boom to bust widens pre-existing market-based gender inequalities. Being a winner or loser in the restructuring of value during the financial cycle is therefore gendered.

The second, and larger, question is the extent to which the cause of the crisis was gendered as a consequence of the gendering of financial decision-making institutions. There are at least two aspects to this question: the gender composition of financial decision-making within firms, regulators and government; and the representation of gendered projects and interests within the relationship between states and finance.

The decision-makers in finance are disproportionately male. The gender imbalance in decision-making is not only found in private finance firms (McDowell 1997; van Staveren 2002) but extends to public bodies including central banks, regulators and governmental committees. There were no women heads of central banks and women comprised only 18 per cent of the central banks' board membership in the Member States of the EU28 in 2013. Among the three EU-level financial institutions, there were no women presidents; there were no women on the board of the European Central Bank, only 7 per cent on the board of the European Investment Bank and 14 per cent on the Board of the European Investment Fund (European Commission 2013a).

The effect of the gender composition of decision-makers on the nature of financial policies, practices and outcomes is mediated in several ways, including: cultural processes; group dynamics; and connections to gendered projects which envisage different kinds of economy and society.

All-male decision-making in private finance firms has been linked to poor and excessively risky decision-making as a consequence of both masculine culture and lack of diversity in group dynamics. Masculine culture and especially the male subculture in the 'City' are linked to a propensity towards high levels of risk-taking and short-term thinking (McDowell 1997). The lack of diversity leads to poor decision-making because it encourages 'group-think' and 'herding' rather than critical thinking (van Staveren 2002). In these ways, the masculine monoculture of finance was conducive to risky and pro-cyclical decisions that inflated bubbles and were careless if not reckless with regard to the consequences. Several studies suggest that increasing the diversity of boards by including women improves company performance (McKinsey & Co. 2007; Erhardt et al. 2003; Warth 2009; Carter and Wagner 2011; Thomson with Lloyd 2011).

Would it make a difference if women were taking these decisions? Would Lehman Sisters have been sufficiently less reckless about risk than Lehman Brothers to have made a difference to the financial crisis? Would the application of quotas of 40 per cent of each gender on corporate boards, as is the case in Norway (Hoel 2008; Storvik and Teigen 2010) and under discussion in the UK (Davies 2011; McKinsey & Co. 2007) and EU (European Commission 2012a; Armstrong and Walby 2012; Fagan et al. 2012), make a difference to the quality of financial decision-making? Can the use of quotas prevent exclusivity and essentialism (Childs et al. 2010; Dahlerup and Freidenvall 2005; Mansbridge 2005)? The answer to these questions depends at least in part on whether the boards of private finance companies are the location for making the key decisions as to financial risk and whether all achieve 40 per cent of women. If these are the most important sites, then changing the nature of the decision-making processes by including the talents of women could improve the quality of decisions.

However, if the most significant factor lies elsewhere, for example in the capacity and power of the state to regulate finance, then the gender composition of the boards of private finance companies is less important. If the most important decisions are made by states, in terms of what to allow finance to do, how financial organizations should be structured and the nature of the policy architecture, then the focus should be on states and their regulatory bodies.

Accordingly, if states are important then the question about the gender of decision-making does not disappear but is displaced to another location. The question becomes: by what gendered process is the composition of the boards of the regulatory committees and central banks determined? How are gendered projects and gendered interests represented in these processes? In short, the question of the gender composition of financial decision-making becomes transposed into the larger question of the gendered projects that are embedded in gendered governmental programmes of finance. This larger question is addressed in chapter 6, which focuses on democracy.

Regulating Finance

What would be involved in regulating finance to mitigate its inherent instability and tendency towards crisis and to prevent or reduce the cascading of the crisis into the real economy? There have been many proposals to reform policy related to finance, including

official policy statements and commissions led by: Turner, director
of the UK FSA (Turner 2009, 2010); Villers for the UK govern-
ment (Independent Commission on Banking 2011); the House of
Commons Public Accounts Committee (2012b); the UK Treasury
Select Committee in its report on issues of supervision and regu-
lation in the context of the banking crisis (House of Commons
Treasury Committee 2009); Crockett, general manager of the
Bank for International Settlements and chairman of the Financial
Stability Forum (Crockett 2000); Haldane, director of financial sta-
bility at the Bank of England (Haldane 2010; Haldane and May
2011); the European Commission (2011c); de Levoisière for the
EU Commission (de Larosière 2009); the G20 (G20 2009); the
World Bank (Buvinic 2009; Caprio et al. 2008); and Stiglitz for
the UN General Assembly (Stiglitz 2010). Four main types of proposed policy reforms are identified here:

- *regulate better*: better policing and implementation of existing rules
  to reduce evasion, avoidance and abuse (House of Commons
  Public Accounts Committee 2012b; House of Commons Treasury
  Committee 2009); greater transparency in financial transactions
  (G20 2012; OECD 2013); better and increased regulation of
  banking and financial markets (Independent Commission on
  Banking 2011; Krugman 2008; Stiglitz et al. 2010); a shift to
  macro-prudentialism in the governance of the financial architecture (Crockett 2000; Haldane 2010);
- *collect tax*: preventing tax avoidance and evasion by reforming the
  intersection of financial and taxation regimes (G20 2009, 2012;
  OECD 2013); introducing a tax on financial transactions, sometimes called the Tobin tax (Attac 2015; European Commission
  2011c);
- *de-financialize*: reducing the size of the financial sector relative to
  the 'real' economy (Krugman 2008);
- *deepen democracy*: increasing the democratic component of the governance of finance (Stiglitz 2009, 2010), including gender balance
  in decision-making on company boards and governmental oversight committees (Armstrong and Walby 2012).

Regulate better

There are four aspects to the better regulation of finance: better
policing and implementation of existing rules; greater transparency
to aid policing of rules; reform of banking and financial regulation;

and the introduction of greater 'macro-prudentialism' so the system is regulated as a whole.

There should be better policing to implement existing rules more effectively; the existing systems are too lax on crimes and acts of omission by the rich and powerful at the expense of the general public. Banking supervisors should identify banks at risk before they collapse; tax authorities should identify and prosecute tax evaders; and police specializing in fraud cases should catch and prosecute fraudsters. The relevant authorities (e.g. police and the criminal justice system; Serious Fraud Office; FSA; HM Revenue and Customs; central banks), already charged with the policing of criminal levels of fraudulent behaviour and with the supervision of banking, should do their jobs better (House of Commons Public Accounts Committee 2012a, 2012b; House of Commons Treasury Committee 2009). The development of better international standards of banking supervision, from the EU to the Bank of International Settlements at Basel, is required. The regulation of individual rogues depends upon enacting laws to make certain activities illegal or on establishing codes of practice to render practices illicit. The location of the boundary between legal and illegal activities varies over time and place and is determined variously by technical expertise, politics and power, as are the vigour and efficiency with which these rules are policed (Conley 2012; Dorn 2010; Engelen et al. 2011; Levi 2008 [1981], 2013 [1987]). Rules include those concerning: theft and fraud; banking and financial markets; corporate governance; tax evasion; and government budgets. Since the crisis, regulators have increasingly fined companies which provide inaccurate information to customers in the 'misselling' of pensions, insurance and mortgages. These penalties include sanctions against individuals for large-scale corporate accounting fraud, both pre- and post-crash, which have led to jail sentences and large fines (Accounting Degree 2014). There have been several enormous fines paid by finance companies as a consequence of their rule-breaking. The largest was a reported $13 billion paid by JPMorgan to settle a series of civil claims over its misselling of mortgages prior to the crash in October 2013 after it was pursued by the US Department of Justice (Wall Street Journal 2013a). Several other multi-billion-dollar fines have been issued and criminal probes conducted in the US against many of the major financial companies (Wall Street Journal 2013b). There have also been several multi-million-pound fines handed out by the Financial Conduct Authority in the UK for financial misconduct. These fines include £86 million in the first three months of 2014 and £474 million in 2013 for manipulation of the inter-bank Libor rate, misleading financial advice, market abuse and other forms of financial transgression (Financial Conduct Authority 2014a, 2014b).

There should be increased transparency in financial transactions. Financial systems should be restructured so they are sufficiently transparent to enable the relevant authorities to see infractions of the rules easily. Increasing transparency and eliminating secrecy (for example, the identity of the owners of bank accounts and companies) would enable authorities to identify tax dodging and money laundering as a necessary first step in addressing infractions of the rules. The plans of the Organisation for Economic Cooperation and Development (OECD) to increase transparency and reduce corruption should be supported and implemented. Financial transactions should be recorded and placed on balance sheets to limit the growth of shadow banking and the extent to which complex financial arrangements are placed outside the view of auditors and regulators (House of Commons Treasury Committee 2009; G20 2012; OECD 2013).

There should be better and intensified regulation of banking and financial markets.

The many proposals include: increasing the ratio of capital held to loans provided in the Basel regulations; quality of collateral; reducing the impact of individual bank failure on other financial institutions and the wider economy by procedures for resolution, such as making banks smaller, so no bank becomes 'too big to fail'; separating retail from investment (casino) banking to reduce risk to the public; and state guarantees for small accounts of individuals (Independent Commission on Banking 2011; Krugman 2008; Stiglitz et al. 2010). The more substantial of the proposed reforms, such as separating retail from casino banking, would have the potential to reduce the reach and significance of finance.

Proposals to improve regulation of financial markets include: slowing the volatility of speculation on stock markets by making it illegal to borrow (rather than buy) stocks in order to sell them short; determining which innovations in financial derivatives are allowed; requiring registration of exchanges of financial instruments to make them transparent and open to scrutiny; scrutiny by credit-rating agencies; regulating new financial products such as mortgages, pensions and credit cards (Blackburn 2002; Krippner 2011; Turner 2009); and reducing international trade imbalances (Wolf 2009, 2014).

Macro-prudential principles should be included alongside

micro-prudential forms of regulation of financial systems. Macro-level regulation is a priority since the financial crisis was caused by the systemic failure of the financial system rather than the failure of one big bank or even sector. Aggregate risk is not the same as adding up the individual risk of every firm; it has an emergent character. For example, diversification at the level of the firm does not necessarily mean that the sector as a whole has diversified. The latter requires a set of reforms including: modularization, so that failure in one firm or sector does not spread to the rest of the system (e.g. splitting retail from casino banking); anti- rather than pro-cyclical risk regulation, since the risk for the system as a whole is greatest at the top of a financial cycle, just at the time when the risk for individual firms appears low; and ensuring that the financial regulator is buffered from the pressures that encourage norm-following and risk-taking so that it can take the necessary precautions (Crockett 2000; Haldane 2010).

The macro-prudential approach has been developed by analysts at the Bank of International Settlements in Basel (Crockett 2000) and also at the Bank of England (Haldane 2010). It involves complexity-based understandings of finance as a system, such as the notion that changing the structure of the system through greater modularization would improve the stability of the system as a whole. There are different principles of engagement, from 'taxing' and 'regulation' to increasing the resilience of the system by increasing its modularity, robustness and incentive structure (Alessandri and Haldane 2009; Haldane and May 2011). The shift to macro-prudentialism is potentially a major change of approach. However, by 2013 it was more developed at the 'ideational' rather than the practical level (Baker 2013). Since the advent of the financial crisis some central bankers have challenged the simple 'efficient markets' thesis, but this is still less than a comprehensive shift. Thus, Tucker (2011: 3–4), the deputy governor of the Bank of England for financial stability, states that 'for financial stability' he encourages 'thinking of markets as inefficient, riddled with preferred habitats, imperfect arbitrage, regulatory arbitrage, herding, and inhabited by agents with less than idealised rationality'. This might appear to be refreshing thinking, but there is a caveat in that it applies only to financial markets: 'for monetary policy, in most circumstances a reasonable default assumption is that core markets are more or less efficient most of the time'. Macro-prudential regulation is built on a rejection of the notion that the market is self-equilibrating, and requires the support of the state. Meeting these challenging conditions depends on the wider social and political context.

Collect tax

The development of tax avoidance and evasion as an integral part of finance should be reversed. There should be changes to financial and taxation systems to reduce 'tax dodging' by rich individuals and companies. Increased transparency is part of this proposal since reducing the scope of secrecy jurisdictions (tax havens) reduces the capacity of the rich to hide from tax collectors. However, the extent of progress achieved through the current modest increases in transparency is debated. Full disclosure of financial information in individual accounts (rather than being limited to information about those already under criminal investigation) would be a larger step.

Even more significant would be measures to prevent the use of accounting devices which shift profits to countries with lower rates of taxation. Such measures include: changing company law so profits are taxed in the country where the business is done rather than where paperwork is electronically finalized; harmonizing tax regimes to reduce the scope for financial companies to engage in 'regime shopping' with its ensuing race to the bottom; and embedding fair taxation rather than tax avoidance as a principle of social responsibility for companies and a necessary condition for receipt of government contracts (G20 2012; OECD 2013; House of Commons Public Accounts Committee 2012b; Harris 2013; Shaxson 2011).

Effective regulation of finance requires rethinking the regulations concerning corporate governance as well as finance per se. Corporate governance and company law regulates: the conditions under which legal personhood can be attached to a collective entity such as a company; the limitation of liability for debts for registered companies; conditionality over (gendered) governance structure and composition; the extent to which a company active in one jurisdiction can be registered in a different one for purposes of company law or taxation, with consequent variations in the fragmentation or concentration of accountability; the extent to which 'private equity' can operate; the existence of takeovers of companies through leveraged buyouts; and the extent to which 'codes of practice' produced by trade bodies are voluntary or compulsory (Armstrong and Walby 2012; Clark 2009; Shaxson 2011). One reform would be to prevent leveraged buyouts by private equity. More important would be the reintegration of company governance so a company is registered, taxed and governed in the same location in which it does business, since this would prevent some of the worst excesses of tax dodging by finance companies. Financial and fiscal regulatory matters overlap significantly when it comes to collecting taxes. This overlap arises because one of the reasons for complex financial arrangements which cross national frontiers is to minimize payment of taxes by corporations and rich people. Tax evasion is illegal but most tax dodging appears to take the form of legal tax avoidance, which can be affected by measures to reduce tax havens and secrecy jurisdictions (Palan et al. 2010; Shaxson 2011). However, pressure to reduce tax avoidance and evasion through increasing cooperation, harmonization and transparency has had limited success (Genschel and Schwartz 2011; Dorn 2012), even though countries such as the UK have substantial control over many tax havens. This is because many havens occupy the curious status of being both British and not-British at the same time. Companies can thus choose to be either according to whichever works to their advantage in the particular circumstances (Shaxson 2011). This situation could be avoided by a reform to close tax havens and secrecy jurisdictions.

There should be a tax on financial transactions (Tobin tax). This would mean that finance contributes in the same way as all other industries to the provision of public infrastructure and collective well-being, as well as reducing the incentive to move funds merely in pursuit of tax advantages (Attac 2015). Most proposals have been for a very small rate of tax on financial transactions of one tenth of one percent (0.1 per cent) or one hundredth of one percent (0.01 per cent) of the value of the transaction. This rate is much lower than the value-added tax (VAT) collected on most non-financial transactions, which is around 20 per cent in many countries. The Directive proposed by the European Commission (2011c, 2013d, 2014) to establish a financial transaction tax in the EU is discussed in chapter 6.

De-financialize

De-financialization is necessary to reduce the scale and power of finance to a level consistent with human well-being. Not only are some banks still currently 'too big to fail', but the finance system itself is becoming 'too big to save' (Sassen 2009). Some individual banks have financial liabilities greater than the entire annual GDP of the UK economy; collectively, the finance system is several times larger than the 'real' economy. This imbalance distorts society and economy. Another financial crisis is likely unless finance is downsized and regulated. It is necessary to reduce the scale, autonomy and power of finance: to de-financialize.

It is especially important to reduce the financialization of basic needs. The precariousness of access to basic needs disproportionately affects women and the poor; those already most disadvantaged by systems of inequality. Financialization does not merely reflect inequalities generated elsewhere, for instance in the labour market, but exacerbates them. Housing is an example of a basic need which, as a consequence of financialization, has become too expensive for many women and the poor to afford without either parental capital or state subsidy through housing benefit. Alternatives include the building of publicly owned rented housing to stabilize the price for this basic need (an example of this practice is found in Enfield, UK; Chakrabortty 2014).The significance of affordable housing is highlighted in cases of domestic violence where the dissolution of the household is a necessary part of ending the violence but where the difficulty in accessing housing limits women's capacity to take this route.

Deepen democracy

The biggest reform challenge is the democratization of decision-making over finance. The principles that Stiglitz enunciated to the UN in his vision of reform included the entitlement of those whose lives were affected by finance to participate in decisions over the governance of finance (Stiglitz 2009). Those who may be subject to the losses generated by finance should be included or represented in its governance. It is technically possible to regulate finance to reduce its capacity to destabilize the real economy. There is a large repertoire of tools available, ranging from stricter implementation of existing rules to both minor and major reform of the architecture of institutions governing the financial system. The challenge is the application of these tools, which requires deepening democracy.

The most substantial reforms would contribute to de-financialization by reducing the scale and reach of finance capital and by allowing greater public control over the creation of money. Several of these potential reforms are relevant to both financial and fiscal issues, including: the separation of retail and casino banking; making leveraged private equity buyouts illegal; reintegrating company governance so that governance and taxation are in the same country as a business; closing tax havens and secrecy jurisdictions; and taxing international financial transactions.

A further call for democratic control is at the heart of the proposal to treat money as a public rather than private good, by controlling the process of creating money through a central bank subject to democratic control, rather than continuing the current practice of allowing private banks to create it through their issuance of debt (Huber and Robertson 2000; Ingham 2004; Mellor 2010). The argument is that since the public aspects of the financial system are necessary to support the creation and exchange of money, then this should be recognized by greater public control over the creation of money. The democratic regulation of finance is increasingly becoming a matter to be addressed in public debate.

While Stiglitz did not directly refer to women in his reference to democratic control, others have. The European Parliament and Commission have called for gender quotas to ensure women's presence on boards of directors of major firms, including finance companies, building on the success of such mechanisms to ensure women's presence in parliaments. Gender equality could be written into financial and fiscal governance in ways that are both straightforward and consistent with existing regulatory frameworks. This would be an example of gender mainstreaming in that it meets goals of gender equality at the same time as it improves the efficiency of the mainstream body to deliver on its own goals. There could be greater consultation by governmental and financial bodies with gendered civil society organizations, such as gender budgeting groups. There are several avenues for such developments, including: gender balance in decision-making; and gender equality to be incorporated into the goals of the financial institution or financial agreement.

Gender balance in decision-making can be written into the governance agreements of financial entities, such as financial scrutiny committees, boards of central banks and corporate boards more generally. Its application can be enforced in different ways: through corporate guidelines (on a 'comply or explain' basis); using employment law (recognizing the right to employ the minority gender when there are equally qualified candidates); and/or using company law to enforce quotas with sanctions for non-compliance (e.g. fines or company dissolution through non-registration).

Gender equality could be included as one of the goals of financial bodies and financial agreements alongside others. This can be done by directly naming gender equality as one of the goals amongst others such as fiscal balance and inflation targets; and it can be included indirectly through setting goals such as full employment which have a positive impact on gender equality. Gender equality could have been included as one of the goals of the 'Six Pack' agreements (see chapter 5) that placed conditions on those Member States in receipt of financial aid as a result of budgetary crisis. Gender equality could be included as a principle in the constitutions of the new institutions being created as part of the reform of the financial architecture.

The implementation of these reforms would therefore constitute a radical restructuring of the financial architecture and the total system. While there is a strong project to deregulate the economy further, based on the deeply flawed but still popular thesis of 'efficient markets', it is nevertheless possible to identify a coherent programme of reforms of the financial architecture that would entail democratic control over finance. The likelihood of such primacy of democracy over finance to reduce the tendency towards crisis requires investigation of relevant political forces and institutions. For this discussion, see chapter 6; here, it can be concluded that the technical means to regulate finance to reduce crises are available; whether or not they are applied is the remaining, political, question.

Conclusions

The capacity of finance to destabilize the real economy could be reduced if there were effective state regulation. Such macro-prudential regulation (Crockett 2000; Baker 2013) could include: controls over capital flows (Keynes 1936; Stiglitz 2002); modularizing the financial system through limits on the size of financial firms and splitting retail and casino banking (Haldane 2010; Haldane and May 2011); increasing the ratio of capital to loans; and reducing tax evasion and avoidance (Shaxson 2011). Potentially, this means that finance can be democratically controlled in the interest of the wider economy and society, even though this is not currently the case, especially in the UK. This deepening of democracy is gendered: in the composition of bodies governing finance in finance firms, central banks and governments; and in the goals of financial entities.

The proposed new framework for the analysis of finance in society includes five dimensions: the conceptualization of finance; its relationship to the economy (industrial capital, employment and state budgets), polity (state and international financial institutions), and violence (especially war) and civil society (especially political projects); and the nature of the social system as a whole.

Finance should be conceptualized as a social relationship, as a social system, rather than as an object, as argued in all frameworks except the orthodox. Finance is a form of profit-seeking and a form of capital, as noted by the political economy framework. The distinction and relationship between the three stages of investment identified by

Minsky, building on the work of Keynes, identify the nature of the financial system that is simultaneously a necessary part of capitalism and a source of its instabilities, which range from minor bubbles to major crises. Finance is a site of power struggles at the heart of capitalism between the producers of goods (capital and labour) and producers of money (central and private banks and financial institutions). This struggle challenges the notion that exploitation takes place primarily at the point of production. The significance of finance grows as processes of financialization spread its influence through economy and society. States can regulate finance so as to mitigate these instabilities but the extent to which this occurs depends on wider social processes. Keynes, Schumpeter and Minsky were correct in their rejection of the equilibrium nature of orthodox economics that rests on Smith, Hayek and Friedman. However, they underestimated the extent to which the social relations of finance are embedded in wider systems of power.

The significance of finance for society depends upon the relationship between finance and democracy. Can the state regulate finance in the wider social interest or do finance and its related political projects capture the state? The answer to this question lies at the heart of the differences between the four frameworks: for the orthodox, state action in relation to finance constitutes interference which makes matters worse, not better, for society; for political economy, capital is likely to capture the state, though not inevitably so; for the heterodox, state action is necessary to turn capital into the servant rather than master of society, and they consider such action possible though contingent; and for Polanyi, societal response is likely and is necessary to contain the excesses of the commoditization of money. A deeper analysis of the relations between finance and democracy is addressed in chapter 6.

It is important to remember that the cause of the crash was finance. The fragility, volatility and precariousness of finance could be, but have not yet been, fully addressed.

4

Economic Crisis: Recession

Introduction

The financial crisis cascaded into the 'real' economy to cause a deep recession. Economic output fell; employment fell; productivity fell; and living standards fell. Most economies in Europe and North America had not recovered the level of output, standard of living or level of unemployment that obtained before the 2008 crash by 2015. However, profits and the value of property and stocks have recuperated in most of these countries. The economy has been restructured: inequality has grown; gender relations have changed form; and people have lower living standards.

Conventionally economists define recession as at least two consecutive quarters of decline in output. In the analysis presented here, the loss of employment, increase in unemployment, decline in living standards and increase in poverty are also included as important aspects of recession. The cuts in public expenditure (see chapter 5) further contributed to the recession. There are significant differences between countries in the depth and trajectories of their recessions.

The distributional consequences of the recession have been uneven. The oft-used slogan 'we're all in it together' is not supported by the evidence. The losses were distributed along traditional class lines; but not only by class. There were complex and uneven gender effects which varied across the different phases and between countries. The first phase of the recession (caused by bank failure) was differently gendered from the later phase of zero growth (caused by public expenditure cuts). The changes taking place challenge dualistic typologies of gender regimes since women were not pushed back into the home. Inequalities related to ethnic and citizenship status were exacerbated.

Economic growth policies to get out of recession have consequences for the structuring of future rewards from work (Hay 2013). Economic growth is often treated as a shared goal and its pursuit treated as a justification for government action; dissenters from this position are marginalized. However, the best strategy to increase economic growth is disputed. For some, the strategy is to remove regulations further in order to encourage entrepreneurship; for others, it is a matter of improving regulation to keep markets free from corruption and bias. Alternative economic growth strategies are differently gendered in both their core assumptions and consequences.

Cascade

The recession was the consequence of the cascading of the crisis in finance into the real economy. The losses in the real economy were enormous; estimates range from 10 per cent to 500 per cent of the annual value of the UK economy. The Bank of England's director of financial stability, Haldane, estimates that the initial value of lost output in the UK due to the financial crisis was around £140 billion, or 10 per cent of GDP (Haldane 2010). If the losses persist, as a result of economic growth not returning to its original trajectory, then the cost of the financial crisis rises to between £1.8 trillion and £7.4 trillion for the UK, or between one and five times annual GDP (Haldane 2010: 3). If only the fiscal costs of the wealth transfer from government to the banks during the bailout are considered, then the figure is lower but still large: around 1 per cent of GDP, which is approximately £20 billion for the UK (and $100 billion for the US). However, Haldane recommends using the larger figures on the grounds that consideration of only the direct fiscal costs underestimates the damage the financial crisis caused to the wider economy.

Haldane's estimates for losses at the global level are proportionately larger. The crisis reduced world output in 2009 by around 6.5 per cent ($4 trillion). If the losses persist, then the loss in output rises to between $60 trillion and $200 trillion for the world economy (Haldane 2010); the upper figure is equivalent to around three years of world output.

Haldane's conclusion is that the UK and other countries cannot afford financial crises. Banks do not make enough profits to match the cost of the crises they create, and taxing banks to compensate the country for the losses they cause the economy would exceed the profits made by the banks. We cannot afford the current banking system; its radical reform is therefore necessary.

What Recession?

In most of Europe and North America there was a deep recession in 2008 and 2009 following the financial collapse. During the one year of 2009, GDP fell in the European Union (EU28) by 4.4 per cent and in the US by 2.8 per cent (Eurostat 2014a). The UK experience was average for the EU, with a fall of 4.3 per cent in 2009 and across the whole of the recession period a fall of 7.2 per cent from peak to trough (ONS 2013a). Although the fall in economic output (GDP) in the UK had ceased by 2014, with a modest return to economic growth, its economy in 2015 remained smaller than before the Great Crash, with a smaller annual economic output than was the case pre-crash. The total output of the economy (GDP) in June 2013 was 3.9 per cent below its pre-recession peak in the first quarter of 2008 (ONS 2013a). There have been four phases in this period of reduced economic output: first, the dramatic fall in output during 2008 and the first half of 2009; second, a small rise in output during the latter part of 2009 and early part of 2010; third, a period in the latter part of 2010 until the middle of 2012 in which the rate of change in output fluctuated around zero, with half the quarters showing increases and half of them decreases; and fourth, since 2013, a return to economic growth. Government economists use the term 'recession' to mean a decline in economic output, measured as GDP, for two consecutive quarters (amounting to six months) (Hardie and Perry 2013). Earlier figures released by the Office for National Statistics (ONS) had reported three consecutive falls in output in the last quarter of 2011 and the first two quarters of 2012, thus constituting a second 'dip' to the recession (Hardie and Perry 2013); but revision of the figure for the first quarter of 2012 to zero, in the light of revised Blue Book figures for the National Accounts, means this period is now described as 'flat' rather than constituting a second dip (ONS 2013a; Hardie et al. 2013). The first phase of the recession was produced by the financial crash (discussed in chapter 3). The second phase, of some recuperation, was linked to the Keynesian boost (discussed in chapter 5). The third phase, when output change fluctuated around zero, was linked to the cuts in public expenditure (chapter 5). In the fourth phase, from 2013, some growth re-emerged and employment rates increased to at least previous levels; however, the overall size of the economy by 2015 was still smaller than it had been prior to the crash.

The conventional focus for analysis is the output of the economy as a whole. However, GDP per capita (for each person, as compared with the GDP of the whole country) is also relevant; indeed, for people's experiences, it is more relevant. During 2008–9, GDP per capita fell by 7 per cent. The reduction in GDP per capita has been slower to recuperate than that of the economy as a whole: in spring 2013, it was 6.3 per cent lower than before the recession, as compared with 3.9 per cent for the economy as a whole in 2013 (ONS 2013a).

Some countries, such as the US, recuperated from the recession more rapidly than others, such as Greece and Spain, that had ongoing recessions in 2015, with the UK being in the middle of this distribution (Eurostat 2014a).

While economists usually use 'economic output' when measuring changes in the economy, other aspects of the economy that are relevant to people, such as employment, unemployment, wages and living standards, are also important. These aspects are considered next.

Decline in employment and rise in unemployment

Unemployment rose across the EU28 (from 7.0 per cent in 2008 to 10.8 per cent in 2014) and in the US (from 4.6 per cent in 2007 to 9.6 per cent in 2010) as a consequence of the financial crisis (Eurostat 2014b). Indeed if unemployment is used as an indicator of recession, rather than the convention of falls in output, then there would have been two dips to the UK recession. The first rise in unemployment rates was driven by the financial collapse. This collapse led to failure in the provision of credit to the 'real economy' (the 'credit crunch'), which generated bankruptcies of businesses and increased unemployment (Bell and Blanchflower 2009). The second rise in unemployment rates was linked to the start of the period of cuts in public expenditure.

Changes in the rates of unemployment, employment and economic inactivity are investigated using data drawn from the EU Labour Force Survey, a large, nationally representative sample survey conducted in all EU Member States (ONS 2009, 2012, 2013g). The data concern people of working age, which is taken to start at 16, the end of full-time compulsory schooling, and to finish at 64 (the age of entitlement to the state retirement pension for women in the UK has been rising from 60 to 65 to become the same as men, and will in the future rise for both men and women towards 68 (HM Government 2011)).

Unemployment rose rapidly during the recession from 5.2 per cent in the first quarter (January–March) of 2008 to a first peak of 8.0 per cent in the first quarter of 2010, falling only slightly to 7.7 per cent, before rising to a second and higher peak of 8.4 per cent in the last quarter of 2011, and very slowly declining thereafter to 7.6 per cent in the third quarter of 2013. Hence the unemployment rate in 2013 remained significantly higher than the pre-crash rate. The definition of unemployment being used is the standard international one (i.e. a person must have been seeking work at some point in the previous four weeks and would be able to start work within the next two weeks).

The employment rate fell from 72.9 per cent in the second quarter of 2008 to a first low of 70.3 per cent in the first quarter of 2008, rose a little to 70.8 per cent, before falling to 70.2 per cent in the third quarter of 2011. It then rose to 71.8 per cent in the third quarter of 2013 (lower than the pre-crash level) and further increased to 73.5 per cent in the first quarter of 2015 (higher than the pre-crash level).

However, the number of hours worked in the economy had recuperated to the pre-crash level by the latter part of 2012, and by the end of 2013 was higher than the pre-crash amount. Hours worked were 949 million in 2008 (January–March), falling throughout 2008 and 2009 to a low of 905 million in 2009 (June–August), but unevenly recuperating to 949 million in 2012 (August–October), and rising to 967 million in 2013 (August–October), thereby exceeding the pre-crash level (ONS 2013g). The implication is that those people who are in employment are working longer hours.

The third category of 'economic inactivity' comprises those who are variously: in education; retired; temporarily or long-term sick; or looking after the home and family. It thus combines those who are busy with activities other than earning money (education and care-work) with those of working age who are not looking for work for other reasons. It also includes people who would like a job but do not meet the standard international definition of being unemployed. In the third quarter of 2013, this last group represented 26 per cent of all those who were considered economically inactive. The economic inactivity rate rose from 22.9 per cent in the second quarter of 2008 to 23.5 per cent in the first quarter of 2010 and then slowly and unevenly declined to 22.2 per cent in the third quarter of 2013. The rate of economic inactivity at the end of 2013 was thus slightly lower than before the crash.

The financial crash and subsequent policy changes continue to impact upon employment, unemployment and economic inactivity. While the peak in unemployment due to the crisis has passed, the rate of unemployment was higher, the rate of employment lower and the rate of economic inactivity lower at the end of 2013 than they were pre-crisis.

Decline in real wages

There has been a significant decline in the level of real wages since 2008 and 2013 in the UK. The average annual rise in earnings 2008–13 was smaller than the average rate of inflation. Before 2008, wages (total and regular pay) had been rising more rapidly than inflation (as measured by the Consumer Prices); between 2008 and 2013, inflation (measured by the Consumer Price Index) was higher than earnings (measured as total weekly earnings) by between 0.9 per cent and 4.0 per cent per year (when comparing the third quarter of each year, August–October) (ONS 2012). This sustained reduction in living standards is unprecedented in the UK post-war period. After 2013, the decline in real wages slowed, largely because the rate of inflation fell to historic lows, reaching zero inflation in 2015, at least partly because of the fall in the price of oil (ONS 2015a).

There has been a decrease in wages and an increase in profits. The proportion of the GDP going to wages declined during the crisis period 2008–13 while there was an apparent increase in the proportion going to profits. Indeed, the proportion of GDP going to wages appears to have fallen to one of the lowest levels since records began (ONS 2013c). It is possible that part of the change may be as a consequence of an increase in the proportion of national income going to the self-employed (Stumbling and Mumbling 2013). Nevertheless, during the crisis, profits rose and wages declined.

Decline in productivity

Productivity in the economy declined in the crisis period, 2008–13, following a very long period of increase. Labour productivity is considered to be a key indicator of economic performance. It measures the amount of real (inflation-adjusted) economic output (real gross value added, GVA) per unit of labour (worker, job or hour worked). The preferred measure of unit of labour is that of hour worked (ONS 2013d).

During the crisis period 2008–13, productivity fell at an average annual rate of 0.8 per cent. This figure uses the preferred measure per hour worked, but productivity is also declining when measured per worker. Before the crash in 2008, productivity had been increasing: productivity per hour worked had been increasing at an annual rate of 2.9 per cent between 1988 and 2008, and of 2.4 per cent between 1973 and 1988 (ONS 2013e).

The decline in productivity did not reverse when the recession was over, but continued through 2013 onwards. The Bank of England's Monetary Analysis Directorate (Barnett et al. 2014: 114) considered that it was linked to 'persistent causes related to the financial crisis' that were linked to 'reduced investment in both physical and intangible capital, such as innovation, and impaired resource allocation from low to high productive uses' as well as cyclical factors.

The output of the economy is smaller than it was pre-crash but the number of hours worked in the economy is higher. Workers in the economy as a whole are thus working more hours but producing less output. They are working on more precarious contracts (Standing 2011). The changes linked to the Crisis during the period since 2008 have resulted in a significant and enduring decline in productivity.

Gender and the Recession

Did women bear the brunt of the recession? Financial crises are gendered around the world (Baden 1996; Buvinic 2009; Pearson and Sweetman 2011; Fukuda-Parr 2009; ILO 2009; Sparr 1994; Young et al. 2011). But exactly how are they gendered? There are conflicting accounts of the effects of the recession caused by financial crisis on men as compared with women. These range from statements that men have lost more jobs than women (OECD 2010) to diametrically opposed statements that women have lost more jobs than men (Rake 2009), with many more nuanced positions in between (Villa and Smith 2010; Rubery and Rafferty 2013; Karamessini and Rubery 2013).

The OECD (2010) headlined an account of the gendered effects of the crisis as a 'mancession'. It reported that:

Unemployment in the OECD area is predicted to reach some 10% in 2010, up from about 5.6% in 2007. Men have been hit harder than women: across the OECD area, male employment has fallen by 3% since the recession started, while the decline for women stood at a tenth of that, at 0.3%. Hence the 'mancession' tag bloggers and commentators have used to characterise the jobs crisis.

In contrast, Pearson and Sweetman (2011) and Rake (2009) declare that women were more vulnerable to job loss than men in the Global South and UK respectively. Rake (2009), in relation to the UK, and Pearson and Sweetman (2011), more widely, argue that women are vulnerable to job loss due to their weaker position in the labour market than that of men. This positioning stems partly from the gender division between paid employment and domestic care-work and is partly due to discrimination. These authors conclude that women are disproportionately the victims of the crisis.

However, some argue women's employment may be more secure than that of men because of contingent gender industrial segregation, whereby women workers are disproportionately concentrated in those industries which are less affected by unemployment (Villa and Smith 2010; FGB and Lyberaki 2011). Further, Villa and Smith (2010) found that women's jobs were more affected in the second wave of the recession than in the first and that patterns varied according to the sex segregation of occupations and industries across the EU.

A more nuanced position is that the gendering of job loss depends on the pattern of sex segregation found in those industrial sectors most affected by the recession and that this varies both spatially and temporally (Walby 2009). For example, women workers in export processing zones in the Global South were particularly affected by unemployment as a result of the early downturn in demand for their products in the Global North (Buvinic 2009). At the same time, women in other parts of the Global South economy were less affected (Walby 2009).

This debate recapitulates the discussion of the extent to which gender inequality in the economy is driven by the gendered division between production and reproduction (Scott et al. 2012) or takes a more complex shape due to practices of segregation (Jarman et al. 2012), discrimination, and divisions between full-time and part-time work (O'Reilly and Fagan 1998). This debate as to the nature of the gendering of crisis has reverberated through analyses of previous recessions (Rubery 1988) and cuts in state welfare provisions in other countries under pressure from international financial institutions (Elson and Çagatay 2000; Lim 2000; Sparr 1994). It is investigated empirically in relation to the 2008/9 recession in the next section.

What happened to gendered relations in the economy?

There is an empirical question regarding who bears the brunt of the recession. Were 'we all in it together' or not? In what way did the crisis affect gender relations? How are changes in the economy expressed in changes in gendered rates of employment, unemployment and economic inactivity? Unemployment among men and women increased during the recession in different ways in different countries of the EU (Eurostat 2014b).

Table 4.1 presents gendered rates of unemployment, employment and economic inactivity, at three-monthly intervals, from early 2008 to late 2013 for the UK. The data are drawn from the Labour Force Survey as reported by ONS in *Labour Market Statistics* unless otherwise specified.

The period 2008–13 saw the restructuring of gender relations in employment, unemployment and economic inactivity. The changes varied by gender, by industry, by public/private sector and by timing. Patterns of gender segregation in employment by industry, occupation and public/private sector meant that one or other gender suffered unemployment depending on which industry or sector was losing jobs at particular times.

The rate of unemployment rose among both men and women but women's rose more over the period 2008–13. Women's unemployment rate rose by 50 per cent from 4.8 per cent in the second quarter of 2008 (2008 Q2) to 7.2 per cent in 2013 Q3, while men's unemployment rate rose by 38 per cent from 5.6 per cent in 2008 Q2 to 8.0 in 2013 Q2. Thus, in 2013 the gender gap in unemployment remained skewed in women's favour but to a lesser extent than in 2008.

Men's unemployment rose more rapidly than women's during the first phase of increased unemployment produced by the financial crisis and peaked at 9.1 per cent in 2010 Q1. Job loss was largest in industries where men were concentrated during the first period of the recession. These industries included construction, where job losses were especially large (e.g. 7.9 per cent between September 2008 and September 2009 as compared with 2.1 per cent for all employment). Men's employment rate fell from 78.8 per cent in 2008 Q2 to a low of 74.9 per cent in 2010 Q1, recuperating to 76.8 per cent in 2013 Q3, and to 78.4 per cent in 2015 Q1 (ONS 2015b), but still below its pre-crash level. Further, one third of those men working part-time in 2013 Q3 were doing so because they could not find full-time jobs.

Women's unemployment grew more slowly, following cuts in public expenditure, to a later peak of 7.6 per cent in 2011 Q4 and

Table 4.1 Unemployment, employment and economic inactivity, by gender, 2008–13

	Unemployment rate men	Unemployment rate women	Employment rate men	Employment rate women	Economically inactive % men	Economically inactive % women
2008 Jan–Mar	5.6	4.8	78.9	67.0	16.3	29.5
2008 Apr–Jun	5.8	4.8	78.8	66.7	16.3	29.5
2008 Jul–Sep	6.4	5.3	78.3	66.5	16.3	29.5
2008 Oct–Dec	7.1	5.6	77.9	66.2	16.1	29.4
2009 Jan–Mar	7.9	6.2	77.2	65.8	16.1	29.6
2009 Apr–Jun	8.8	6.5	76.0	65.9	16.5	29.5
2009 Jul–Sep	9.0	6.5	75.5	65.8	16.9	29.4
2009 Oct–Dec	8.9	6.6	75.3	65.6	17.3	29.6
2010 Jan–Mar	9.1	6.7	74.9	65.6	17.4	29.6
2010 Apr–Jun	8.7	6.8	75.5	65.7	17.2	29.3
2010 Jul–Sep	8.4	7.0	76.0	65.3	16.9	29.6
2010 Oct–Dec	8.6	7.1	75.7	65.6	17.0	29.3
2011 Jan–Mar	8.4	7.0	75.8	65.6	17.1	29.4
2011 Apr–Jun	8.4	7.2	75.8	65.4	17.0	29.2
2011 Jul–Sep	9.0	7.5	75.1	65.4	17.3	29.1
2011 Oct–Dec	9.0	7.6	75.4	65.6	17.0	28.9
2012 Jan–Mar	8.7	7.6	75.8	65.8	16.9	28.7
2012 Apr–Jun	8.5	7.5	76.3	66.0	16.5	28.6
2012 Jul–Sep	8.2	7.4	76.5	66.5	16.5	28.1
2012 Oct–Dec	8.1	7.3	76.6	66.6	16.4	28.0
2013 Jan–Mar	8.3	7.3	76.2	66.6	16.7	28.0
2013 Apr–Jun	8.3	7.2	76.2	66.7	16.7	28.0
2013 Jul–Sep	8.0	7.2	76.8	66.8	16.3	27.9
Change 2008 Q2 to 2013 Q3	*+2.2*	*+2.4*	*–2.0*	*–0.2*	*0*	*–1.6*
% change 2008 Q2 to 2013 Q3	*+38*	*+50*	*–3*	*–1*	*0*	*–5*

Source: ONS (2009, 2012, 2013g)

2012 Q1. The greater loss in women's jobs was related to the decline in public sector employment, where more women are located than men. This sector shrank from representing 21.5 per cent of total employment in September 2010 to 19.4 per cent in September 2012, and may shrink further as a consequence of planned reductions in public expenditure. Women's employment rate fell from 67.0 per cent in 2008 Q2 to 65.3 per cent in 2010 Q3, recuperating to 66.8 per cent in 2013 Q3, and rising to 68.6 per cent in 2015 Q1 (ONS 2015b), which is higher than pre-crash levels and the joint highest since comparable records began.

Labour activation policy

There has been a drive to remove people from receipt of 'welfare' payments in the hope they will find employment. The entitlement to income support without seeking employment was significantly diminished for two groups of women in the period 2008–14: lone mothers with young children; and older women aged 60–4. Other groups affected include those claiming benefit on the grounds of disability and long-term sickness. During a period of recession, these changes may move people from being legitimately economically inactive (due to age, disability or caring for young children) to unemployment as well as to employment.

In the UK, lone parents have been able to choose to be full-time carers of dependent children and receive income support. This capacity has been changing such that parents of increasingly younger children are being required to seek employment. In 2012, entitlement to income support without seeking employment was restricted to only those lone parents with children younger than 12, reducing to 10 years in 2009, 7 in 2010 and 5 by June 2012 (ONS 2012: Table 10.1). Parents of children above this age need to be actively looking for employment to receive income support; in other words, they are considered to be unemployed rather than economically inactive.

The age at which women are entitled to claim a state pension has been increasing. A woman who is 60 years old and does not have employment is no longer eligible for a state pension, and to be entitled to income support she must be looking for work, that is, to be unemployed. The age at which women can claim a state pension has been rising from 60 towards 65 years so that it will match the age at which men currently become eligible. This equalization will be followed by a further increase in the pensionable age for both men and women in the future. The original timetable for the introduction of changes in state pensions was significantly speeded up by the Pensions Act of 2011 (HM Government 2011).

Policies to promote women's employment, while increasing in frequency and scope, are not uniformly applied across all social groups. For instance, women living in households with a high earner are not subject to these labour activation policies (Armstrong et al. 2009). The applicability of policies therefore varies according to factors such as women's (assumed) access to other sources of income, which, in turn, intersect with other sources of inequality.

Has the recession pushed women back into the home and 'economic inactivity'?

Is the crisis increasing domestication? Does the loss of women's employment and public services mean women are becoming increasingly economically inactive as they are pushed back into the home?

Economic inactivity is the term used for all people of working age who are not in employment or unemployed (looking for employment). It includes those engaged in unpaid care-work, those who have retired (but are of working age) and those who are leisured. Economic inactivity does not necessarily mean that a person is not busy doing productive things; only that they are not in or looking for employment. People's positioning within a category depends upon their response to survey questions posed by an interviewer who asks those who are not in employment whether they are actively looking for work. Only those respondents saying they are looking for work (regardless of whether or not they are claiming unemployment benefits or jobseeker's allowance) are included in the category of unemployed.

The relationship between the categories of employment, unemployment and economic inactivity was very different for men and women during the crisis period of 2008 to 2013. The rate of employment for men declined and their rate of unemployment increased; almost in mirror image. There was a small increase in men's rate of economic inactivity towards the height of the employment crisis in the middle of the period (from 16.3 per cent in 2008 Q2 to 17.4 per cent in 2010 Q1), but this had subsided to the pre-crash level (16.3 per cent) by 2013 Q3.

Women's employment rate declined and their unemployment rate increased but their rate of economic inactivity did not significantly rise during the crisis: it was 29.5 per cent in 2008 Q2; 29.6 per cent (its highest level) in 2009 Q2, 2010 Q1, Q2 and Q4; thereafter falling to 27.9 per cent in 2013 Q3. Thus women's economic inactivity rate fell from 29.5

per cent to 27.9 per cent during the period 2008–13. Women's unemployment increased but their economic inactivity did not. Women's employment fell and then recuperated. Women thus stayed in the labour market during the crisis period 2008–13, being either employed or unemployed. The crisis did not increase women's economic inactivity; it did not push women back into the home. Indeed, to the contrary, there was a decrease in women's rate of economic inactivity.

So what was happening 'in the home'? There was a reduction in public services, as shown in chapter 5, which is likely to have increased the amount of domestic care-work performed in the home. However, this increased domestic care-work did not prevent women seeking employment. Therefore it appears that there has been an intensification of care-work in the home and a deterioration in the experience of work–life balance for women (Gregory et al. 2013). At the same time, the increasing casualization of employment is adding further pressures for women combining their paid work and home life (Hofäcker and König 2013).

The implication of this pattern is that dualistic models of gender relations which treat women's work as either care-work or paid work, or as either production or reproduction, are too simplistic to capture adequately the changes induced by the crisis. Instead, the outcome is better understood as comprising changes within the public gender regime, from social democratic to neoliberal, rather than as a shift from a public to domestic gender regime. This discussion of an alternative way to model gender relations is discussed further in chapter 7.

Economic Growth Out of Recession

There are two main approaches to economic growth that concern regulation: deregulation to remove bureaucratic obstacles to growth on the assumption that markets are inherently efficient; or regulating markets to improve their functioning by removing distortions caused by corruption, monopoly, discrimination and power. These alternative strategies are intrinsically distribution strategies since the nature of the economic growth shapes who is likely to be more highly rewarded. All economic growth strategies are thus 'pre-distribution' strategies in that they create a set of positions in the economy which give rise to distributional effects.

During the period from 2010 to 2015, in the UK and elsewhere, there were government efforts to reduce the regulation of a range of markets. Regulations were conceptualized negatively as 'red tape'; in other words, as unnecessary bureaucracy. The 'red tape challenge' invited proposals to remove regulations that were seen to be encumbering business. In 2014, the prime minister announced the cutting of 800 regulations, many concerning health and safety and the environment in the small business sector, out of the government target of 3,000 regulations to be amended or scrapped (Cabinet Office 2014). Moves on deregulation were supported by the government's Business Taskforce (2013). This body called for the cutting of 'red tape' in a wide range of areas, including markets for services and arrangements for data protection and financial reporting for companies. It also opposed the extension of rights to pregnant workers.

The contrasting position is that regulation is necessary to make markets less distorted and thereby facilitate economic growth. This strategy includes regulation to prevent the development of monopolies and prevent distortion of labour markets through discrimination. The approach is underpinned by the theory that preventing such market distortions facilitates economic growth by removing obstacles to the development of full employment. In this strategy, social justice is a necessary component of a productive economy.

These economic growth strategies are differently gendered. There is a substantial body of equalities legislation, largely originating in the EU, which is relevant to the labour market. This legislation has sometimes been conceptualized as 'red tape' which disrupts efficient market function since it interferes with the decisions of employers. However, it is better conceptualized as necessary to reduce the discrimination against women (and other minorities). The legislation reduces distortions based on power that interfere with merit-based labour markets, and thereby improves their efficiency. Further, legislation to promote the reconciliation of employment and care-work (e.g. regulating working time to ensure maternity, paternity and parental leaves and supporting flexible working practices) enables the continuous employment of mothers and other carers and hence contributes to human capital development as well as the efficiency of labour markets.

Women's participation in employment without effective regulation of the market for labour may result in a growth of low-wage, low-skill and precarious employment, which leads to low productivity. Part-time working in the UK tends to be a distinct sector constituted by largely low-level employment rather than comprising reduced-hours working spread across the full range of skill levels. Improving the productivity of part-time working in the UK requires greater regulation to ensure women can remain attached to the same employer despite leave for childbirth.

Regulation of labour markets to reduce discrimination and facilitate full employment thereby contributes to the goals of both social justice and high-productivity economic growth.

Most of the discussion about economic growth out of recession has been focused on fiscal issues. It has concerned the tension between cutting public spending to reduce the government budget deficit and increasing public spending to boost the economy and provide social investment in human capital. These fiscal issues are addressed in the next chapter (chapter 5). The focus here is on policies concerning regulation that can contribute to economic growth.

The best route for economic growth out of recession is through the full utilization of women's labour, effective policies for full employment, removal of labour market discrimination, and the enhancement of policies to facilitate combining employment and care-work. An increase in employment and improvement in its quality would provide a significant boost to the economy. It would also widen the tax base and reduce fiscal pressures.

Two key areas concern laws to reduce discrimination and to regulate working time. The first is to improve the implementation of existing regulations to prevent discrimination against women and minorities in the labour market. Examples of such measures include: removing fees for complainants' use of employment tribunals to test the justice of their complaints (TUC 2014); providing free legal advice to complainants and employers with regard to the merit of complaints prior to tribunal through an extension of the Equality and Human Rights Commission's remit and funding; and increasing sanctions against employers who are discriminatory. The second is to develop the laws regulating working time to make it easier to combine employment and care-work and reduce the likelihood that mothers lose attachment to their employers when having children. The facilitation of combining paid and care-work could be achieved by, for example: removing conditions (e.g. length of employment) which restrict entitlement to maternity, paternity and parental leave; and extending the length of these leave periods.

Conclusions

The simple concept of recession treats it as a decline in economic output that is inevitably followed by economic growth. This notion appears to assume the existence of automatic stabilizers in the economy which act as negative feedback loops to recuperate the system's equilibrium. The Schumpeterian model whereby recession is an occasion of destruction and creation which changes the structure of the economy might seem the more appropriate one for the recent crisis. However, the restructuring has not produced revitalized economies. In the UK at least, it has on the contrary lowered the rate of productivity, lowered the standard of living and deepened inequalities. This is despite recuperation in rates of employment and rates of profit. Total output per year has not yet recovered to pre-crash levels even though economic growth appears to have been somewhat restored. The losses to the real economy from the financial crisis are ongoing in 2015.

There have been four phases in economic growth: crash, small recovery, flat, and resumed growth. The Great Crash generated reductions not only in economic output but also in employment rates, in real wages and in productivity. The hours worked have recovered so those in employment are working for as many hours as they were prior to the crash. However, unemployment remains high and living standards have fallen significantly as inflation has been greater than the rise in wages over the period as a whole, despite the drop in inflation 2013–15.

The recession has been gendered but in complicated ways. The early and later parts of the recession in the UK generated by the financial crisis were gendered in different ways: men lost jobs more than women in the early part and women more than men in the later period. This difference is a consequence of the gender segregation between industries (e.g. men's concentration in construction) and between public and private ownership. Women did not leave the labour market even when they lost jobs. Indeed women's rate of economic inactivity fell. The sources of women's livelihoods are not more domestic than they were pre-crash. Men initially lost more jobs during the bank crash and then women more than men as public expenditure was cut. However, women have become unemployed rather than economically inactive. This is partly due to government policy, which has restricted women's entitlement to benefits: pensions for the over 60s and benefits to stay at home with young children for lone mothers. Domestic work may have intensified but women remain in the labour market. Economic hardship and inequalities have increased.

The outcome of the crisis has not been for women to 'return' to the home, to a more domestic form of gender regime, but rather a retreat from the institutions of gendered social democracy in the welfare state. A more neoliberal form of public gender regime is emerging.

5

Fiscal Crisis: Austerity

Introduction

The centre of the crisis is disputed. The attribution of responsibility and blame for starting the crisis is at stake in this dispute. The hegemonic position is that the crisis is centred on government expenditure which produced the budget deficit, and hence that the appropriate response is austerity, meaning cuts in public expenditure. The counter-hegemonic position holds that the budget deficit is a consequence rather than cause of the crisis. In this latter position, the fiscal crisis is seen as an outcome of the crisis in the real economy which itself was a result of the crisis in finance. The crisis cascaded from finance to the real economy, causing a rise in government budget deficits. Interpreting the increase in the deficit as a fiscal crisis led to 'austerity'.

'Austerity' is the condition in which limitations in state social expenditure are legitimated by a perceived need to reduce government deficits. Austerity has become the hegemonic response to the crisis despite significant objections. The debate on austerity, on reducing the budget deficit and, in particular, cutting public expenditure, has become the focus of mainstream politics. Finance is no longer the centre of public debate even though there are still unresolved issues and unimplemented agendas on its regulation.

Fiscal 'crisis' and 'austerity' are marked by contestations over distribution. These are not only class based. They include the scapegoating of minoritized groups that are identified by their ethnicity, nationality and migration status. In the current crisis, the significance of the gender dimension of this contested distribution is beginning to become visible.

While the growth of fiscal deficits has been common to most countries in Europe and North America, the scale and consequences have varied significantly. Again, the UK experience is in the middle of the distribution, with Germany among those least affected and Greece and Spain among those most affected.

The emerging debate on the fiscal crisis concerns the contested strategy for economic growth out of recession. Public expenditure is seen as either a detriment to economic growth, by using up resources on welfare that could be better used elsewhere, or as necessary for enhancing growth, through its investment in human capital.

What Deficit?

Where did the deficit come from? Is it the cause of the crisis or the consequence of the crisis? If the deficit caused the crisis then there is pressure to narrow the deficit. If budget deficits are a consequence of the crisis then it is necessary to look elsewhere for the causes and solutions. In the UK, the chancellor of the Exchequer holds that the increase in the public debt and budget deficit is the cause of the crisis: 'the soaring budget deficit had its roots in an unsustainable increase in public spending in the eight years before the crisis' (Osborne 2013). In contrast, for the International Monetary Fund (IMF) (2011: 3), the increased public debt is a consequence of the crisis: most of the increase in public debt in the UK 2007–11 was 'revenue loss associated with output losses from the financial crisis'.

The account offered by the IMF is better supported by the evidence. The UK government suffered substantial loss of income due to the decline in taxes arising from the recession in output and employment, which itself was an outcome of the financial crisis. Lost income from taxation rather than extra expenditure constituted the larger part of the increase in the government budget deficit. The size of government debt increased largely as a result of a recession-induced decline in income from tax receipts combined with increased expenditure on unemployment benefits. In addition, significant funds were expended by the government to prevent UK banks from collapsing during 2007 and 2008. The bailout of the banks, including Northern Rock in September 2007 and the Royal Bank of Scotland in 2008, cost around 1 per cent of GDP (Haldane 2010). Further, the burden created by this debt increased as a result of a rise in the interest rate charged on government debt by financial 'markets'. The extent of the rise in interest rates was related to 'perceptions' held in the financial 'markets' regarding the ability of governments to maintain the payment of interest on their debts. This assessment was visible in the grades attached to borrowers by credit-ranking agencies. A vicious circle is then created; the closer a country gets to defaulting on its debts, the lower its credit rating and the higher the interest rate charged on its debts. The outcome is an increase in the transfer of funds from citizen-taxpayers to finance capital in the form of interest payments on the national debt. In 2008 Iceland came close to default and received a bailout from international agencies, followed by other countries including Ireland and, by 2010, Greece. The possibility of default was treated as a crisis, as an emergency, and was thereby held to justify rapid changes in government policy.

The budget deficit is different from the national debt; though the two are often confused. The budget deficit is the annual gap in the government budget between income and expenditure. The national debt is the total of debt accumulated over many years. The cost of interest payments on the national debt depends on the size of the accumulated debt, not on the size of the annual budget deficit. Historically, the UK has had very varied levels of public debt. It rose during the eighteenth century to a peak at 237 per cent of GDP in the early nineteenth century, during the Napoleonic Wars, and then fell for a century. It rose during World War I and again in World War II, fell to around 25 per cent in 1992, before rising during the financial crisis and its aftermath. In 2014, public debt was less than 100 per cent of GDP and therefore far below the peak it once reached. The current cost of the interest payments on the national debt is around 3 per cent of GDP. Thus, historically, the current level of national debt is not exceptional and the cost of maintaining it constitutes a small proportion of GDP (Chantrill 2014).

Keynes (1936) argued that expenditure by the government would help to prevent the deepening of a recession. Government spending would help economic growth. This Keynesian position creates a trade-off between enlarging the deficit (which would add a little to the national debt) and deepening the recession. The development of Keynesian thinking (Hutton 1986) has led to a series of subtle distinctions in social democratic approaches to economic growth, which offer varied reasons for different balance points (Corry 2013). The analysis becomes more complex when the goal of reducing inequality is added to the goal of economic growth. Iversen and Wren (1998) develop this analysis of trade-off into a three-cornered 'trilemma' between the goals of budgetary restraint, income equality and employment growth: progress towards two of these three goals might be possible, but not all three at the same time.

In 2008/9, many governments, including the UK's, chose to increase public expenditure in order to reduce the depth of the recession in output and employment. In this they were successful.

In May 2010, the policy was reversed and public expenditure cut. The newly elected UK government, a coalition of Conservatives and Liberal Democrats, chose the other policy and prioritized reduction of the deficit over reducing the depth of recession. This was not part of the manifestos on which these parties had fought the election. Instead, it was legitimated by the fiscal crisis in Greece and the possibility that the UK might experience a similar one. In a series of budgets and reviews (from the 2010 Comprehensive Spending Review to the Welfare Benefits Up-Rating Bill of January 2013), public expenditure on benefits and services was reduced and taxation changed with the aim of reducing the deficit (Osborne 2010; House of Commons 2013). Most of the reduction in deficit was intended to be achieved by a reduction in public spending and a much smaller proportion by an increase in taxation.

At a later date the government narrative changed, such that by 2015 it was held that reducing the deficit by cutting 'unnecessary' welfare expenditure would free up resources for the private sector and thereby improve economic growth. This narrative rejects the earlier acceptance of a trade-off between government spending and economic growth and replaces it with the very different view that reducing spending would increase economic growth.

Public expenditure has consequences for both distribution and economic growth. Arguments over the deficit, its nature and its consequences for the economy, have implications for both inequality and growth, each of which will now be discussed.

Contested Distribution

There is tension between capital and democracy. If a country were democratic, then the majority of citizens could vote to transfer profits and property to themselves, thereby potentially undermining capitalism itself. However, they rarely, if ever, do this in practice. Instead, the tension is addressed by strategic or historic compromise (Berman 2006; Korpi 1983). For Gramsci (1971), hegemony was the temporary consensus created around a perceived shared interest in a context of unequal power in capitalist societies. Several forms of compromise are possible as outcomes of this struggle and several different points of equilibrium have thus emerged (Esping-Andersen 1990).

The tension between capitalism and democracy can be stabilized in different ways: finding a balance point in a trade-off whereby profits from private property are balanced by redistribution through welfare; and by the development of a form of economic growth delivering benefits for both capital and labour simultaneously, as in the 'social investment state' perspective. Class is not the only dimension of distributive struggle; gender, ethnicity and nation are also important.

Social democracy has been an example of such a compromise (Berman 2006), articulated by Marshall (1950) in relation to citizenship, by Crosland (1956) on the future of socialism, by Korpi in relation to class struggle (1983) and by Giddens (1998) as the Third Way. The slow emergence of a social democratic project during the late nineteenth and early twentieth century was followed by its institutionalization in political parties, occasional access to governmental power, and some progress in building enduring institutions in the social formation (Berman 2006). This process was uneven and varied across Europe, with setbacks from the 1980s. In Sweden and other Nordic countries the key political settlement leading to the institutionalization of social democracy in government and society occurred during the 1930s (Korpi 1983). In the UK, this development was weaker and later, with greatest access to governmental power in 1945. From the mid-1970s, this was contested by a neoliberal project (Hay 1996) which became institutionalized in government in 1979, offering a very different form of compromise between capitalism and democracy.

A focus on fiscal matters, on the balancing of tax and welfare benefits, is shared by many analysts despite contrasting orientations regarding the appropriate balance between income and expenditure. O'Connor (1973), analysing the 'fiscal crisis of the state', found a tendency for state expenditure to grow more rapidly than the ability to raise taxes. Pierson (2001b) considers the increase in welfare must cease and give way to conditions of 'permanent austerity'. Schäfer and Streeck (2013), though from a different route, concur with the view there is now an 'age of austerity' due to the balance of forces. However, Taylor-Gooby (2013a) argues that the balance point can be placed differently because there is greater support for funding expenditure than is commonly assumed. These approaches to fiscal policy place the question of the proper balance between taxation and state expenditure at the centre of contemporary discussions as to the priorities of social democratic politics and policies.

Inevitable or discretionary austerity?

'Permanent austerity', Pierson (1998, 2001b) argues, is a consequence of the state's inability to generate further income in the context of structural pressures to increase expenditure. According to Pierson (1998: 540), 'Welfare states everywhere face considerable strains' concerning the 'undeniable difficulty that governments now face in funding their social policy commitments'. He suggests that 'the intensity of fiscal pressures is clearly growing' so that 'Governments appear increasingly unable to respond to new demands.' The pressure on the welfare state is seen as the inevitable result of the structural transformation of advanced industrial economies:

> three profound transitions have been taking place as the advanced industrial economies become post-industrial ones: the slowdown in growth of productivity (and consequently economic growth) associated with a massive shift from manufacturing to service employment; the gradual expansion, maturation and 'growth to limits' of governmental commitments; and the demographic shift to an older population. Each element of this 'triple transition' to post-industrialism represents a powerful and continuing source of pressure on the welfare state. (Pierson 1998: 541)

The government 'commitments' concern expenditure on programmes to ameliorate social risks; the most costly of which are health care and pensions (Pierson 1998: 545). Increasing government income from the usual sources is regarded by Pierson (1998: 546) as politically difficult:

> the pain of taxation has grown over time as rising social expenditures required government officials to reach further and further down the income distribution in search of revenues. Mature institutional welfare states require a heavy tax burden on average and even below-average income households, which necessarily produces growing political tension.

These issues are compounded, in Pierson's view, by the growth in government debt, decline in fiscal slack, and increasing 'pre-commitment' of fiscal resources, which mean the state's capacity to take on new initiatives or programmes that require resources is reduced. Pierson (1994, 1998: 552) argues further that these irresistible forces are meeting an immovable object in confronting the resilience of the welfare state. This resilience is due to the electoral support found amongst the welfare state's many beneficiaries, and to the institutional stickiness of political systems in which there are both veto points and path-dependent processes that 'tend to lock existing policy arrangements into place'. While Pierson's account of austerity pre-dates the recession that started in 2008, it shares two key themes with writings on government budgets after the crisis: the presumed need to balance the government budget; and the narrow foci of government revenue on income tax and of government expenditure on welfare benefits.

The analysis of Schäfer and Streeck (2013: 1, 2) parallels that of Pierson in its concern for fiscal constraints and the balance point between government income and expenditure, which depends upon political forces. Indeed, they deepen the account with the proposal of additional limits to democratic choice: 'The current financial and fiscal crisis has only exacerbated the long-term shrinking of the room governments have to manoeuvre', while 'growing international tax competition has rendered it more difficult to raise taxes on companies and top income earners'. However, they differ in their interpretation of the political forces in play. Schäfer and Streeck (2013: 9) propose that the build-up of public debt since the 1970s was not the consequence of democratic political pressure for expenditure, because during this period trade union membership declined and economic liberalization grew. They argue: 'however this process [of accumulation of public debt] may be interpreted or explained, it cannot possibly be conceived as having been driven by a rising influence over policy by democratically organized citizens'.

Schäfer and Streeck (2013: 10, 16), in seeking an explanation elsewhere, point out that as 'debt has increased and the fiscal room for manoeuvre has diminished, electoral turnout has fallen', especially among the 'less well-off' and the unemployed, alongside increasing inequalities. These authors suggest that financial markets have become a political constituency that keeps the state under surveillance and pressure: 'international investors ... unrelentingly police sovereign commitments to austerity – and, if necessary, will make their discontent felt by raising the interest rate on new loans' (Schäfer and Streeck 2013: 19, 20). The 'subsidies to financial speculators' are made to 'appear as assistance to poor states' by 'international central banking'; thus 'popular agitation around the international politics of public debt tends to express itself in terms of nations versus nations, rather than people versus the financial markets' (Schäfer and Streeck 2013: 21). Schäfer and Streeck therefore accept the traditional terrain of argumentation, the balance between tax and public expenditure, but they include financial markets as an additional political force affecting the location of the balance point.

This approach to austerity is thus concerned with the balance between government income and expenditure so as to reduce or avoid government budget deficits and satisfy the political forces. While elegantly argued, there are omissions and limits to this approach; it is too narrow in focus, even with the additional consideration of the pressure exerted by financial markets. It is too narrow in: marginalizing or ignoring the gendering of income and expenditure; in underestimating the significance of tax dodging on an industrial scale; in neglecting state expenditure beyond welfare, such as spending on war; in neglecting the regulatory capacity of the state to level the playing field or tilt the field in favour of one sectional interest or another. However, more importantly, it is wrong to accept that the terrain of argument should be that of the balance of government income and expenditure, as if imbalance here were the cause of the crisis, rather than one of its many consequences.

Taylor-Gooby (2013a), while recognizing the forces that have given rise to 'austerity', does not conclude that the current balance point is so fixed. He acknowledges that there is a double crisis in state budgets, partly stemming from the financial crisis and the decision to cut expenditure to reduce the budget deficit and partly from the long-term process of the ageing of the population, but he does not agree that the room for democratic manoeuvre is so limited. He argues that there would be political support from the public for the small increases in taxation required for specific key expenditures: to end child poverty, taxes the equivalent of 0.7 per cent of GDP; for investment in child and elder care, transfers from the 1.1 per cent of GDP currently 'spent' on tax relief for non-state pensions; and, to take care of the pressures on health and education, increases of 0.4 per cent of GDP in taxes per decade. In this way, Taylor-Gooby rejects notions of 'irresistible forces and immovable objects'; even though he also argues on the shared terrain of the proper balance of taxation and public spending. He argues that the balance point could be different and that the obstacles in reaching it are not insuperable. Taylor-Gooby thus concludes that there is no economic or political necessity for 'austerity'.

Tax

Fiscal tensions are the outcome not only of changes in public expenditure but also of changes in government income from taxation. The narrowing of the government budget deficit can be achieved by increasing the taxes collected as well as by reducing expenditure. However, most of the attention on the fiscal balance has focused on cutting public expenditure rather than on increasing income from taxation. Taylor-Gooby (2013a) rightly points to the relatively small scale of the rise in tax that would be needed to balance the budget. The literature on the nature of such increased income from taxation is, however, rather separate from that looking at the ways and means of achieving this increase; only income tax receives much attention and it is usually in a negative manner. There are other ways to raise income from taxation and they overlap with the consideration of finance that was addressed earlier.

There are several ways in which the amount of tax collected can be increased other than raising the rate of existing taxes. These include: reducing tax dodging, whether legal avoidance or illegal evasion; and introducing new taxes such as a financial transaction tax or 'Tobin tax'. These issues lie at the boundary between the financial and the fiscal. There is overlap because contemporary tax dodging often includes complex manoeuvres developed by the finance industry and, at the same time, financial services and products are exceptional in their capacity to escape taxation.

The scale of uncollected taxes is large. The UK HM Revenue and Customs estimate that 'the tax gap stood at £35 billion (7.9% of all tax due) in 2009–10', although, according to the UK Public Accounts Select Committee, 'other estimates suggest the figure is much greater' (House of Commons Public Accounts Committee 2012b). Despite the deficit and the public concern with tax avoidance and evasion, there have been cuts in the numbers of tax inspectors in the UK as a result of central government budget cutbacks.

The development of complex financial arrangements to avoid, evade or dodge tax has been extensive. The arrangements include the use of tax havens (secrecy jurisdictions) and complex cross-border movement of funds to take advantage of differences between tax regimes. There is complex fragmentation of the legal headquarters of companies, tax residence and the actual location of the business as companies seek to reduce their tax liability. There is substantial lobbying of government on behalf of rich clients to change laws so as to facilitate tax avoidance (Palan et al. 2010; Hacker and Pierson 2010; Shaxson 2011). The collection of tax is historically very varia-ble (Piketty 2014), with substantial implications for social inequality.

There have been calls to reduce secrecy and increase transpar-ency in order to tackle the avoidance and evasion of taxation. There have been some small changes in terms of an increase in bilateral exchanges of information in the case of individuals where there is suspicion of tax offences. However, there has been no systematic exchange of information or systematic use of sanctions against states that protect the secret operations of their banks. The implementation of the agenda on preventing tax dodging has only just started and is far from complete.

Transforming State Transfers

There are several ways in which state social expenditure could be reduced without detrimental consequences for social inequality if a preventative perspective were adopted. This perspective has been articulated in various ways, including 'pre-distribution' (Hacker and Pierson 2010) and 'prevention' (Public Services Commission 2011). The examples here concern areas where state subsidies for the poor have effectively become transfers to private firms. This includes, for example, subsidies for housing and low wages.

The first example is that of social housing, that is, housing either built and owned by the state or in the form of state-supported mutuals and rented accommodation. The UK currently transfers significant sums of money to private landlords via housing benefit, which subsidizes the rents paid by the working poor as well as unemployed people. The money given to the private sector through housing benefit could instead be invested by the local state or state-supported mutuals in building new homes. This investment would have four effects: increased housing stock, which is currently in short supply; lower rents; long-term reductions in state expenditure on housing benefit; and a boost for jobs and thereby economic growth.

There is a parallel example in the minimum wage. The UK currently transfers significant sums of money to private employers via tax credits in order to top up wages that are beneath poverty level, especially for low-income individuals in households with dependent children. If the minimum wage were to be raised to a living wage then the need for government transfers, which represent state subsidy for the private sector, would be reduced.

Gendering the Fiscal

The fiscal is gendered. Changes in the balance of public expenditure and the income from taxation have gendered distributional consequences. Not only do they have gendered effects but the causes of changes in expenditure and taxation are also gendered.

Public expenditure is gendered because the development of state provision of education, health and care-work is gendered (O'Connor et al. 1999; Daly and Rake 2003; Esping-Andersen 1990, 2009). The public institutions providing these services socialize labour that was previously organized under domestic relations in the home and performed disproportionately by women. The jobs in education, health and care-work are disproportionately carried out by women, in sex-segregated occupations, so an increase in employment in these institutions increases female employment (Gottfried 2013). The provision of education, health and care through publicly funded institutions thus changes gender relations in the economy by reducing domestic labour and increasing paid employment for women (Orloff 1993; Walby 2009). The change in the typical relations under which women obtain their livelihood increases economic independence for women as it increases their direct rather than mediated access to money income. Women are disproportionate users of the public provision of education, health and care. Women disproportionately support these services and articulate this in their political preferences (Manza and Brooks 1999).

The growth of public provision of education, health and care together with income support for the old, sick and unemployed is often known as the development of the welfare state. The political project of social democracy is associated with its development. Hence, both the welfare state and social democracy are gendered. The development of the welfare state is the development of a gendered welfare state. The development of social democracy is the development of a gendered social democracy (Walby 2009). The welfare state project of social democracy has simultaneously been a class-based project of the working class. It is therefore both a feminist and labour project (Walby 2011a). The strongest welfare states have developed in those countries with the strongest development both of labour and feminism and of their alliance (Huber and Stephens 2000, 2001). This is a project within both civil society and the state.

In the UK, this project was slowly and successfully implemented as political democracy developed, with key milestones being the increase in entitlement to vote in 1918 and the election of the Labour government in 1945. The expansion of the project continued until 1979. After the 1979 election, several tendencies conjoined to weaken the labour part of the welfare state project. However, the feminism continued to grow in strength even after 1979, in, for example, expanding the welfare principle into the provision of services to prevent domestic and sexual violence against women. Only in 2010 was this expansion halted. Contestation over the welfare state is articulated through the fiscal since its development concerns public expenditure. The nature of the gendering of the fiscal is varied over time.

Tax is a gendered transfer of resources. Taxation is gendered because the rich usually pay more tax than the poor and men are usually richer than women. The more income a person has, the more income tax they will usually pay; the more expenditure a person makes, the more 'value-added' or 'sales' tax they will usually pay. The processes of increasing or decreasing taxation are gendered. Increasing taxation decreases gendered inequalities whereas decreasing taxation increases these inequalities. There are many nuances in this gendering, which are associated with the detail of specific forms of taxation. For example: tax on petrol is gendered since men drive more than women; tax on alcohol is gendered since men drink more than women; and exemptions from the payment of VAT, or sales tax, for children's clothing are gendered, since women more than men buy children's clothing. Reducing tax evasion and tax avoidance would be gendered since the extra funds would disproportionately come from men. Changes in the details as well as overall level of taxation are gendered. Tax is a feminist issue.

Logically, any government budget deficit could be narrowed by either cutting expenditure or collecting more tax. Narrowing the deficit by cutting expenditure increases gender inequality; while narrowing the deficit by collecting more tax reduces gender inequality. The ratio between cutting public expenditure and increasing tax income is gendered. The fiscal is a gendered and feminist issue.

In UK budgets since the election in May 2010, there have been changes in public expenditure and taxation that, on balance, have reduced expenditure more than they have raised taxation. These have been analysed for their gender effects using the technique known as 'gender budgeting' or 'gender impact assessment' (Women's Budget Group 2013, 2014). This technique disaggregates data into categories that are known to be gendered and then compares the categories (Himmelweit 2002). Gender budgeting techniques demonstrate that the consequences of the post-2010 changes to benefits, tax credits, indirect tax and income tax are gender unequal. For instance, analysis of the 2010 budget by the House of Commons Library found that of the £8.1 billion net personal tax increases and benefit cuts, £5.8 billion (72 per cent) was to be paid by women and £2.2 billion (28 per cent) by men. Changes in indirect taxes 2010–11 were found by de Henau and Santos (2011) to be to the detriment of women: the reductions in fuel duty benefitted men and the affluent more than women and the poor, since men and the affluent drive more than women and the poor; the rise in VAT hurt women and the poor most, since, despite certain exemptions, their purchases are more likely to be subject to VAT than those of men and the affluent.

The cuts to public services, education, health and care have greater impact on women than on men. The disproportionality is partly because women are more likely to use these services, such as child-care; and partly because women are more likely to be employed in the public than the private sector and hence suffer most from public sector wage freezes and cuts in jobs (Women's Budget Group 2013). This argument applies to a range of types of expenditure, including also the cuts in budgets for services to prevent domestic and sexual violence against women (Towers and Walby 2012).

These changes to government budgets also increase other inequalities. The Institute for Fiscal Studies report by Browne and Levell (2010) contests the chancellor's claim that the June 2010 budget was 'progressive'. These authors showed that the distributional effect of tax and benefit changes being introduced between June 2010 and April 2014 would be regressive since low-income households of working age would lose the most.

The gendering of budgets is contested (Lahey 2009; Women's Budget Group 2010, 2014). The Fawcett Society took the government to the High Court in 2010, alleging that it had failed in its legal duty to consider the gender inequalities that would be produced by its policy measures in the 2010 budget (Fawcett Society 2010). While the legal challenge failed it nevertheless established the government's obligation, under its own equalities legislation, to conduct equality impact assessments of its budgets (Conley 2012). Thereafter, major government statements involving spending cuts have been subject to differing assessments of their impact on gender. The government's own 'equalities impact assessment' by HM Treasury (2010) suggests that the pooling of income in households makes it hard to offer more than a minimal gender analysis. However, the Institute of Fiscal Studies (Browne 2011) argues that a reasonable account is feasible. This claim is supported by a range of studies (e.g. House of Commons Library 2010, 2013; Women's Budget Group 2013).

The reduction of the deficit by reducing public expenditure rather than raising taxes is gendered. Women are more likely than men to use, support and be employed in the public services supported by this state expenditure, while they are likely to pay less tax because their income is lower than that of men. This is a significant gender restructuring. The year 2010 was a turning point in the gendering of the fiscal in the UK. Fiscal policy prior to 2010 had tended to narrow gender inequality; thereafter it increased it.

Contested Economic Growth Strategies

The immediate aftermath of the financial collapse and deepening recession in output and employment saw a brief moment of policy consensus on the use of the Keynesian tool of increasing state expenditure to increase aggregate demand and thereby soften the depth of the recession. However, following this brief period of consensus, the division in perspective on securing economic growth increased. On one side, neoliberals sought deep cuts in public expenditure with the stated intention of freeing up resources for use in profitable locations in the private sector. On the other side, social democrats found a new form of expression of their traditional approach to economic growth in the concept of 'social investment', in which state investment in human capital development was seen as the way forward. These are gendered strategies even though this is rarely made visible.

Brief Keynesian boost

Some governments tried to stimulate their economies to prevent the recession turning into depression and deflation. The UK, along with several other governments, attempted to mitigate the emerging recession during 2008 and 2009 by providing a stimulus to the economy along Keynesian lines. In November 2008, the European Commission announced an economy recovery package of €200 billion, and in February 2009, the US signed a $787-billion stimulus package into law. The G20 group of larger, more developed countries pledged measures worth $1.1 trillion in April 2009. The measures included tax reductions such as the UK government's temporary reduction in VAT from 17.5 per cent to 15 per cent in November 2008. There were also interventions to support those industries deemed to have been particularly affected. For example, car manufacturing in the UK, France and Germany received a subsidy to support the scrapping of old cars in order to encourage the buying of new ones.

Prioritizing full employment is a policy which generally tends to benefit women (Braunstein and Heintz 2008). However, in this case, assistance targeted the industries of construction and car manufacture, which comprised mainly male employees. The boost was therefore gendered since it supported the economy at a time when it was men who were most at risk of losing their jobs.

This Keynesian policy phase did not last long, but it did serve to demonstrate that such a response was possible. However, the boost applied an industrial policy that worked to the detriment of gender equality. The use of alternative industrial policies would have benefitted men and women more equally. These policies include investment in the green economy to speed transition to a low-carbon economy, in the infrastructure to socialize care-work, and in knowledge-intensive services (Walby et al. 2007). While the last of these tends to be gendered in complex ways (Perrons 2005; Durbin 2011; Shire 2007; Walby 2011b), it nevertheless produces more jobs for women than does the car industry. Instead, the short-lived boost fed into an industrial policy which supported the gender-segregated industrial structure.

Neoliberal growth theory

From 2010 the UK government increasingly cut state spending on public services. There were two narratives to support this strategy, each linked to economic growth, but in different ways. Initially, the cut in spending was legitimated as a way of reducing the deficit that otherwise risked the government defaulting on its debts; the difficulties in Greece were held up as an example of what needed to be avoided. Later, the cuts in spending were justified as the means to free up resources for use by the private sector to generate growth. This was based on the assumption that only activities in the private sector create economic growth. By 2015, the growth agenda constituted the dominant legitimation of economic and fiscal policy. This approach is based on the 'efficient markets' thesis and is in contradiction of Keynesian thinking regarding the best way to achieve economic growth. It assumes that cuts to government spending will increase growth, whereas the Keynesian perspective assumes such cuts will decrease growth.

Alongside the programme of cuts in public spending was a further strategy of privatization of public services to move them from state to market provision. Some public services, including health care and services to prevent violence against women and girls, were deemed essential and therefore were not to be significantly reduced. These services were instead subject to privatization and marketization, whereby public money was used to fund the services but they were to be provided through processes of competitive tendering by the private and third sectors. Health care and services to prevent domestic and sexual violence were to be delivered by non-state entities potentially for profit (Towers and Walby 2012).

Social investment state

Within the EU an alternative economic growth theory and practice have been taking shape, which variously draw upon: historic legacies of Nordic social democracy (Esping-Andersen 2002); heterodox economic theories of human capital (Becker 1964; Heckman 2006); the concept of the knowledge economy; and traces of feminism (European Commission 2013b). This is becoming known as the 'social investment state' model of economic growth (Morel et al. 2012).

This model for economic growth focuses on the skills held by human beings, otherwise known as human capital (Becker 1964). As the economy develops beyond agriculture and industry, knowledge becomes increasingly important for economic growth. Hence, in encouraging the processes that develop skills, education and knowledge become central to the promotion of economic growth. Some of these skills are acquired in childhood (Heckman 2006) and others are accumulated throughout life. Investment in the education of girls in particular spurs economic growth by increasing their human capital and thereby their high-quality employment (Klasen 2002; Thévenon et al. 2012). This means that state expenditure on education and training can be conceptualized as investment that contributes to economic growth rather than as welfare or distribution for purposes of social justice (European Commission 2013b; Morel et al. 2012). There has been a significant development of public expenditure on childcare, which is in alignment with these goals.

There are some critical commentaries on the coherence of the model as currently developed. Nolan (2013) finds it difficult in practice to ascertain the boundary between social expenditure for social investment and that for welfare purposes. Jenson (2009) is critical of the social investment perspective for leaving out an explicit focus on gender equality. She finds the de-gendering occurs at least partly due to the focus on children. Children are the target of investment for development of their human capital, which displaces the needs and concerns of adult women. The social investment analysis also tends to focus attention on the development of human capital even though, implicitly if not explicitly, it does contain a broader understanding of economic growth.

However, it is possible to address these concerns by making the gender dimension more explicit and drawing on a range of analyses of social investment in particular areas (such as the minimum wage and social housing, discussed earlier). The development of the framework for a gendered economic growth strategy is briefly explored here and more fully in chapter 7.

Developing a gendered economic growth strategy

The core of social democratic economic growth is the alignment of the goals of justice and growth, which simultaneously promotes both social inclusion and full employment. In practice, it is through gendering the traditional social democratic growth strategy of full employment that this can take place, since women are the largest available and under-utilized source of labour (Walby and Olsen 2002; Walby 2007b). Three elements are involved: a social investment state; a forward-looking industrial policy; and regulation of labour markets to make them efficient instead of discriminatory. This means: state social investment in human capital formation through the provision of the necessary infrastructure of publicly funded and provided education and care for children, the elderly and the sick; industrial policy that looks forward to the knowledge economy, where there is gender balance of beneficiaries, instead of looking backward to protect the carbon-producing industries of car manufacture and road building, where more men are employed; and the regulation of labour markets to reduce discrimination that limits their efficiency.

Transnational Financial Institutions

These developments are enmeshed in a wider series of changes that extend globally, if unevenly so. Practices promoted or enforced by international financial and trade institutions including the IMF, the Bank of International Settlements and the World Trade Organization (WTO), as well as by the European Union, have implications for the nature of decision-making in individual states. International and transnational bodies are relevant for the development of financial and trade policy, for example in the ongoing attempts to liberalize trade in services. The relevance of international bodies is especially visible in times of financial crisis when limits to banking are reached. International financial institutions are then called upon to provide governments with emergency loans, which generally arrive only with significant conditions attached.

The drive to liberalize services, to put public services out to competitive tender on the market, is supported by the WTO Directive on the liberalization of services. This Directive, in turn, was embedded in the EU Directive on the liberalization of services. The EU Directive allows Member States some flexibility in deciding which services are of 'economic interest', which are to be marketized fully, and those having a 'general economic interest', which can be shielded from some of these competitive pressures, so there are differences in the actions of Member States (Penna and O'Brien 2006). This liberalization is gendered since employment in and use of public services are gendered.

The financial crisis has been destabilizing the European Union. The funding of the government budget deficits in some EU countries became the subject of intense financial speculation. This was exacerbated by the volatile judgements of ratings agencies, and thus interest rates on these debts were suddenly increased to levels considered unsupportable. The political issues this raised within the EU were compounded by the interaction of fiscal arrangements with the new currency of the EU, the Euro, which around half of the twenty-eight Member States have adopted. Several solutions have been proposed, two of which are discussed here: the Six Pack and the Excessive Deficit Procedure; and EuroBonds.

The 'Six Pack' was introduced by the EU in 2011 to establish the framework and conditions for loans and regulate the emerging debts of countries in the Eurozone. EU Member States were facing possible defaults on their government budget deficits because of the level of interest charged by the financial markets and the size of the annual deficits and accumulated debts. The hope was to limit annual government budget deficits to 3 per cent of GDP and the accumulated debt to less than 60 per cent of GDP through the Six Pack of five Regulations and one Directive. Countries that fell beneath this threshold were subject to the 'Excessive Deficit Procedure' (EDF) whereby the Commission set 'medium-term objectives' which were intended to 'correct' their finances. Unlike other EU actions, this one had a 'reverse qualified majority voting' system introduced which meant that a country had to win a majority of votes to overturn a Commission order; an unprecedented degree of centralization of EU power. Those Member States that received loans incurred increased EU-level control over their economies. In the case of Greece, for example, which received loans from the EU and IMF in 2010 and

2012, a board (representing the European Commission, the European Central Bank and the IMF) known as the Troika oversaw the implementation of a structural adjustment package called an Economic Adjustment Programme (European Commission 2013c). Some elements, such as the increased capitalization of banks and improved tax collection, are focused on general aspects of financial and economic efficiency. However, others appear to introduce or deepen specifically neoliberal principles, through increased competition and reduced regulation. These latter elements included policies to: cut 'red tape'; liberalize the professions, energy sector and transport system; and privatize a range of government-owned assets, from gas production to lotteries.

A different and longer-term solution, set out by the European Commission (2011b), was to pool resources within the EU by the creation of Eurobonds (in the form of 'Stability Bonds') to keep the interest rate on government debts to reasonably low levels. Such pooling of debt was intended to provide an effective bulwark against attacks by the hedge funds, which threatened potential government defaults by increasing the interest rates on government debt to unpayable levels. However, such a device was considered to risk the creation of moral hazard. It was feared that countries would lack incentive to keep their budget expenditure modest and would leave other, richer countries, especially Germany, to foot the bill disproportionately. It was felt that to avoid such moral hazard a more harmonized set of fiscal and financial arrangements across the EU in which to embed the Bonds was necessary (European Commission 2011b). This type of solution, which involved the deepening of European Union institutions and the ever closer engagement of Member States, was consistent with the original plan for the European Union. The plan foresaw the use of economic crises to promote the political integration required to achieve the primary objective of preventing war ever again in Europe (Haas 1958; Hallstein 1973 [1969]). This proposal for Eurobonds was rejected in the form suggested (Stability Bonds), but it is likely to return in a new but equivalent form at the next financial crisis. The policy question remaining unanswered is the nature of the deal that offers both the pooling of financial risk and the deepening of EU institutions in a manner acceptable to the prevailing dominant political forces. This deal will be gendered and will embed practices more conducive to one form of gender regime than others. The outcome may take different forms and will depend upon the balance of forces and arguments in the conjuncture at the time of the next crisis.

What would a pro-gender equality Six Pack look like? What should be the appropriately gendered component of the institutional measures necessary to support Eurobonds? First, the measures would adopt the principles of the gendered social investment state. This would entail the public provision of investment in human capital, including education, care services for children and the elderly, and health care. The provision of public services would be protected since this is an important component of a social democratic public gender regime; rejecting the assumption that privatization is always better. Second, the measures would adopt the principles of the gendered regulatory state. This would entail the provision of regulations for equal treatment in labour and other economic markets and regulations to facilitate the combination of employment and care-work. Third, the measures would ensure gender balance in financial and economic decision-making, including on corporate boards, central banks and committees to regulate finance at Member State and EU levels.

The Six Pack and its EDFs place the economic governance of debt-burdened EU Member States under the surveillance of transnational bodies which are better known for their neoliberal rather than EU values and priorities. Nevertheless, the Eurobond approach potentially offers the EU some independence from the priorities of the transnational financial institutions and global capital markets. It also increases the likelihood of EU citizens having a greater voice in deciding their economic future.

Only a transnational polity has the capacity to confront transnational capital. Robinson (2014) has argued that there already is such a transnational state, but it represents the interests of global capital. However, others such as Carroll (2010) have shown that significant regional divisions continue to exist. Further, Habermas (2009) contends that there is a democratic deficit in the European Union because it has become a project of its elites more than of its citizens. Nonetheless, he continues to hold onto a reasoned belief in its potential. The European project may be faltering (Habermas 2009) but it is not yet over (Giddens 2014). The EU is the only polity with the potential to regulate finance capital. But will it do so? These issues will be further discussed in chapter 6 on democracy.

Ways Forward for Fiscal Strategy

There are several ways in which fiscal strategy could be improved in the light of the research discussed earlier. There are four main goals: reduce the fiscal deficit and its destabilizing effects; increase economic growth; deliver social justice by reducing inequality; and deepen democracy. These goals overlap and depend upon each other; in particular, social justice and economic growth are best considered as mutually supportive goals. Each of the main goals could be addressed through several possible actions, as follows:

- First, reduce the fiscal deficit and its destabilizing effects by: collecting taxes rather than reducing public expenditure, by collecting more of the taxes owed by more rigorous implementation of existing law, closing tax havens and reforming company law to reduce the fragmentation that facilitates tax dodging, and introducing a new tax on financial transactions; raising the minimum wage to a living wage to reduce state subsidy of low wages; and fiscal pooling at the EU level to reduce the capacity of financial markets to raise interest rates on government debt.
- Second, increase economic growth by social investment in: social housing to create jobs and reduce subsidy to private landlords; human capital development including life-long education for the knowledge economy; and public care, especially but not only for children, to reduce interruptions to employment.
- Third, deliver social justice by reducing social inequality by making full employment and gender equality goals of fiscal strategy, including in the forthcoming restructuring of the EU financial and fiscal architecture.
- Fourth, deepen democracy, including by reducing gender imbalance in decision-making; and by using gender budgeting to increase awareness of the implications of budgets for gender inequality.

The fiscal deficit could be reduced by collecting more of the taxes owed. Tax dodging could be reduced through more vigorous use of the existing law; and by reforming the law so it is harder to dodge taxes. There could be more effective collection of the taxes owed to the state through more energetic use of existing legal practices and by reducing the generosity with which companies and rich individuals defaulting on their taxes are treated. The number of tax inspectors could be increased rather than reduced. The criminal law, rather than only the softer forms of civil law, could be used to hold tax dodgers accountable. States could act, either individually or jointly, to close the tax havens and secrecy jurisdictions that allow companies and rich individuals to hide their money offshore to avoid and evade taxes, by using the powers they have through shared sovereignty and by banning economic and financial transactions with entities that use tax havens. There could be reform of the laws that allow companies to separate their tax liabilities from their actual place of business and from their legal headquarters, in order to reintegrate and make company tax liabilities transparent, thereby reducing their capacity to dodge taxes. A new tax could be introduced on financial transactions: even very low rates of taxation on financial transactions would raise considerable revenue.

There are several forms of social investment by the state that reduce the deficit and increase economic growth. Raising the minimum wage to a living wage would reduce the state subsidy of low wages. Investment in building social housing would reduce state subsidy of high rents and boost jobs. State investment in life-long education helps develop the human capital needed for growth in the knowledge economy. State investment in childcare and other forms of care facilitates continuous employment among women, thereby reducing gender inequality and increasing human capital and economic growth.

Social justice is developed by making visible the inequalities in budgeting and by fiscal pooling. The routine use of gender budgeting would enable the effects of budgets on gender inequality to be made visible. This could be in parallel with environmental impact assessments for sustainable development and impact assessments for further forms of inequality. Fiscal pooling across the EU, to reduce the significance and cost of fiscal deficits by lowering the interest rates charged by financial markets, is the largest and most ambitious strategy. It would require the development of new political mechanisms to govern these practices. This would be possible only if there were to be a restructuring of the fiscal, financial and democratic architecture of the EU. Some restructuring of this architecture is very likely at the next financial crisis; a crisis which is probable since the reforms to the financial system have as yet been minimal. The inclusion of the goals of full employment and gender equality could be inserted into the new fiscal and financial architecture in this restructuring.

Some of these fiscal reforms, such as reducing tax dodging, could be achieved by the UK acting alone. Others are feasible through EU-level action, though the engagement of the other international bodies including the OECD, G20 and UN, is also significant. The more energetic pursuit of tax avoiders by the UK is possible within the existing law. The proposal for a financial transactions tax has the support of the majority of EU Member States but not the UK. The implication of these fiscal reforms for gender relations is that they would facilitate the development of a social democratic public gender regime.

Conclusions

Austerity has been the response to the perceived crisis in the fiscal domain. Austerity itself has fed the recessionary spiral in the real economy, thereby acting as a positive feedback loop. The deficit was a consequence of the recession in output and employment, which was itself a consequence of the crisis in finance. In this way, the crisis has cascaded from the deregulation of finance, to finance, to the real economy, and to the fiscal and austerity.

There was an opportunity to slow the cascade of the crisis by increasing rather than decreasing government spending. This route of 'Keynesian' boost to the economy was taken only for a very short moment in 2008/9. It was replaced after the 2010 election with austerity, in other words, the attempt to reduce the deficit by cutting expenditure. The opportunity to absorb the cascading crisis by using fiscal levers was rejected after 2010.

The initial narrative used to legitimate austerity was that the possibility of defaulting on the debt was a crisis, a state of emergency or of exception, sufficient to justify government actions which had not been part of the manifestos on which the parties were elected to government in 2010. Later, the legitimating narrative switched to that of economic growth. It was argued that growth would be better achieved by reducing the use of resources by the state on welfare in order to facilitate the growth of private firms.

There has been considerable resistance to austerity by projects seeking social justice. There has also been an emergent counter-narrative that contests the theory of economic growth from the perspective of the social investment state, which itself combines the projects of social justice and economic growth.

The contestations over distribution and over the strategy for economic growth involve gender as well as other social inequalities. Austerity has had a detrimental impact on gender relations by increasing gender inequality. There was a sudden change in the trajectory of development of the gender regime, which had been progressing in the direction of a social democratic public gender regime, to a neoliberal trajectory. Austerity is a tipping point in the trajectory of the gender regime. Gender is central to the crisis. The contestation over the strategy for economic growth is also gendered, as well as involving other forms of social inequalities. The neoliberal growth strategy of reducing state expenditure further increases gender and other inequalities. The social democratic economic growth strategy centred on social investment by the state would decrease these inequalities.

6

Democratic Crisis?

Introduction

The crisis, starting in the deregulation of finance and cascading through banking collapse into economic recession and a state fiscal crisis, has become a political crisis; with the potential to become a crisis in democracy. It is a political crisis in which governments around Europe have fallen, established political parties have crashed and new political projects and parties have emerged. Whether this political crisis cascades into a crisis of democracy is the concern of this chapter. A democratic crisis would mean existing political institutions are no longer sufficient to channel conflict, which would have consequences for the rate of violence and result in a possible systemic crisis.

The cascading of an economic crisis into a democratic crisis is the European nightmare. In the last century, the financial crisis in 1929 cascaded into the economic crisis of depression in the 1930s, cascading in central and southern Europe into a political crisis which then cascaded into a democratic crisis of fascism, holocaust and war. Is it different this time; or will the European nightmare become real?

The European Union was established to prevent recurrence of this nightmare. Its founders sought to create a trans-European polity that would prevent war and holocaust ever again. Whether the EU will achieve this goal depends on the development of the institutional architecture of the EU, involving, for example, its depth of democracy and its financial and fiscal instruments.

This chapter starts by addressing the concept of 'democracy' to ascertain what might constitute a democratic crisis. It proceeds by identifying and appraising the contesting political forces in play. An investigation of the EU as the terrain for a potential tipping point into a democratic crisis is then undertaken.

The Edge of a Democratic Crisis

Five issues need clarification to ascertain whether the crisis is cascading into a democratic crisis. What exactly is meant by democracy? At what point might a political crisis become a democratic crisis? Has the 'depth' of democracy been declining? Is there a 'state of exception' or emergency which has led to the bypassing of democratic processes? Has political conflict cascaded into violent conflict?

What is democracy?

The ideal of democracy is the realization of the will of the people to which each person contributes equally. This is close to Rousseau's (1968 [1762]) notion of 'the general will' and to declarations of the American and French Revolutions in the eighteenth century: 'The law is the expression of the general will. All citizens have the right to contribute personally, or through their representatives, to its formation' (National Assembly of France 1789: Article 6). The practice always falls short but that does not diminish the power and legitimacy of the ideal, which has become widely held (George 2004, 2010; Wright 2010). There are various approaches to the procedures and institutions which are necessary for the actual achievement of some level of democracy. This 'procedural' conception of democracy implicates a range of mechanisms to secure representation, and places varying importance on the role of deliberation (Held 1995; Habermas 1996 [1992]; Majone 1996; Potter et al. 1997; della Porta 2013).

The failure of existing political institutions to prevent the financial crash and its ensuing crises re-opens this long-standing tension in the conceptualization of democracy between 'the will of the people' and 'a set of institutions to deliver the will of the people'. The first conceptualization is close to the popular understanding of democracy: if political institutions do not deliver the will of the people then they are not delivering democracy. This interpretation of democracy may represent an ideal which is never fully realized, but it has nevertheless become a widely and deeply held value. The second conceptualization concerns procedures and institutions. Minimally, a country is democratic if it holds elections, has more than one political party, has a free press and allows citizens to form associations in civil society. There is variation in the depth of democracy produced by different political institutions.

The procedural approach to democracy is dominant during relatively settled periods. However, in times of crisis, the more fundamental question is raised: why has the will of the people not been realized through the actions of the political institutions? What aspect of the political system has prevented this realization; and what would a truly democratic system look like? The legitimacy of political institutions is questioned in times of crisis and the architecture of the system of political institutions comes to be challenged.

Distinguishing between political and democratic crises

Democracy involves political contestation. In contemporary political forms this includes, but is not confined to, contestation between multiple political parties. These parties are situated in a broader field of organized political actors ranging from those in civil society projects to those involved in designing and executing governmental programmes. Political parties usually refine and entrench political projects in a more institutionalized organizational form than is the case for the more fluid projects of civil society. Political parties articulate alternative political projects that aspire to be governmental programmes.

This institutionalization is an asset in more settled times, since it facilitates the incremental, cumulative development of a political project and the development of the commitment and allies necessary to carry it forward. However, at times of rapid change and crisis, this entrenchment can be a weakness, since parties can be slow to adapt to new circumstances which require adjustment of old agendas and the creation of new ones. Hence, in times of crisis, old political parties may fall out of favour with voters, at the same time as new political parties are formed to offer new agendas. Financial, economic and fiscal crisis can thus cascade into political crisis for old political parties while creating opportunities in the political landscape for new ones. This is not a crisis in democracy. It may be a crisis for old political parties but it only becomes a democratic crisis if political conflict cannot be channelled through political institutions.

Existing political parties are challenged when important concerns arise which are not part of their established political agendas. Their slowness or outright failure to address these new issues to the satisfaction of the public and electorate has generated a crisis for these old parties. This has led to new political agendas and organizational forms, ranging from 'grassroots' and non-governmental organizations (NGOs) to political parties, at local, national and transnational levels. The new social media, including the internet, have facilitated these developments. In some cases, there has been a turn away from state-oriented political institutions, such as political parties, towards new projects, communities and institutions which are linked horizontally rather than vertically (e.g. eco-communities; peer-to-peer lending instead of borrowing through banks). In addition, a range of new political parties has developed which are located both to the left and to the right of the older traditional parties from which they have sapped support.

Sometimes a tension occurs between grassroots horizontal practices and 'pre-figurative' politics to create new ideas (Graeber 2002) on the one hand and developing state-oriented political institutions (Wallerstein 2011b) on the other hand, as in the World Social Forum (Smith and West 2012). The theoretical debate can be dichotomized into these two major positions but there are many nuanced positions between them. The analysis here disperses this tension across a wider spectrum of politics found in civil societal projects, political parties and governmental programmes (see Walby 2009, 2011a for a fuller discussion). Civil society projects are themselves varied in their orientation to and capture by the state: many grassroots organizations are autonomous and proud of their independence from the state; trade unions are independent bodies with varying political activities and engagements; while some NGOs may campaign actively on some issues but be quieter on others according to their dependence upon government funding. Political parties may be oriented towards the state for the achievement of their projects, but in times of crisis old parties may implode and new ones start up in ways responsive to new agendas related to the crisis. However, some parties struggle to move beyond long-established positions that have become deeply institutionalized even if these positions are no longer relevant. Governmental programmes may become so deeply institutionalized that they are immovable even if irrelevant or harmful, but they may also be relatively free-floating and open to capture by well-resourced lobbyists. Social formations change more slowly in response to these and other pressures. It is useful to make distinctions not only between civil society and the state, but between civil societal projects, political parties, governmental programmes and social formations. The concept of 'project' is deployed to mean a set of ideas and practices that are oriented towards social change. 'Project' is used in preference to 'frame' or 'discourse' since these are both more focused on ideas and less focused on impetus for change.

Contemporary democracies, at least in Europe and North America, have various types and levels of institutionalization in their political projects. This variation facilitates the fluidity necessary for the responsiveness of political institutions to new circumstances. A crisis for a specific political party or government is not a democratic crisis. A democratic crisis is when the political institutions are no longer sufficient to channel political conflict.

There has been a significant growth in new or revived political parties in Europe since the financial, economic and fiscal crises. These have arisen across the full political spectrum. Particularly important are those parties to the left and to the right of major parties and those that make claims on behalf of particular political subjects such as national, ethnic or religious groups.

In the UK, for example, this process has included the emergence of two nationalist and one left party: the United Kingdom Independence Party (UKIP), the Scottish Nationalist Party (SNP) and the Greens. UKIP, to the right of the major centre-right party of the Conservatives, calls for the UK to reduce in-migration and to repatriate powers or withdraw from the European Union. The SNP calls for the independence of Scotland from the UK and is situated in the social democratic space that was traditionally occupied by the Labour Party. The voting in the UK General Election in May 2015 demonstrated the increased electoral significance of both these parties. The close division in the vote in the referendum on independence for Scotland in September 2014, with 45 per cent for independence and 55 per cent for continued union, showed the strength of Scottish nationalism. In addition, the Greens, positioned to the left of the Labour Party, have been gathering increasing support in 2015.

Many other EU Member States have similarly seen the emergence of new parties to the left of the traditional centre-left and to the right of the traditional centre-right in elections after 2009 (European Parliament 2009, 2014). In the May 2014 elections of the European Parliament there was a significant emergence of and growth in parties to the left and right of existing centre parties, including ethno-nationalist positions. For example, in Greece, there has been the emergence of both Syriza, a new party to the left of the traditional centre-left grouping, and Golden Dawn, a new party to the right of the traditional centre-right grouping. In Spain there has been the formation and strong growth of Podemas, to the left of the traditional social democratic party. There has also been growth in parties on the right, including the Front National in France. However, by February 2015, only Syriza in Greece had formed a government.

Is the depth of democracy declining?

The financial crisis has exposed the lack of democratic control over finance and the consequences of this lack for economy and society. Yet the absence of democratic control over finance is not considered relevant to many traditional concepts of democracy. Indeed, in many conventional approaches to democracy, the range of institutions over which there should be democratic control for a country to count as democratic is typically quite narrow and excludes finance. If the definition of democracy were broadened to include the range of institutions over which the democratic principle held sway, then the reduction in the democratic control over finance would be understood as a decline in the depth of democracy.

The traditional approach to the political institutions required to deliver democracy specifies a relatively narrow range of institutions focused on free competitive elections, free association and political parties, and a free press. But some electoral systems, while democratic in this traditional sense, enable little more than the alternation of elites or 'polyarchy' (Dahl 1971; Robinson 1996; Fung and Wright 2003).

A relatively narrow set of requirements for democracy is proposed by Freedom House (2014), which lists several political rights and civil liberties, including: free and fair elections of the head of government and legislature; the right to organize in different political parties and other associations; political choice free from domination by non-democratic or corrupt forces; and transparent and accountable governments.

Walby (2009) distinguishes three levels of depth of democracy rather than a simple dichotomy between democratic and not democratic. These are constituted through ten issues:

1 no hereditary or unelected positions, including a monarch and members in either chamber of Parliament;
2 no colonies, that is, no governance of territories that do not also meet these criteria;
3 no powers of governance held by additional non-democratic polity such as organized religion;
4 universal suffrage, de facto as well as de jure;
5 elections, especially those that are free, fair and competitive; in

a context of free speech and free association and developed civil society associations;
6 low cost of electioneering, either by law or by custom;
7 electoral system with proportional representation;
8 electoral system with quotas for under-represented groups such as women;
9 proportionate presence in parliament of women and minorities;
10 range of institutions (e.g. welfare services) governed by the democratic polity.

In the first, shallowest, form of democracy, non-elected governance positions have been eliminated and replaced by representatives elected by universal suffrage in the context of free association in civil society. This is the traditional understanding of democracy.

In the second, middle, level, attention is paid to the nature of the procedures to secure representation of women and minorities. This level goes beyond shallow forms of representational practice such as voting to encompass the presence of women and minorities in the deliberative forums, including the legislative assembly or parliament, as well as in the civil society institutions that underpin democracy at the level of the state. The presence of women and minorities in political institutions has been found, after much investigation, to be necessary for there to be representation in practice (Phillips 1995; Childs et al. 2010; Mansbridge 2005). Without the presence of women the deliberations that are an important part of democratic procedure would occur with fewer contributions from perspectives more frequently held by women. This proposal draws on Habermas' (1996 [1992]) concept of deliberative democracy, in which argumentation is a necessary part of the process of democracy in a plural society in order to have the possibility of reaching agreement or compromise between different positions aligned with different social groups. The decreasing gender imbalance in political decision-making is an important component of deeper forms of democracy.

The third, deepest, level in the typology of forms of democracy is reserved for those polities that extend the principle of democratic governance to the widest range of institutions. The governance of major public services, such as finance, health, education and care services, through procedures that are democratically accountable, rather than through procedures focused on increasing profits for private owners, is of significance for the depth of democracy. Privatization is considered to reduce the depth of democracy since it removes institutions from democratic governance. When the definition of democracy is deepened in this way then regulations can be seen as forms of democratic control rather than mere bureaucracy. Regulation is activity by the state to intervene in markets to make them more effective and fair. The 'red tape challenge' is an exercise in the recalibration of the balance between democracy and capital, away from democracy, and towards capital. The neoliberal project of deregulation is a project of de-democratization. This repositions thinking on both bureaucracy and markets. Bureaucracy is the systematic application of rules by authorities and is necessary to achieve democratic governance. The 'efficient markets' thesis is mistaken since, left unregulated, 'markets' become riddled with corruption, fraud, rent-seeking and distortions as those in positions of power change markets to suit their own interests. Regulation by democratic states reduces such distortion of markets by the corrupt and powerful. The achievement of democratic depth requires the regulation of finance in the interests of the majority, not the minority. Deregulation and privatization are processes of de-democratization.

There have been contrary movements in the depth of democracy since the 1980s: there has been increasing depth in relation to the presence of women and minorities in parliaments; but decreasing depth in terms of the reduction of democratic control over finance and public services.

State of exception: legitimation of bypassing democratic procedures

A crisis can be described as an emergency, an extraordinary situation or an exceptional state. In a crisis, it is not uncommon for there to be a call for the use of emergency measures in a short time span, even if it means bypassing the usual procedures. The concept of 'state of exception' is used to address this set of circumstances in the context of the diminution of democracy during declared crises. It occurs when a government declares a 'state of emergency'.

A 'state of exception' (Agamben 1998, 2005) is the declaration by the executive branch of the government that it is necessary for it to take control over all the levers of power, regardless of prior law and agreed political procedure, because an emergency has arisen that is sufficiently serious for this to be necessary. It is a concept that sits on the border of politics and law: the suspension of the juridical order by political decree. Agamben argues that the power to declare a 'state of exception' lies at the core of the power of the executive since it is the power to declare the limits of law and political procedure. Whatever agency is able to declare a state of exception has ultimate power.

Agamben offers a set of examples to illustrate his point. One follows the Al Qaeda attack on the US when, on 3 November 2001, President Bush issued a 'military order'. This order authorized the indefinite detention and trial by military commissions of non-citizens suspected of terrorism, which was the basis for the Guantanamo camp. Another example is that of Nazi rule in Germany from the 1930s until 1945. Others concern the fate of various European democracies that declared war during the twentieth century. Agamben's exploration of the theory and practice of the 'state of exception' shows how this practice, which is far from uncommon, allows executives to use a declaration of crisis, whether justified or not, to undermine democratic procedure.

The discussion of the development of the concept and practice of 'securitization' by Buzan et al. (1998) and Buzan and Hansen (2009) has similarities with that by Agamben (1998, 2005) on the 'state of exception'.

> 'Security' is the move that takes politics beyond the established rules of the game and frames the issue as a special kind of politics or as above politics. (Buzan et al 1998: 23)

> Security is about survival. It is when an issue is presented as posing an existential threat to a designated referent object (traditionally, but not necessarily, the state, incorporating government, territory, and society). The special nature of security threats justifies the use of extraordinary measures to handle them. The invocation of security has been the key to legitimizing the use of force, but more generally it has opened the way for the state to mobilize, or take special powers, to handle existential threats. Traditionally, by saying 'security', a state representative declares an emergency condition, thus claiming a right to use whatever means are necessary to block a threatening development. (Buzan et al. 1998: 21)

The focus here is on the process by which something can be construed as such a serious threat that it requires actions that bypass the normal democratic procedure. The construction of security for Buzan is a discursive process of making claims. It can potentially be played out on a number of policy terrains rather than being restricted to the traditional security concern of military threats.

Indeed, the UK national security strategy names several potential threats as being of greater risk than that of invasion by foreign military forces (HM Government 2010). Terrorism is regarded as the most significant risk, which has wide-ranging implications for the due process of justice (Aradau and van Munster 2009; Hudson 2009). Even an increase in organized crime is considered more of a risk to UK security than a foreign invasion (HM Government 2010).

The language of 'emergency' and 'crisis' was used in the UK to justify the transfer of billions to the banks and finance sector during the financial crisis in 2008 and to cut billions from state expenditure on welfare benefits and public services in the fiscal crisis of 2010. Immediately after the May 2010 election the new government, a coalition between Conservatives and Liberal Democrats, declared, using the example of Greece, that there was a crisis. The new government claimed that this 'crisis' gave rise to a need, previously unforeseen, to cut public expenditure; even though this was not part of the mandate on which the government had been so recently elected.

Analysis of the 'state of exception' and of 'securitization' assists theorization of the processes under which democratic and judicial procedures are diminished or set aside when crises are declared by executive authorities. The ability to declare that a situation has crossed the threshold into being a crisis that threatens existential security is an extreme form of power. It is a form of power that can threaten democracy.

Crisis, democracy and violence

If political institutions become unable to channel conflict then the political crisis is likely to cascade into violence and become a crisis in democracy. The theorization of the boundary between political and violent conflict has been developed in the work of Arendt (1970), Gramsci (1971), Mouffe (1993) and Walby (2009), while empirical evidence on these issues in Europe has been collected by della Porta (1995) and in the UK by Bagguley and Hussain (2008) for the riots in the early 2000s and by Mansley (2014) for the most recent period.

For Arendt (1970) politics constitutes the highest level of social organization; political disagreement is regarded as a virtue. Agonistic politics are good for society in that they involve the active channelling of conflicts into politics, treating enemies as opponents, where they may find compromise or resolution and thereby avoid violence and chaos. Mouffe (1993) likewise argues it is important for democracy that antagonism is given expression in political conflict mediated through mainstream political institutions. When agonistic conflicts have ceased to be the substance of mainstream political debate and the issues addressed by mainstream political institutions are ones that are merely technocratic or managerial, then democracy suffers.

In such contexts of the inadequate expression of major conflicts in politics, Mouffe argues, there is a danger of the development of fundamentalist politics based on non-negotiable values at the heart of ethnic, religious and nationalist identities.

The re-ordering of the relationship between politics and violence is addressed in the work of Weber (1968 [1922]), who considered that states became modern when they had developed a monopoly over legitimate violence in their territory. In these circumstances the territory they controlled was pacified; though the state could and did exercise its monopoly of violence. Tilly (1990) sought to demonstrate the acuity of Weber's thesis. He investigated the relationship between states and violence over a thousand-year period of European history and concluded that violence became slowly ever more concentrated in the state.

For Gramsci (1971) the use of violence by the state was less stable than implied in Weber's thesis. Governance was secured through hegemony that rested on a mixture of consent and coercion. In settled times hegemony is maintained through an appearance of consent. In a crisis that hegemony is challenged; cracks emerge and conflicts become more visible so that consent is no longer assured. At such moments the ruling bloc is likely to respond with coercion to replace consent as the method by which hegemony is maintained. Coercion may re-stabilize the situation so that consent re-emerges as the basis of hegemony. Alternatively the use of coercion may make visible power hierarchies and inequalities to such an extent that hegemony is not restored but further destabilized. In such a case the crisis may become systemic.

In much contemporary social theory, violence emerges for analysis only at the edges of society; it is relegated to the margins, appearing only in the actions of criminals, terrorists and occasional inter-state wars (Malešević 2010; Walby 2013b). This is a mistake, since violence is a long-standing and central aspect of society, though hugely varied in form and extent. There are important patterns in the deployment of violence. For example, the levels of different forms of violence co-vary, meaning that if there is more of one form of violence in a country then there is likely to be more of other forms. This is shown in Walby's (2009) cross-national analysis of the correlation between homicide rates, use of capital punishment and government spending on the military. Further, violence regularly appears during particular kinds of political protest and contestation (Tilly 1978; della Porta 1995).

Several European countries have experienced violent political protests against the austerity response to the fiscal crisis. This is especially the case in southern European countries, such as Greece, where the fiscal crisis has been especially severe and the rates of unemployment, especially among youth, have risen to extremely high levels. During the summer of 2011, one year after the introduction of austerity, there was extensive rioting in the UK (Guardian 2012).

Mansley (2014), in an analysis of violence during political protest in the UK, found that the level of violence used by both protesters and police had increased since the financial and economic crisis of 2009. This upturn followed a decade during which such violence had been declining. There had been a process of 'hardening' of police tactics over the period since 2000. Initially this change had led to a reduction in violence by protestors. However, in the most recent years, the loss of legitimacy by the state as a consequence of the financial and economic crisis led to an increase in violent protest. Mansley's model thus subtly combines changes in the wider environment, the crisis, with changes in policing tactics, their hardening, to explain the recent increase in the deployment of violence by both police and protestors. Thus it is not simply that crisis leads to violence during protest; it is the loss of legitimacy by the state during the crisis in combination with harder police tactics.

Is there a democratic crisis?

The fiscal crisis has cascaded into a political crisis. The old political parties and their agendas are being displaced by new ones. In 2015 there are several indications that the political crisis is beginning to become a democratic crisis, though it is not yet clear how far these processes will go.

There is a substantial challenge to the constitutional settlement of the UK: the movement for independence by Scotland; and the growth of a right-wing movement that seeks to curb immigration by leaving the EU. The Scottish nationalist movement has become a powerful force in Scottish politics but narrowly lost the referendum on independence in 2014. Its strength created controversy over the constitutional settlement, regarding the distribution of powers between the different nations and regions and Westminster, which is having continuing repercussions. UKIP has become a powerful force in UK politics. It is channelling experience of economic stress into resentment against immigration and contributed to the decision of the Conservative Party to promise to hold a referendum on the UK membership of the European Union if they won the 2015 election. There has also been a growth in violence during political protest as the legitimacy of democratic institutions has been undermined.

In 2015 this is not yet a crisis in democracy since, despite the increase in violence and the challenges to the de facto constitution of the UK, the political institutions are still significant in channelling conflict. It is not clear whether this will last. The outcome will depend in particular on the political forces in play and developments in the European Union. These issues are considered next.

What Political Forces?

There is a historical precedent in the regulation of capital by the state in the Bretton Woods institutional system set up in 1944, fifteen years after the Great Crash caused by finance capital in 1929. Following the Crash, the ensuing Great Depression, rise of fascism and World War II, social democratic forces emerged triumphant to enforce their claim to regulate capitalism, including finance, for the good of the society as a whole. The post-war settlement, the compromise between capital and labour, included strong regulations on finance capital. It led to an unprecedented thirty years of economic growth, increasing prosperity, increasing state welfare provision, the partial transformation of the gender regime, and reductions in class and gender inequalities.

What are the political forces relevant to the crisis as it now cascades through the political system, and how strong are they today? These forces include not only the traditional categories of capital and labour, and their divisions, but also political forces shaped by gender, nation and ethnicity. They are shaped by processes changing the environment on which they contend, including those of Europeanization and globalization. Key questions are whether the state could potentially regulate finance in the wider social interest and, if it could do so, whether finance and its related political projects have so captured the state as to make this regulation unlikely in practice. Chapter 3 on finance identified the technical reforms that would be necessary to re-stabilize finance so that it no longer threatens the stability of economy and society, but left open the question as to whether such reform was likely. This issue is addressed here, situated in the wider question of the role of political democracy in the several stages of the crisis, including the economic and fiscal as well as financial crises.

A range of projects and complex political forces, including both those opposing and those supporting regulation, are active in the field of finance. There are links between financial and economic position and political projects but no simple relationship between them, since the way people perceive their interests is shaped by social processes and struggles. As defined here, drawing on Walby (2009, 2011a), a project is a collective process within civil society that creates new meanings and goals for action while drawing on a range of both rhetorical and material resources. The process includes the ideational elements contained in concepts of 'discourse' and 'narrative' but goes beyond these to include 'practices'. It is different from the concept of social movement in that it is not confined to 'protest' but encompasses practices that are less visible, such as lobbying, and more institutionalized. A project is not the expression of essentialized identities such as those of gender, class or ethnicity; rather it includes the reconstitution of goals, practices and subjects through joint activities and discussions. Projects thus have a complex relationship to the social systems constituting their environment.

It is necessary to identify the projects in both immediate and broader form; to ascertain the political constituencies involved in these projects and draw boundaries around them. It is necessary to assess the balance of power between the different political projects and their associated forces. These projects are variously institutionalized. The 'state' itself can be identified at different levels: countries; the EU; and transnational/UN. The different forms of institutionalization of the political forces in different kinds of states affect the capacities of these forces.

The neoliberal project

The rhetoric of the neoliberal project centres on the claim that reducing regulation benefits all, including both capital and labour, since it improves the competitiveness and efficiency of markets. During the crisis there have been attempts to unsettle the hegemonic position of the 'efficient markets' thesis underpinning the deregulatory project of neoliberalism which contributed to the financial crisis (see chapter 3). However, since the efficient markets thesis maintains its hold on a wide range of institutions that produce knowledge, including the discipline of economics (Mirowski 2013), it has proved hard to dislodge from its hegemonic position.

There remains a question as to whether the various fractions of finance and industrial capital actually share the same interests in the deregulation of financial markets. The deregulation allowed extraordinary levels of profit for finance capital but the instability of finance has created problems for industrial capital. Insofar as finance capital has penetrated and therefore controls industrial capital then the theoretical division of interests is unlikely to surface in politics. However, if and where this process is incomplete, tensions may develop between these interests. Indeed this tension is visible in the differences between EU Member States in the extent to which they seek to regulate finance: the UK, where finance is strong, seeks less regulation than other Member States, such as Germany, where industrial capital is strong. The tension between finance and industrial capital thus surfaces in disagreements between Member States over EU-level policy.

The projects associated with the interests of finance can be either narrowly or broadly identified. In the narrow sense, there are public relations staff and lobbyists connected with finance companies that seek to influence legislation and codes of practice. Finance companies have lobbied against the regulation of their trade, as documented by Tett (2009). Attempts to reduce the secrecy of tax havens that allows for tax evasion and avoidance are contested by finance companies in the interests of their rich clients (Palan et al. 2010). The City of London Corporation, an association working in the 'square mile' of London where many finance companies have their headquarters, is well funded in order to represent the interests of these firms in government and elsewhere (Shaxson 2011). There has been resistance to attempts to reform and restructure financial practices. Such resistance is evident in representations to the press and political committees (Morgan 2010) and in considering the entity formed to run the nationalized banks (UK Financial Investments), which was set up at arm's length from democracy to comprise City personnel and principles of action (Engelen et al. 2011).

In a broader perspective, finance is often aligned with a project that can be variously described as promoting deregulation, market fundamentalism or neoliberalism (Harvey 2005; Greenspan 2008; Soros 2008). The neoliberal project has grown in ascendancy to become a governmental programme and embedded within social formations. It has captured think tanks, political parties, states and international financial institutions. It has challenged the basis of alternative political projects, attacked trade unions and welfare states, and reduced the depth of democracy (Harvey 2005; Walby 2009). The project has become sedimented in parties of the centre-left as well as right (Arestis and Sawyer 2005; Mudge 2008).

The social democratic project

Projects seeking the regulation of financial and economic markets can be broadly or narrowly defined. In the broader sense, there is a social democratic project, supported by trade union, labour, feminist and environmental organizations, positioned to advocate regulation of the economy in the wider public interest. These coalitions increasingly include a gender component in the analysis which reflects the shifts in their gender composition (Walby 2011a). While analysts of social democracy have rarely discussed finance as being one of its targets (Cramme and Diamond 2012), this is beginning to change. The UN Commission headed by Stiglitz to report on a proposed new global financial architecture suggested that all those who might suffer the consequences of financial failure should share in the governance of financial institutions (Stiglitz et al. 2010).

There are organizations seeking to reduce tax dodging, ranging from NGOs such as UK Uncut to expert networks such as the Tax Justice Network (2007). There has been considerable opposition to austerity and the restructuring of the welfare state which has involved a wide repertoire of actions, including lobbying, strikes and demonstrations (Taylor-Gooby 2012, 2013b). There are organizations, such as the Trades Union Congress, False Economy and the Women's Budget Group, that seek to make visible the unequal impacts of the neoliberal restructuring of the state following post-crisis attempts to reduce the budget deficit (Conley 2012).

There is a thesis that rising unemployment can generate progressive political resistance; that polarization in economic conditions generates radicalism. However, historically, there is some evidence to the contrary; unemployment can demobilize, as was the case in the 1980s (Bagguley 1991; Korpi 2002, 2003). An opposing thesis is that high and increasing unemployment generates the scapegoating of minorities, as occurred during the Depression in Europe in the 1930s.

There is now social democratic contestation over the leading ideas that underpin the neoliberal project. Even within economics there are counter-hegemonic positions including, for example, that of macroprudentialism (Crockett 2000; Haldane and May 2011). There have been indications of an ideational shift taking place in specific institutions, such as the Bank of International Settlements (Baker 2013), but these changes have not yet become hegemonic.

Contesting forces

Ascertaining the character and balance of current political forces associated with these projects for and against regulating finance capital is difficult. The Occupy movement suggests that it is 1 per cent against

99 per cent. However, while it is possible to make some distinctions between the various constituencies and projects concerning the regulation of finance, there are challenges in identifying a simple division between the beneficiaries and the losers of finance. The process of financialization has implications for the nature of the constituencies engaged in politics. In some instances the boundaries between what once may have been distinct categories of supporters and opponents of finance capital and its political projects have become blurred. The financialization of industrial capital reduced the distinction between financial and industrial fractions of capital while at the same time increasing the power of finance.

The financialization of everyday life increases the involvement of many individuals in the web of interests of finance as the range of financial products is extended to a wider variety of consumers. For example, the development of mortgaged housing and the sale of council houses gave some households an interest in rising house prices, though this was not in the interests of all. The development of pensions entwines workers and pensioners with finance capital. As Aglietta (2000b: 147) asks: 'What is the meaning of, and what are the prospects for, a stage of capitalism whereby pooled savings of labour, whose investment is delegated to professional managers, become the paramount shareholder?' The process of blurring of the boundaries between those who are exploited by finance and those who are its beneficiaries is not unique to finance capital; wage labourers exploited by capitalist employers simultaneously may benefit in the form of higher wages from the success of their employer. Nevertheless, financialization has significant consequences for the constituencies that might otherwise have supported political projects seeking to regulate finance capital.

The relationship between finance and the state depends on whether states are democratic or captured by finance. Both outcomes are possible. In the UK social democratic period between 1945 and 1975, which followed the turbulence of the financial crash of 1929, fascism, holocaust, war and reconstruction, there was significant regulation of finance in the interests of the wider economy and society. This was a period of unprecedented financial, economic and social stability; economic growth and development; increased democratization; reduced violence and warfare; increasing personal freedoms; and decreasing inequalities of many kinds. It was a period in which the balance of political forces was in favour of the regulation of finance.

This social democratic regulation of finance was challenged by the development of the neoliberal project, with its market fundamentalism, deregulation, and attacks on alternative projects in trade unions, collective bargaining, welfare states and social democracy. As financialization developed, extending into everyday life through mortgages, pensions and credit cards, and into industrial capital through the fragmentation of company forms and shareholder value, finance capital increased its power through the associated political project of neoliberalism. The neoliberal project captured many political parties, states and international financial institutions, spreading as a global wave around the world to become embedded in governmental programmes and social formations. However, there remain significant variations in the extent to which this has occurred. There are also significant outposts of alternative thinking and practice.

Globalization has tilted the terrain of contestation towards capital and away from labour. If finance were global and democratic institutions only national it would be difficult to achieve democratic control over finance. Globalization is a potential challenge to democratic institutions embedded at a country level because, as capital becomes global while democratic institutions tend to remain located at the level of national states, it becomes harder for democratic states to control finance and other forms of capital. As capital becomes more mobile than labour it can go 'regime shopping' for the laws and regulations that best suit its interests and, in so doing, provide incentives for states to reduce their requirements from capital. This process applies in particular to finance capital, which is the most mobile form of capital.

However, there are important caveats to the argument that capital is global while democratic institutions are national. Globalization is not new; capitalism has already been global for at least a century and, more probably, for several (Wallerstein 2011a [1974]). Globalization thus did not prevent previous rounds of regulation of finance. Some form of regulation of finance and trade has existed for as long as there have been global hegemons (Arrighi 1994). Perhaps most important was the regulation of capital flows agreed at Bretton Woods in 1944. There is no necessary reason based on spatial scale and globalization to prevent such regulation from happening again. Further, because finance needs to touch to ground in some way, it requires a territorial base from which regulation could emanate (Sassen 2001). More importantly, it is not only finance that is global but also financial institutions. Finance needs institutions in order to operate: to regulate its markets; to police fraud; and to protect its property. There are several such global financial institutions, including: the IMF, World Bank, International Bank of Settlements and WTO. There are many regulatory agreements, including the Basel agreements regulating banks. The regulation of these institutions of finance governance constitutes the terrain for further democratic interventions.

Globalization does not prevent the democratic regulation of finance; though it does affect the terrain, or fitness landscape, on which the argumentation and contestation between the projects of finance capital and democratic forces occur. Finance is organized through institutions just like other forms of social relations; hence it could, in principle, be regulated, just like other institutions. The question here is more specific: can the regulation of finance through international financial bodies respond to pressures from democratic forces and institutions, not only capitalist ones? Or is the outcome of the crisis moving in the opposite direction, towards increased control over governments by international financial bodies and, through them, by finance capital?

The success of the neoliberal project in the UK has partly been a result of the decline in the power of the social democratic project. The post-war social democratic project drew on a constituency based in trade unions rooted in skilled manual work in an industrial era of mass production. It has suffered from the decline of its key constituency, trade-unionized male workers in manufacturing, whose numbers had declined along with their industries. The halting of the forward march of labour noted by Hobsbawm (1978) was partly the result of structural changes in the working class due to the decline of its traditional industrial base in heavy manufacturing. However, there is a new basis for social democracy in the transformation of the gender regime and the institutionalization of feminism in civil society and the state. It is this re-gendered social democratic project that the neoliberal project contests. The transformation of the gender regime creates new material positions for women, which shape their forms of association and their perceived interests.

Women on average have different experiences from those of men as a consequence of gender divisions so, on average, hold different political priorities. The most significant change in this regard has been the growth in female employment (Manza and Brooks 1999). The implications of this are amplified by the location of the employment disproportionately in care-work in the public sector (Knutsen 2001). 'Care-work' is used broadly to encompass health, education, childcare, care for the elderly and services to prevent violence against women. The increase in employment has led to only small reductions in domestic care-work, thereby generating a general interest among employed women in the public provision of care-work. Women's expression of their perceived interests is mediated by their increased engagement in and development of civil societal projects, extending into the state. Women now comprise half the membership of trade unions (Visser 2006, 2013; Department for Business, Innovation and Skills 2014; RMTLondonCalling 2014) and are increasingly represented in parliament (Inter-Parliamentary Union 2014) and in the gender equality policy architecture (Walby et al. 2012b). The development of alliances and coalitions (Ferree and Hess 2000; Vargas and Wieringa 1998; Woodward 2004; Moghadam 2005) further enhances their influence. There remain significant variations between countries in the representation of women and in the alliances that are made (Ferree 2012; Kantola 2010; Lombardo and Forest 2011; McBride and Mazur 2010). These variations include the extent to which gender equality agendas are mainstreamed (Walby 2005) and the nature of the intersection of different projects (Verloo 2006; Walby et al. 2012a, 2012b).

The significance of the gender component of social democratic projects can be seen in voting for parliamentary politics and in engagement in strike action as members of trade unions. There is a significant gender gap in voting for political parties, with women, especially young women and employed women, increasingly likely to vote further left than men. In the UK in 2014, while women overall are slightly more likely than men to vote Labour, younger women, 18–39, are significantly more likely to do so (YouGov 2014). In the US elections in 2012, the gender gap was the largest in US history, with a 20 percentage point gap in favour of Obama, the Democratic candidate for the presidency (Gallup 2012). This gender gap is found in many of the more industrialized countries, as female employment has increased (Inglehart and Norris 2000). This is associated with employed women being more likely than men to have positive views towards public service provision (Manza and Brooks 1999) and to state welfare (Huber and Stephens 2000). The increased employment of women stands out as the most important explanatory factor at both micro (Iversen and Rosenbluth 2006; Finseraas et al. 2012) and macro levels (Abendschön and Steinmetz 2014).

The reduction in public services is being contested (Taylor-Gooby 2012, 2013b). The UK has seen a surge in industrial militancy after 2010 from public sector trade unions which now have female majorities. Coordinated strikes by public sector unions in defence of pensions in 2011 and 2012 led to more days of strike action in those years than any others since the crisis began (ONS 2012: 14). The contestation over public expenditure concerns jobs that are disproportionately held by women (in the public services) and services (health, education, care services) that are disproportionately used, and politically supported, by women (Walby 2011a). Gender relations are an important part of the politics of the opposing projects of social democracy and neoliberalism.

The social democratic project is being re-gendered. While the male constituency is declining along with the industries that generated the workers who joined trade unions, the female constituency is growing as women are increasingly employed, especially in the public sector, in the welfare state. These women are the emerging political constituency leading the social democratic political project. Their position in the public gender regime, and additionally in the public sector, generates interests that are in alignment with social democracy. This is especially the case when those women have, or act in solidarity with those women who have, dependent children, since this generates interest in the state provision of childcare and education, in addition to health and elder care. Women are increasingly accessing organizational and discursive resources and taking up political opportunities in both civil society and state-oriented projects.

Hence the political forces relevant to the wider democratic agenda hinge on gender, because of the re-gendering of the social democratic project. Feminist contributions to the social democratic project continued to build the institutions of the gendered welfare state (such as childcare and services to prevent violence against women). However, this process is being halted by forces associated with the financial crisis as cuts in public expenditure are reducing these services. The neoliberal project is gendered in its target of reducing gendered public services.

The changing balance between the power and influence of neoliberal and social democratic projects is key to understanding the depth of democracy and the capacity of the state to regulate finance and other forms of capital in the wider social interest. During the 1980s the neoliberal project gained ascendancy as the social democratic project lost ground with the slow demise of the male skilled manual workers whose trade unions had comprised such a core part. This was a period leading into the current crisis in which there was a reduction in the depth of democracy on class-based issues and the deregulation of finance. The tension between finance and industrial capital over the deregulation project as it applies to finance is not yet resolved. Finance capital is stronger in the UK than in many other EU Member States, and it is the UK that most strongly argues against regulation of finance in EU-level discussions. Thus the tension between finance and industrial capital over the regulation of finance has become an issue in the politics of the EU. The social democratic project is gaining a new constituency of support among employed women and particularly those women in public sector employment. The cuts in public expenditure following the fiscal crisis have put this gendered social democratic project at the front line of class-based political conflict.

The Crisis and the EU

The EU has become a pivotal node in the political and democratic crisis, with implications for its Member States. Can the EU respond to the pressures generating the political crisis so that it does not cascade into a democratic crisis?

The institutional structure, or the architecture, of the governance of the EU economy has been destabilized by the crisis, especially the fiscal phase. The 'austerity' response to Member State government budget deficits is not only destabilizing Member State governments but reverberating through the EU-level architecture. Since the causes of the financial crisis have been only partially addressed, another wave of financial instability can be expected at any time. There is now the prospect of Member States exiting the EU, thereby taking the crisis to a new level: Greece has been on the brink of exit several times during its fiscal and austerity crisis; and the UK was promised a referendum on EU membership by the Conservatives if they were to win the 2015 election. There is thus the possibility of a major fissure in the EU in the near future (writing in early 2015). This would have major repercussions for the capacity of the EU to act as a polity in terms of both its internal governance of economic and equality issues and its external influence in the world. However, the EU has traditionally thrived on crises, turning these into opportunities for the deepening of its institutional architecture. The next crisis could be an opportunity for the deepening of the financial and fiscal architecture of the EU; or it could lead to fragmentation. It is likely to be a tipping point in the process of Europeanization (Giddens 2014; Liddle 2014).

Addressing the question of the role of the EU in the potential cascading of the political crisis into a democratic crisis requires analysis of: democracy and the EU; the fiscal crisis of Member States and EU-level policies to address it; and the actual and potential capacity of the EU to regulate finance capital.

Democracy and the EU

What does democracy mean for the EU? Traditionally, democracy has been considered to be greater when decisions are taken at levels that are closer to citizens than when they are taken further away from individual citizens; in the former the links between citizen and decision-making are shorter than in the latter case. This understanding of democracy has underpinned the principle of 'subsidiarity' in the EU, under which decisions should be taken closer to the citizen at Member State level rather than further away at the EU level, unless there are clear reasons why only the EU level can address the issue at hand. If the challenge to be addressed is national, then the Member State is usually the correct level for action; if the challenge is global, then it is sometimes more appropriate for the EU level to be activated. The capacity to respond at the EU level is thus necessary for the EU to be able to defend the interests of its citizens in relevant circumstances, but only in those circumstances. The argument over the location of 'subsidiarity', which affects whether the Member State or EU level is the more appropriate site of political action, is hence an argument about what constitutes deeper democracy in the EU.

Assessing democracy in the EU depends partly on the interpretation of the relationship between three levels of governance: Member State, EU and global. The conventional approach to democracy assumes that the closer the state to its citizens, the more democratic it is, generating a presumption that the Member State level is the preferred one for the exercise of democratic will. However, such an approach is challenged in a global era by forces that are global in range, not least those of finance and industrial capital. It is necessary to have democratic institutions with a greater spatial reach than those of Member States in order to match more nearly, and be able to contest and negotiate with, global capital. The EU is potentially a polity having the capacity to negotiate with global capital more effectively than the smaller polities of Member States.

Assessing democracy in the EU also requires addressing the issue of whether political power is zero-sum or not, so that the relationship between the EU level and the Member State level of governance can be understood. On the one hand there is an argument that there is a limited amount of political power and that this is held either by the nation-states or by the EU (Moravcsik 1993): if the nation-states have power, the EU does not; and if the EU has power, the nation-states do not. On the other hand there is the view that the pooling of sovereignty by nation-states enhances the likelihood of their obtaining their goals (Milward 1992). This rejects the zero-sum notion of political power on the grounds that by giving up power at the Member State level there is an increase in power at the EU level which increases the overall political influence of EU citizens. The argument that the expansion of the powers of the EU is a deepening of democracy thus rests on rejecting the zero-sum account of political power and adopting the view that pooling of sovereignty by Member States increases the depth of democracy for EU citizens.

There is continuing political debate about the proper division of power between the Member State and EU levels, which is evidenced by the 2014 elections to the European Parliament. The principle of 'subsidiarity' requires that decisions are taken at Member State level unless there can be justification that the EU level creates greater benefit. The location of the 'subsidiarity boundary' is the subject of controversy; it was not fully settled by its formal negotiation during the revision of the Treaties that create the powers and act as the de facto constitution of the EU. The governance of the Single European Market is located at EU level while the governance of most welfare issues is located at Member State level. From a gender perspective this means that regulation of equality in employment is primarily an EU-level matter while provision of state welfare in relation to care-work is primarily a Member State matter. Further, each EU-level entity contains a different balance of the interests of the EU as a whole and of the separate Member States. The entities with the strongest EU-level focus are the directly elected European Parliament, the European Court of Justice, the European Commission and the European Central Bank. Other entities, such as the Council of European Ministers, more fully express the interests of the Member State governments. At a global level the EU is legally one entity in engagement on trade issues in the WTO but operates only as a coalition of states in many UN institutions.

As discussed in chapter 5, the crisis has come to involve the fiscal, in particular the balance between income and expenditure in government budgets. The fiscal has traditionally been located as a matter of Member State rather than EU-level competence under the principle of subsidiarity. The response to the crisis has challenged the location of the fiscal as a Member State matter, since the EU level has been involved in conditional loans to governments in fiscal crisis. Is the movement of the location of decision-making over fiscal matters away from Member States to the EU level a reduction in democracy or a deepening of democracy? It is a deepening if it is essential to fulfil the will of the citizens; but not otherwise.

As discussed in chapter 3, the crisis started with a financial crisis that was caused by the deregulation of finance. Finance operates globally, as well as having a terrestrial presence in particular countries (Sassen 2001). Finance is potentially a matter of EU-level competence since it can be considered a matter relevant to the Single European Market. However, in practice, before the crisis the EU had little involvement in the governance of finance, which had been largely left to a mix of Member States and transnational bodies. The response to the crisis has involved some development of EU-level regulations over financial entities. This increased capacity of the EU level is contested by some Member States under the principle of subsidiarity. The increased power of the EU level over finance is a deepening of democracy if this is the will of the people; but not otherwise.

Crisis has a role in the theory of the development of the EU. The EU was established after the 1939–45 war with the aim of building a political architecture so that never again would there be war and holocaust in Europe. The intention was to prevent the re-emergence of the militarist nationalism that had devastated Europe. The statesmen of the time did not think that there was sufficient political will to establish the necessary institutions immediately but held a theory for their development. This theory was to create economic institutions at the heart of Europe which would require political institutions to stabilize them; economic institutions being inherently unstable without associated political institutions. There would be pressure to deepen the political institutions at each of the inevitable future economic crises. In the long run this crisis-led process of the deepening of political institutions would establish peace in Europe. This is known as the 'spillover' theory of European integration (Haas 1958; Hallstein 1973 [1969]). If this spillover theory of the EU is correct, then the current crisis is an opportunity to deepen the institutions of the EU in a way that further removes both the prospect of war within Europe and the threat to its survival as a single polity.

However, much contemporary analysis of the EU focuses on issues relevant to the economy rather than on the original concern for peace. From this perspective, the concern is with the model of capitalism emerging from the conflicts exacerbated by the crisis, which in turn has implications for democracy. Here, the goal pursued is that of sufficient economic integration to ensure that EU Member State economies can flourish in a globalizing and increasingly competitive world. This integration has been centred on the creation of a Single European Market by reducing the practices that act as barriers to trade between Member States. The EU has developed a distinctive version of capitalism entailing full employment and social inclusion. This 'variety of capitalism' (Hall and Soskice 2001) contrasts with that in the US, which has fewer state interventions to regulate markets and consequently greater inequality and social exclusion. There is variation among the EU Member States in the extent to which the former, more social democratic variety or the latter, more (neo)liberal variety of capitalism is hegemonic. There is also variation in terms of the preferred model of capitalism. The tension between neoliberal and social democratic approaches to capitalism is endemic in processes of economic governance in the EU, and the balance between these approaches changes over time and especially in times of crisis. While there is still attachment to the social democratic model of economic growth through the pursuit of full employment and social inclusion, there has been an increase in the priority accorded to the neoliberal model of economic growth through the pursuit of deregulation and increasing the proportion of economic activity coordinated by markets rather than states. Following the economic crisis that resulted from the financial crisis, the EU has offered at least two strategies to support the re-emergence of economic growth: the '2020 Strategy for smart, sustainable and inclusive growth' in 2010 (European Commission 2010) and the attempt to negotiate a free trade agreement with the US, the Transatlantic Trade and Investment Partnership (TTIP) (European Commission 2015); and the 'Social Investment Package' in 2013 (European Commission 2013b). The 2020 strategy (European Commission 2010) was a move in a neoliberal direction. Its neoliberal character is seen, for example, in the failure to mention the significance of promoting gender equality and reconciliation of working and family life as a route to full employment. The TTIP negotiations have raised fears that environmental and equality concerns will be downgraded in a new trade agreement that might give corporations greater powers. By contrast, the Social Investment Package (European Commission 2013b) emphasizes investment in human resources, such as provision for socialized care-work, which has further positive consequences for gender equality.

Fiscal crisis

The political struggles over the best way to address government budget deficits are key to the current confrontations that might lead to a democratic crisis. Large government budget deficits enable finance capital to charge very high interest rates on the deficit as a consequence of the potential for 'markets' to withdraw and bankrupt the state. The 'austerity' response of some governments, whether to placate finance 'markets', as a condition of loans, or to reduce state expenditure, risks high levels of poverty. However, increasing deficits in order to stimulate economic growth in times of recession is also a well-established, if contested, 'Keynesian' governmental practice. The financial crisis led to an increase in government budget deficits in many EU Member States. As discussed in chapter 5 on the fiscal crisis, the cause of the deficit is politically contested. While even the IMF has conceded that the major part of government deficits was due to a decline in tax revenues as a consequence of the recession, which, in turn, was caused by the financial crisis, the hegemonic political position has centred on the contribution of pre-crisis governmental spending.

The EU dimension to the fiscal crisis stems at least in part from the common currency, the Euro, used in nineteen of the twenty-eight EU Member States. The shared currency limits the range of options available to individual Member States to address this crisis (e.g. by ruling out devaluation) and increases the responsibility for action by EU-level institutions, particularly the European Central Bank and the European Commission. The European Commission attempted to limit Member State government deficits through increasingly severe rules and interventions at the same time as finding ways to offer loans, albeit with stringent conditions attached, to those Member States in greatest difficulty (European Commission 2011a, 2013c). This process has entailed a shift in power from the Member State to the EU level in decision-making on fiscal matters.

The package of rules about deficits, known as the 'Six Pack' (see chapter 5), introduces several new regulations concerning Member State government budget deficits in an attempt to limit the size of deficits in all Member States, but especially those in the shared currency zone, the Eurozone (European Commission 2011a; Lapavitsas et al. 2012). In addition, there have been special arrangements for the states in greatest difficulty, with loans secured from the EU and the IMF, governed by the Troika, a committee representing the IMF, European Central Bank and European Commission. The conditions attached to these loans extend well beyond promises to repay the loans and, at least in the case of Greece, included requirements to reduce the level of welfare spending, reduce protections to workers, raise taxes, revise collective bargaining arrangements and privatize state assets (European Commission 2013c). The measures are parallel to the traditional, neoliberal, 'structural adjustment' conditions attached to IMF loans to countries in fiscal crisis in the Global South

(Greer 2014). These new procedures constitute a substantial reduction in the democratic capacity of the Member State governments in receipt of these loans.

The depth of the austerity caused by these fiscal policies has led to significant political challenges. These challenges have been articulated through both the traditional political repertoire of creating new political parties, holding demonstrations and conducting strikes, and through a spillover into violent protest, riots and clashes with police using hard tactics. The austerity has been particularly severe in Greece, where unemployment, especially among youth, has risen to exceptionally high levels. The political conflict has become correspondingly deep with the rise of both the neo-fascist Golden Dawn political party and the left-wing Syriza (Kouvelakis 2011; Spourdalakis 2014). In 2015, Syriza was elected to form a new government that sought to renegotiate the conditions on the loans.

These loans and fiscal measures are only a temporary solution to the immediate difficulties of the cascading crisis. Under discussion has been the development of Eurobonds (and similar devices) in which the EU itself guarantees loans to Member States without the assistance of the IMF. The European Commission (2011b) issued a Green Paper to discuss the feasibility of introducing 'Stability Bonds'. Such bonds would potentially reduce the problem of the pressure on governments in deficit facing punitive interest rates or loss of control of their fiscal processes to the Troika. The bonds would place the full might of the Eurozone, and potentially the whole EU, behind the Member State under pressure from the financial 'markets'. This process would ensure protection from the threat of default and, by removing the threat of default, drive down the interest rate and the cost of maintaining the deficit. However, the bonds would mean that the 'solvent' EU Member States, for example Germany, would be seen as 'supporting' those Member States in deficit. The Commission proposal was rejected in 2011 at least partly because of the fears of governments of 'solvent' Member States, including Germany, that it would result in there being no effective check on the growth of budget deficits in other Member States for which the EU as a whole, and the solvent states in particular, would become responsible.

Eurobonds remain a potential means of defeating the power of finance to threaten democratic governments with interest rates so high that they would default. However, such potential can only be realized with agreement on the nature and extent of the regulation of Member State budgets at an EU level. This would involve substantial further pooling of sovereignty over financial and fiscal matters to strengthen the EU level sufficiently for it to address finance. The financial and fiscal architecture of the EU would need to be restructured, with implications for its associated political institutions. If this restructuring were to occur in the same context as that obtaining at the time of writing in 2015, then the balance of political pressure would be likely to embed targets and regulations over Member State government budgets that would be probably be neoliberal (following the logic of the Six Pack).

At the next wave of financial instability (which is likely because the causes of the 2008 financial crisis have not been fully addressed) it is probable that some version of the Eurobond proposal will re-emerge on the political agenda. It is of course theoretically possible for very different conditions to the current ones to be included in a future restructuring of the financial and fiscal architecture of the EU. For example, it would be possible to institutionalize the goals of full employment, social cohesion and equality, including gender equality, in the new financial and fiscal architecture. The conditions embedded in the institutionalization of any new settlement will depend on the balance of forces at the time of the next crisis.

Financial regulation

The crisis was generated by the failure to regulate finance. The EU efforts to reform these regulations are necessary to prevent a further round of crisis; but they are politically contested. The EU has engaged in a programme of regulatory reform of the financial services sector, including: the supervision of the financial sector; strengthening financial institutions and providing a framework for their recovery; increasing the transparency of financial markets; and increased protection for consumers of financial products (European Commission 2011c). The legitimacy of this programme has been drawn from the powers of the EU level enshrined in the Treaties, most recently the Treaty of Lisbon, to create and protect a Single European Market. European public opinion typically supports these actions. However, the responses of Member State governments are divided; in particular there is opposition to some of these attempts at financial reform, led by the UK.

European public opinion supports EU action against the effects of the financial and economic crisis. This is shown in the Eurobarometer (European Commission 2011d) findings from the polling of opinions across the EU. In autumn 2010, there was support for the view that a range of measures to tackle the crisis would be effective: 77 per cent for stronger coordination of economic policy among EU Member States; 75 per cent for closer supervision by the EU of large financial groups; and 71 per cent for a more important role for the EU in regulating financial services. There was support by 88 per cent for tougher rules on tax avoidance and tax havens, and by 80 per cent for the regulation of wages in the financial sector (i.e. bankers' bonuses). Further, 82 per cent of Europeans wanted the EU to play a stronger role in developing new rules for the global financial markets.

In 2011, the European Commission (2011c) proposed a Directive to establish a financial transaction tax in the EU. This was for three purposes: to harmonize developments for national tax measures to prevent fragmentation of the single market; 'to ensure that financial institutions make a fair contribution to covering the costs of the recent crisis'; and 'to create appropriate disincentives for transactions that do not enhance the efficiency of financial markets thereby complementing regulatory measures aimed at avoiding future crises' (European Commission 2011c: 2). The proposal was for a very low rate of tax on financial transactions of one tenth of one percent (0.1 per cent) of the value of transactions in securities (shares and bonds) and one hundredth of one percent (0.01 per cent) for financial derivatives. This rate is much lower than the rate of around 20 per cent for the VAT on most non-financial transactions. The Commission anticipated that the tax would raise around €57 billion a year.

The Commission draft Directive followed calls for the development of a proposal for a financial transaction tax by the European Parliament in March 2010 and 2011 and by the Council of Ministers in March 2011. Eurobarometer (European Commission 2011d: 13) reported that 61 per cent of EU citizens supported the introduction of a tax on financial transactions. Some individual countries have adopted the tax, including France in August 2012, and there have been announcements of the development of such legislation by Spain, Italy and Portugal (European Commission 2013d). However, the European Commission proposal was rejected by the UK, which led opposition by some other Member States. London has a very large finance sector which is very influential over the UK government (as discussed in chapter 3).

The Commission (2011c) stated that the legal basis for their proposed Directive lay in Article 113 of the Lisbon Treaty on the Functioning of the European Union, which allows for harmonization legislation necessary for the proper functioning of the internal market without distortions. Conflicting legal opinions by lawyers for the Council and for the Commission surfaced in the media. Reuters

(Jones 2013) reported that the legal service of the Council of the European Union had found that the introduction of the tax would exceed EU powers over taxation, while EurActiv (2013) reported that the legal service of the European Commission had refuted this interpretation, stating that their proposal was in conformity with EU and international law. The UK government filed a legal challenge to the Commission's proposal for a financial transaction tax with the European Court of Justice; losing the case in 2014 (European Court of Justice 2014). The UK's opposition to the tax refers to the principle of subsidiarity; that the tax would be an inappropriate intrusion of the EU level into an arena that was properly the competence of the Member States. Opposition from other Member States was more often expressed as reluctance to proceed without global-level agreement.

The Commission proposal received the support of several Member States, including France and Germany, but met opposition from others, including the UK. After much political and legal debate, the plan in 2014 was for a core group of eleven Member States, not including the UK, to establish a harmonized system of financial transaction tax in 2016 (European Commission 2013d, 2014).

The EU has developed a modest programme of reform to improve financial regulation. There have been significant divisions in the response of Member States to this; the UK, which has a large finance sector, being particularly resistant. The outcome is that there is as yet probably insufficient regulation to prevent a return of financial instability potentially leading to a further financial crisis. Such a financial crisis would be likely to cascade again into a crisis in the real economy, into a fiscal crisis and a political crisis.

The next financial crisis

There is likely to be a further financial crisis since the regulations on finance necessary to avert this possibility have not yet been adopted. While there have been significant changes to financial and fiscal regulation they do not yet go far enough to stabilize the EU economy from the effects of another financial crisis. At the next crisis it is likely that the issues discussed earlier regarding a new financial, fiscal and democratic architecture for the EU will be hurriedly put back on the political negotiating table, leading to its reconstruction. Either the institutions will deepen or the EU will fragment.

Such deepening of the institutions might include the creation of 'Eurobonds' (Stability Bonds or their equivalent), enabling the EU to create the finance (at low interest rates) necessary to support its Member States in budgetary difficulties against the risk of default that could be created by financial 'markets' generating very high interest rates. The creation of such bonds would generalize the risk of default across the whole EU and, since the risk of an EU default is so unlikely, protect all Member States. This process would depend on the agreement of EU Member States to pool the risks and sovereignty, which would probably require EU-level institutions to have increased influence over Member State fiscal matters. The settlement to deepen the institutions may, or may not, embed the principles of equal treatment, social justice and democracy. The current balance of forces make the inclusion of such principles unlikely even though these are core 'values' of the EU and central to its established model of economic governance and economic growth.

It may be that there will be no agreement to deepen the EU financial, fiscal and associated political institutions. If this is the case then it is likely that by or during the next crisis the EU will fragment in one way or another. Some Member States may leave. If the EU were to fragment it would mean the policies the EU has pursued would no longer have a major polity as their champion. Most attention has been focused on the impact of EU fragmentation on economic growth; with departing Member States potentially losing their position within the Single European Market and experiencing a drop in their economic output as a consequence (CBI 2014). However, fragmentation also has implications for policies on equality and human rights. It is likely that the equal treatment provisions embedded in Treaties and Directives would be less frequently implemented by those Member States that have long been reluctant to embrace them, since there would be less enforcement from a weakened set of EU-level institutions. The EU's position as a champion of human rights and gender equality in global institutions would be significantly diminished.

Has the EU become an instrument of transnational finance capital or is it the only existing polity that has the capacity to contain global finance and subject it to democratic control? The argument here is, on balance, the latter; but it is by a close margin and the question is likely to re-emerge in a critical way at the next crisis. While finance has considerable influence over the UK state, which has sought to protect finance from EU regulation and taxation, it has less influence on other Member States and the EU level. If there is to be a solution to the political crisis and the emerging democratic crisis in the UK or any other EU Member State, it will involve the EU level.

Conclusions

The tension between the ideal of democracy and the actually existing procedures has been made visible throughout the crisis cascading through society. The failure to regulate finance to prevent its potentially destructive instability is a failure of the state. It is a consequence of the reduction in the depth of democracy that is part of the neoliberal project of deregulation.

The crisis is both real and socially and politically constituted. While a formal state of emergency, a state of exception, has not been declared, financial crisis was nonetheless used to justify massive transfers to banks, and fiscal crisis was used to justify austerity at the same time as reneging on electoral manifesto commitments.

There is a political crisis in the sense that many long-standing political parties in Europe have struggled to produce agendas the electorate see as relevant to the financial, economic and fiscal crisis, and have thus declined. Meanwhile there has been the development and growth of new political forms and new political parties. These projects and parties have emerged to both the left and the right of traditional parties; however, only one had formed a government by 2015. The conflict has spilled out beyond traditional forms into violence, both in riots and during mass political protest, but on an ad hoc rather than generalized basis.

The depth of democracy has been changing in contrary directions since the 1980s. For some issues there has been a decline in the depth of democracy, with deregulation and privatization, including the reduction of democratic control over finance and the removal of some public services from democratic control through privatization. For gender issues there has been some increase in the depth of democracy, as changed democratic procedures have facilitated the reduction in the gender imbalance in decision-making arenas such as Parliament.

The political forces in play on this terrain include not only those associated with the traditional categories of capital and labour but also those of gender. The contestation between the neoliberal and social democratic projects over the extent to which finance and other forms of capital are regulated for the common good is central to the crisis. It is also a gendered contestation. The neoliberal project is gendered in that the focus of its agenda for the crisis has become state public expenditure, which is gendered in terms of its distributive and employment effects and in its supporting constituencies. The gendering of the social democratic project is changing with the decline of the industries that had supported a male trade-union-based social democratic constituency and the rise of services that support a gender-balanced trade-union-based social democratic constituency. Gender relations are thus at the heart of the crisis.

The EU has become the pivot for this question of democratic crisis in relation to Europe, including the UK. The EU is both a global actor with potential to regulate finance and a terrain of struggle in the fiscal crises of several EU Member States. The democratic legitimacy of EU decision-making is challenged by opposition to its actions in the fiscal crises of some Member States. These Member State fiscal crises became an issue for the EU level because the Troika of European Commission, European Central Bank and the IMF granted loans to indebted Member States which had harsh conditions that provoked opposition. One route towards the resolution of the fiscal crises of these Member States lies in further pooling of sovereignty in order to gain financial support through the creation of 'Eurobonds'. However, concomitantly, the harsh conditions combined with economic recession reduce the legitimacy of the existing EU-level powers and generate centrifugal tendencies to blame minoritized others for the crisis. Will there be a significant reconstruction of state political institutions through a new political, financial and fiscal architecture for the EU?

The deregulation of finance that caused the financial crisis was part of a broader neoliberal project of deregulation to remove state control over finance and the economy. This deregulation project is a process of de-democratization in that it removes controls put in place by democratic states to regulate capital and markets. Can the effective regulation of finance be established; or has finance grown too powerful for the current set of democratic institutions in the UK, EU and UN to achieve this goal? Within the EU, which governs many aspects of the economies of its Member States, the cascading of the crisis into fiscal matters has led to challenges to the democratic legitimacy of the EU political institutions that have struggled to address the crisis. Whether the EU disintegrates as a consequence of the challenge from political interests linked to finance capital, or restructures into a more capable set of institutions, hangs in the balance in 2015. Dependent on the outcome of this challenge to the EU is the issue as to whether the political crisis generated by the financial crisis will become a democratic crisis.

7
Crisis in the Gender Regime

Introduction

The crisis changed gender relations. Women have lost jobs and suffered from the cuts in public services; but they have not been pushed back into the home. Despite loss of jobs and of public services, women are not leaving the labour market and production and returning to reproduction. The crisis has not re-familialized women despite cutbacks in state-provided services. The changes challenge conventional theoretical frameworks in which women are seen as moving between home and work, reproduction and production, or domestic and public spheres, according to improvement or deterioration in the economy. How can this apparently contradictory state of affairs be understood?

Theorizing these changes in the gender regime is challenging and important. It means addressing the conceptualization of gender, not only at the level of specific institutions, but also more broadly at the level of the gender regime in the country as a whole. Gender relations have changed in each of several institutional domains as the crisis has cascaded through society. Theorizing this process requires a framework that can encompass gendered changes in finance, in public expenditure (the fiscal), in employment (the economy), in the household (the economy) and in the political system. In order to make sense of the different ways in which women are engaged in work, in production and in the public sphere, it is necessary to make distinctions not only between domestic and public gender regimes, but also between neoliberal and social democratic forms of public gender regimes. The gender regime has been abruptly shifted in a neoliberal direction during the crisis but not away from a public form. A focus on the family and an assumed oscillation between de-familialization and re-familialization is insufficient to grasp the complexity and significance of the changes. It is important to consider the application of the distinction between neoliberalism and social democracy, which has been developed within class analysis, to differences in forms of the public gender regime.

The theoretical distinctions between neoliberalism and social democracy are important not only for understanding the changes in the gender regime during the crisis, but also for understanding the implications for the gendered economic growth strategies out of the crisis. The goal of economic growth is used to legitimate policies towards the economy and towards gender relations. But there is more than one potential economic growth strategy.

This chapter starts with a critical review of theories of changes in gender relations relevant to the crisis, followed by discussion of an alternative theoretical framework that develops the conceptual distinctions needed to theorize the changes. This framework is applied to the various stages of the crisis by drawing on the analysis in the earlier chapters of the book.

Theorizing Changes in Families or in Gender?

How are the changes in gender relations due to the crisis to be theorized? All engaged in the debate presented here agree that gender is to be understood as a social relationship rather than a fixed attribute. They agree that practices and institutions can be gendered, not only individual behaviour. Most treat gender as a social system in some way, though some do this more implicitly than explicitly. Gender is a social relationship rather than an essence. Gender has meaning as a social relationship between genders. Gender relations are a system of social relations, in the sense that they are self-reproducing. The practice of gender reproduces gender relations; and in this way is a system. A gender regime is a pattern of gender relations; and can take different forms. Divergences between models of gender relations arise in the identification of the most important institutions for characterizing the relationships between gendered institutions. These divergences lead to differences in the analysis of gender relations in the crisis.

The main approaches to gender relations during the crisis make a distinction between forms of economy where women gain their livelihood in the family and those where they gain this in paid employment. During times of economic hardship there is often assumed to be a change in the direction of the family and household; which is reversed during times of economic growth and development. This argument has been articulated using slightly different concepts and terms, which nonetheless have significant similarities, including: familialization (de-/re-familialization) (e.g. Esping-Andersen 2009); breadwinners (male, or dual-earner households) (e.g. Lewis 1992); and production or reproduction (e.g. Elson 2002; Young et al. 2011).

Patterns of gender relations can have different degrees of familialization (Esping-Andersen 2009; Saxonberg 2013). De-familialization is usually seen as reducing gender inequality. It has been seen as a form of modernization involving individuation and increased choice (Giddens 1992; Beck 1992). De-familialization has been variously defined to mean: 'capacity to form an independent household' (Orloff 1993); 'degree to which individuals can uphold a socially acceptable standard of living independently of family relationships, either through paid work or social security provision' (Lister 1994: 37); or dependent upon the provision of care-work outside the family (Esping-Andersen 2009). These approaches to gender relations share a focus on the form of the family, as the most important institution for the analysis of gender relations.

A different distinction is sometimes made between those households which have male breadwinners and those that have dual earners, which is then seen to be congruent with other variations including that of the nature of state welfare policy. This distinction has been developed by a large body of feminist writers following an early influential text by Lewis (1992). Lewis (1992) proposes that the core distinction is between gender relations where the household tends to be supported by a 'male bread-winner', where the man is the main wage earner, and those where there is a 'dual bread-winner', in which both women and men earn wages; in addition there are intermediary positions. The focus is on the emergence of working mothers (Brush 2002). The model included reference to the role of the welfare state in shaping the extent to which households had either a male earner or dual earners, through state provision of welfare. Many revisions refined the model by, for example: making distinctions as to whether women were treated as wives, mothers or workers (Sainsbury 1996); whether the state supported care through providing a set of services, money to purchase services or money to provide the services at home (Jenson 1997); including lone mothers (Lewis 1997); and including additional components of state regulations including those concerning labour markets, reproduction and sexuality (O'Connor et al. 1999). However, while these later additions nuanced the operationalization of the model, they do little to extend its range because of the assumption that variations in these factors are congruent and hence do not serve to identify significant further types of gender regimes.

A further conceptualization of the distinction is between production and reproduction. The identification of a division between production and reproduction is found in the work of feminist macroeconomists, including Elson (2002), Bakker and Gill (2003), Elson and Çagatay (2000) and Young et al. (2011). These theorists draw a distinction between patterns of gender relations where women's livelihood is centred on unpaid domestic labour and those where women's livelihood is centred on waged labour. Reproduction as well as production is a sector of the economy even though it is not paid or marketized labour. The theorists argue the crisis has led to a reduction in women's productive work and an increase in women's reproductive work as a consequence of the reduction in state expenditure on welfare, which is seen to increase the amount of work women need to do in the home. Women work harder in the home as a consequence of economic crises. Crisis pushes women from productive to reproductive work.

Critique of dualist typologies

The problem with the conceptualization of different patterns of gender as a dichotomy lies in its over-simplification of the varieties of gender regime. The models assume that changes in the family/household/(re)production are closely linked to changes in other aspects of gender relations. In particular, it is assumed that the form of the welfare state is closely aligned to the form of the family/household/(re)production. If the welfare state grows then there is de-familialization; a shift from male-breadwinner to dual-earner or lone-mother households and a shift in the main site of women's labour from reproduction to production.

However, this has not been happening during the crisis. The welfare state has been diminished in scale as a result of cuts in public expenditure, but women have not been re-familialized. There has not been a return to male-breadwinner households; women have not left production to return to reproduction. The evidence is a major challenge to dichotomous theories of gender relations. The proposed close theoretical connection between the form of the welfare state and the form of the family/household/(re)/production is not supported by the empirical evidence of the changes taking place during the crisis. There is a need to move beyond the overly simple and direct alignment, or reductionism, inherent in these models.

It is necessary to replace the dualistic model of gender relations with one that is sufficiently complex to encompass the observed empirical changes. A theoretical model of gender relations that allows for more flexible relations between the institutions of welfare state and family/household is required, rather than assuming their simple alignment. This flexibility is found in the model of the gender regime developed in Walby (2009), revised from Walby (1990, 1997), which contains the conceptual distinctions necessary to theorize the crisis in relation to the gender regime.

Developing the Model of the Gender Regime

In the model of the gender regime used here, there is a distinction between domestic and public gender regimes (Walby 2009), which has parallels with the distinctions already made between de-/re-familialization, male and dual breadwinner regimes, and whether women's labour is focused on production or reproduction. However, there are significant differences; in particular, a distinction is made between different forms of the public gender regime. There is not only a distinction between the domestic and public form but also between different varieties of the public gender regime. The two main varieties are the neoliberal and social democratic forms. A second major difference is the explicit recognition of further elements such that the institutional domains considered comprise the economy, polity, violence and civil society.

More nuanced distinctions between the forms of gender regimes are needed, in particular between public gender regimes that take a neoliberal and those taking a social democratic form. Women can perform waged labour under both neoliberal and social democratic regimes. It is not only a question as to whether the gender regime is more domestic or more public; it depends on the nature of the public gender regime (similar to the distinctions between varieties of capitalism, discussed later in this section). This distinction can and should be applied across all the institutional domains of economy, polity, violence and civil society, not only the economy or political economy. The most important differences between the neoliberal and social democratic forms of the public gender regime lie in the gendered depth of democracy and the degree of gender inequality. The extent to which governance is democratic is closely associated with the level of inequality.

The differentiation between social democratic and neoliberal gender regimes originates in different routes of transition from earlier domestic gender regimes to public gender regimes. The transition from domestic to public regime includes a process in which women increasingly gain their livelihood from free wage labour and decreasingly from unpaid care-work in the home. It requires the socialization of domestic labour, which can take place in different ways, in particular: the provision of services by the state; or the purchase of services from the market. The provision of services by the state is usually the consequence of democratic pressure, involving gendered political projects: this is the social democratic route. When this gendered democratic engagement is absent, it is still possible for the transition from a domestic to a public gender regime to occur, but it is dependent upon the purchase of services on the market: this is the neoliberal route.

The social democratic route to a public gender regime depends upon the effective mobilization of political forces in the context of a democratic polity. The most prominent examples can be found in the Nordic countries of Sweden, Denmark, Norway and Finland. The alliance between feminism and labour that became the Nordic gendered social democratic project was successful in embedding its project in government programmes and in the social formation. The project depended upon the mobilization of forces in civil society, especially but not only in the trade unions, and accessing state power in political systems that had deeper democratic practices than many others. A key component was the development of publicly funded and provided childcare. This provision facilitated women's near-continuous employment, from which benefits flowed to both women and their employers, with a positive economic growth spiral being generated in the 1970s. The growth rested upon the more efficient mobilization of women's labour in paid employment in both private companies and the state than was possible in the more individualized domestic settings. These new relations of production generated economic growth to the benefit of all in the economy. While the main example is the Nordic countries, weaker versions of this trajectory can be found in other Member States of the European Union.

The neoliberal route to a public gender regime depends upon the purchase of services in the market to enable the full employment of women and thereby the transition to a public gender regime. Ultimately this route to the socialization of domestic labour enables the full employment of women. It does not depend upon the development of democratic forces in support of this goal. In this route, the employment of women follows the development of the economy, rather than leads it. It rarely occurs until very high levels of economic development have already been reached. The classic example is the US.

Most countries lie somewhere along a continuum between the Swedish social democratic and the US neoliberal model. The majority contain mixed elements, with some institutions more social democratic and some more neoliberal; amounting to a country-specific gender regime overall.

It is necessary to have a model of the gender regime that includes more than the family and the welfare state. The four institutional domains which the model needs to encompass are: the economy, which includes not only the family but also employment and finance; the polity, which includes not only the welfare state but also democratic politics and the EU; violence; and civil society. Theorizing these different trajectories to the public gender regime requires a model which takes account of the depth of democracy and therefore needs to include the domains of polity and civil society. In their absence it is not possible to theorize the development of the depth of gendered democracy that is needed to explain the different forms of transition.

An institutional domain is a set of social practices through which social life is reproduced. Each domain has an internal coherence that can be demonstrated substantively and argued theoretically. The economy encompasses all aspects of the economy including finance, marketized production and unpaid domestic care-work. The polity encompasses not only the state but all other centralized institutions of governance, including the EU and those organized religions that govern intimacy. Violence is included because it significantly structures social relations and because its various forms, from war to homicide and domestic violence, are coherently interconnected. Civil society is the site of the construction and contested negotiation of meaning, including intimacy, sexuality, associations and social movements. These institutional domains jointly constitute a gender regime, and no one domain has a priori causal or analytic priority. Variations in these institutional domains produce variations in gender relations.

There is an explicit theorization of the macro level of gender regimes in this model of gender relations. This is differentiated from the meso level of gendered institutions and more micro level of gendered practices. Gender relations are constituted at all of these levels and across all of the institutional domains. Gender as a social relationship is a system in that it is self-reproducing; doing gender reproduces gender. Institutions are gendered. Different institutions have differently gendered practices.

Gender relations do not assume an infinite variety of patterns. There is a clustering in the patterns such that if one aspect takes one form then other aspects are likely to take other forms. This is not a simple determinism of a necessary and sufficient type but rather rests on a probabilistic understanding of the patterning of social systems. Gender regimes take a limited variety of forms. These are further limited by their intersection with capitalism and the form of capitalism. In contemporary Europe and North America, and most of the other rich countries of the OECD, these forms of public gender regime can be arranged along a continuum from neoliberal to social democratic.

The distinctions made between varieties of gender regime have similarities with the distinctions that have been made between varieties of capitalism. They share appreciation of the significance of variations in the extent of democratic state intervention to regulate economies. Discussions on the varieties of capitalism draw a distinction between economies coordinated by markets and those coordinated by states (Hall and Soskice 2001; Hanké 2009; Streeck 2009). This distinction parallels that found in discussions on the varieties of welfare state regimes between liberal and social democratic regimes (as well as other sub-types) (Esping-Andersen 1990; Hicks and Kenworthy 2003). However, these debates on varieties of capitalism have often left gender out of focus, though there are important exceptions (Estevez-Abe 2005, 2006; Gottfried 2000; O'Connor et al. 1999; Shire 2007; Waylen 2007). Nevertheless, the distinction between (neo)liberalism and social democracy developed in relation to varieties of capitalism can be fruitfully applied to varieties of gender regime.

Gender regimes intersect with capitalism as well as with other regimes of inequality such as those based on ethnicity. These regimes change each other as they intersect; they mutually adapt, though this may be in an asymmetrical manner. Gender regimes are subject to change as a consequence of these intersections. The intersection does not mean that the systems cease to exist or that they change their form such that they cannot be recognized. The gender regime is not nested within capitalism. It intersects with, but is not subsumed by, capitalism. The gender regime and capitalism are mutually adaptive complex systems which shape each other.

Change does not take place in a simple, unilinear fashion; rather there are rounds of restructuring which layer change upon institutional change. During the crisis there has been a round of restructuring of the previous gender regime by the neoliberal project that has achieved governmental power. This has involved the undoing of social democratic patterns of public expenditure through cuts in the public spending that supported the gendered social democratic institutions. However, there are also some practices that have become so deeply sedimented in the social formation that they have not been substantially reduced even though they have been restructured. This is the case, at least to some extent, for government expenditure on childcare and on services to prevent violence against women. The mechanisms through which public funds flow to support these services are being privatized and marketized. Childcare is provided not by publicly run nurseries but by private nurseries looking after children of parents who are individually subsidized through tax credits. The running of refuges and sexual assault referral centres is put out to tender on the open market, and increasingly run no longer by feminist-oriented specialist service providers, but by generic service providers, such as housing associations, and by global capital, such as G4S (Towers and Walby 2012). The services have been reorganized as well as reduced to become hybrid forms of institutions in which government funds support services delivered by the private or third sector. This is not a simple oscillation between social democratic and neoliberal forms of public gender regime. It is better conceptualized as a round of restructuring in which new layers are built upon already existing institutions created in earlier rounds of restructuring. There is no simple 'return' to the previous state. This process parallels previous analyses of rounds of economic restructuring (Massey and Meegan 1982; Bagguley et al. 1990). This analysis shares the concern to analyse different types of changes in gendered institutions with the new feminist institutionalism (Waylen 2007). This model of the gender regime is developed in more detail in Walby (2009). These conceptual developments are applied next to the stages of the crisis.

Re-Gendering the Economic Growth Regime

A major concern of mainstream politics is how to deliver economic growth; in the context of the crisis this concern has become even more prominent. The analysis presented here challenges the neoliberal

growth strategy and argues that an explicitly gendered social democratic growth strategy is more likely to be successful. This strategy
has three components: regulating markets to improve their efficiency;
social investment by the state to build human capital; and industrial
policy that is forward not backward looking.

Following the financial crisis, Tucker (2011: 3–4), the deputy governor of the Bank of England for financial stability, stated that he
found financial markets to be 'inefficient, riddled with preferred habitats, imperfect arbitrage, regulatory arbitrage, herding, and inhabited
by agents with less than idealised rationality'. This echoes the finding
by Adam Smith in 1776 that 'people of the same trade seldom meet
together, even for merriment and diversion, but the conversation
ends in a conspiracy against the public, or in some contrivance to
raise prices' (Smith 1986 [1776]: 152).

Without regulation, markets are inefficient; they are subject to distortion by corruption, monopolies, discrimination and power. The
neoliberal opposition to regulation produces a contradiction. Policy
cannot produce both efficient markets and deregulation since efficient markets require regulation. The generic policy of deregulation
reduces the efficiency of markets. Without regulation, market failure
in one part of society cascades into the next: insufficiently regulated
financial markets are unstable and damage the real economy.

The regulation of markets is a gender issue. Regulation of labour
markets is necessary to overcome the inefficiency of allocation of
men and women to jobs on discriminatory rather than meritocratic
criteria. Regulation of labour markets is necessary for full employment, in order to overcome the difficulty of combining employment
and care-work by regulating working time and regulating leaves for
maternity, paternity and parenting. In the absence of regulation, the
main carer interrupts their employment, with additional problems of
weakened human capital formation and fertility which drops beneath
replacement levels.

Contemporary economies cannot grow without human capital.
Human capital development is limited without state social investment. The neoliberal opposition to state investment is in contradiction to human-capital-based economic growth. The development
of human capital requires state social investment. The reduction
of public expenditure reduces the production of the human capital
needed for economic growth.

The development of human capital through state social investment
is a gender issue. State social investment is needed to provide the
education that develops human capital and provides the childcare

(and elder care) needed to allow for the full employment of the main carer, who is usually a woman.

Without a forward looking industrial strategy, investment is concentrated in old industries rather than the ones with future potential. Without adequate state procedures, lobbyists from the sunset industries are better able to persuade the state to back their industries than those of the future. The proper identification of future industries is needed for nimble economic growth.

The industrial strategy is gendered. As the crisis cascaded from banks to jobs the government made their counter-balancing investment in the old carbon-producing industries of cars and roads. The alternatives, of green investment in the infrastructure for low-carbon energy, of the knowledge-intensive economy where there is gender balance among workers, and of the care sector needed to modernize the organization of women's labour, did not benefit. The future development of government industrial strategy needs to reconsider its engagement with gendered lobbies and the nature of gendered industrial futures.

Just distribution of rewards and economic growth are often posed as trade-offs in that social justice is treated as an alternative goal to that of economic growth. However, not only does the project for justice rarely become a governmental programme when it is seen as a trade-off with economic growth but the assumption of a trade-off is itself mistaken. As this analysis has shown, justice and growth are entwined rather than being opposed; they co-produce each other. Only if the full set of human capacities is engaged will the economy be successful. Only if there is just allocation of rewards will the full set of human capacities become engaged with the economy. The future distribution of rewards is embedded within the growth strategy – it is a form of pre-distribution. The economic growth strategy needs just distribution in order to succeed.

Economic growth is gendered. Since the rate of economic growth is shaped by social institutions, and since social institutions and structures are usually gendered, the rate of economic growth is shaped by gendered institutions. Changes in the institutions in a gender regime affect the rate of economic growth. A gender regime is not limited to the family or system of reproduction, but extends to all institutional domains: economy (domestic, production for the market, financial), polity, violence and civil society. Each of these intersects with the institutions that affect the rate of economic growth.

There are several locations where aspects of the gender regime affect economic growth. Within each of the institutional domains through which the crisis has cascaded there are significant gender issues. These include: finance, economy, state and democracy.

Finance: preventing destructive instability

Preventing financial crises that wreck the real economy is the priority action for the production of economic growth. Haldane has noted (see chapter 3) that the reduction in economic output caused by banking failures far outstrips any contribution that banks could make to taxpayers, since the losses to the real economy are larger than the value of the financial sector. Gendered action that would reduce the likelihood of further financial crises includes improving the gender balance in decision-making in finance companies by, for example, legislating for quotas on corporate boards when this is not done voluntarily. But more important is the re-gendering of the governmental institutions that have legitimate democratic oversight over finance. This step would ensure the effective democratic control over finance so that it can never again damage the real economy by excessive risk-taking in pursuit of private profit.

Economy: regulating markets for efficiency

Economic growth in the real economy is assisted by full employment and by high-productivity (i.e. highly skilled and high-wage) employment (see chapter 4). Although there has been a return to pre-crisis rates of employment, this has been combined with a reduction in productivity (and wages) and less than full employment, as evidenced by high rates of both unemployment and involuntary part-time working. This is low-productivity economic growth generating less output per hour worked than the pre-crisis level.

Gendered action to improve economic growth would be to regulate labour markets more effectively to reduce the discrimination that distorts them. Reducing discrimination and segregation increases the effective utilization of women's labour by reducing inefficiencies and rigidities in the markets for labour. The practices and institutions of discrimination and segregation impair the functioning of the labour market, reducing its efficiency by preventing the best allocation of labour, hence reducing its competitiveness and the rate of economic growth. Paying women less than the fair rate reduces their incentive to take employment and so reduces the likelihood of achieving full employment. Hence, when effectively implemented, anti-discrimination legislation promotes full employment and economic growth.

Further gendered action to improve economic growth would be to regulate working time in labour markets to facilitate the combination of employment and care-work. This action would contribute to full employment and continuity of employment with the same employer, which facilitates human capital development. Interruptions in employment for intensive care-work lead to the degradation of carers', particularly mothers', human capital. Preventing breaks in the relationship between employer and employee during childbirth and initial childcare thus contributes to the maintenance and increase of human capital, which, in turn, fosters higher levels of productivity. Regulation of working time, through maternity, paternity and parental leave entitlement, thus contributes to economic growth.

Fiscal: social investment state

The provision of socialized care-work increases the labour supply and human capital of mothers and other carers and thereby promotes economic growth (see chapter 5). Socialized care-work includes not only childcare and education, but also social and health care for the old, sick, disabled and frail. The development of state-funded childcare and elder care increases the availability of women for employment and enhances its continuity by reducing gaps for periods of intensive care. This reduction of breaks in employment reduces the deterioration in human capital that usually occurs during such breaks. Thus the provision of socialized care-work increases both the quantity of the female labour supply and its level of human capital, thereby contributing to economic growth. The consequent increase in female employment would increase the tax base and reduce fiscal tensions.

The provision of socialized forms of care-work by the state means that the average female worker has a higher level of human capital than would be the case if the provision of socialized forms of care-work were only to occur when it was profitable to provide this on the market. State funding to ensure the provision of education, health and care services can boost economic growth by increasing the level of human capital as well as increasing the employment rate. Thus a social democratic public gender regime is more likely to contribute to economic growth than a neoliberal form, and both of these public forms are more likely to do so than a more domestic form of gender regime.

If the fiscal tensions are resolved by reducing expenditure on the social investment state, then a demographic crisis will be generated as women reduce the number of children they bear to below the level needed to reproduce the population and labour force, as is the case in many countries in eastern and southern Europe. A demographic crisis reduces the capacity for economic growth.

Democracy: inclusion of all citizens in decision-making

The inclusion of all citizens in political decision-making is the goal of democracy. This democratic principle is legitimate in its own right. In addition, democracy contributes to effective decision-making. There is considerable variation in the extent to which women and gendered projects are included in democratic procedures. The greater the depth of democracy then the more the voices and projects of women are included. An improvement in the gender balance in decision-making results in more effective and appropriate decisions.

Economic growth is a widely shared goal. But the interpretation regarding how it is best achieved varies and the nature of the strategy adopted pre-structures the distributional effects of the growth.

Women's effective political citizenship makes the provision of socialized care-work, parental leaves and equal treatment laws more likely, since it increases the likelihood that women would have an effective political voice in developing such policies. The gendered depth of democracy affects the gendering of financial governance, the gendering of labour market regulation and the gendering of fiscal priorities. These aspects affect the likelihood of financial crisis, the achievement of full employment, the accumulation of human capital and hence of economic growth. Gender equality in democracy contributes to increasing economic growth.

Social democratic public gender regime, not de-familialization

This account of a social democratic economic growth strategy is centred on the 'gender regime', not on 'family'. There are some points of overlap but also important points of difference. There is overlap in the provision of public funds to socialize childcare and other aspects of care, including elder care and education: this supports both a 'social democratic public gender regime' and also 'de-familialization'. There is overlap in the regulation of working time to facilitate the work–life balance that allows the combination of employment and care-work. But there are additional components in the social democratic public gender regime strategy for economic growth that are absent in a de-familialization strategy. The framework of 'gender' brings into focus issues of: gender balance in decision-making in finance; regulating the labour market to prevent the distortion arising from discrimination; and deepening democracy to facilitate the articulation of projects supporting gender equality and women's full inclusion in economy and society. The two approaches share a common core around re-balancing women's labour in care-work and paid work; but the gender regime approach goes further than the narrower de-familialization approach to include a wider range of social institutions, and hence is a more fruitful framework in terms of generating both economic growth and gender justice.

Conclusion: Gender as the Pivot of the Crisis

All phases of the crisis have been gendered, albeit in varying ways. In finance the absence of women from both company and political decision-making had deleterious consequences for the quality of decisions. The various phases of job loss in the economy were differently gendered in that it was largely men affected in the initial phase which followed the banking collapse, and slightly more women in the phase following austerity. The impact of austerity is disproportionately experienced by women and the poor as cuts are made to benefits and welfare services. The challenges to democracy are gendered, though this gendering is often hidden by the relative invisibility of women in joint projects at the intersection of different strands of inequality.

Gender has become the pivot of the crisis as its major articulation has become fiscal tensions and attempts to reduce public expenditure. The fiscal has become the centre of the political crisis, and these fiscal tensions are deeply gendered. Public social expenditure is gendered in that it is disproportionately spent on public services that are disproportionately used by women, disproportionately employ women and are disproportionately politically supported by women. The contestation over the budget deficit is gendered in that the reduction in public expenditure rather than collecting more taxes is a gendered practice which increases gender inequality. While some key public services, such as for childcare and services to prevent violence against women, continue to receive government income, their provision is being privatized. This gendering of public expenditure is the outcome of a gendered political project to socialize domestic labour and to move from a domestic gender regime to a social democratic form of gender regime. This project has been slowly and cumulatively, if unevenly, successful in building the institutions of the welfare or social investment state and regulation of the labour market for several decades, at least since 1945. This progress came to an abrupt halt in 2010 with the new government's decision to narrow the budget deficit predominantly through cuts in social expenditure. These cuts represent the end of the slow move towards a social democratic public gender regime and its replacement by a sudden turn to a neoliberal public gender regime. They are contested.

While women are still relatively absent from decision-making, there had been a slow and cumulative progress to their increased presence. This increased political engagement was one of the causes of the changes in the gender regime. The crisis is marked by contestation over the potential increase or decrease in the depth of gendered democracy. While there have been attempts to remedy the relative absence of women in economic financial decision-making that was contributory to the crisis, the privatization of gendered public services contributes to de-democratization. There has been an increase in feminist activity in civil societal organizations including trade unions; however, this can be hard to see when feminist political forces are engaged in joint and intersecting projects with labour and other social democratic forces. The forthcoming gendered democratic challenge at the next round of the financial crisis will probably result in the financial and fiscal architecture of the EU being subject to further restructuring. It is far from clear whether the EU's commitment to the value of gender equality will be institutionalized during this process.

The strategies for economic growth out of the crisis are gendered. The strategy of deregulation and reduction in public services has detrimental consequences for the ability of women to access high-quality jobs, and hence for the maintenance and development of their human capital. The consequent economic growth delivers its rewards to the few, not the many. There is an alternative strategy into economic growth that draws on the inclusion of all potential workers into high-quality jobs. This is a gendered strategy for economic growth which depends upon the mobilization of the state as a source of social investment in human capital, as well as a source for the regulation of markets that is necessary to prevent their distortion by discrimination, monopoly and power. The social democratic public gender regime is more conducive to economic growth than the neoliberal public gender regime because of its implications for the quantity and quality of female labour. This regime reduces interruptions to employment due to intensive care by providing socialized care-work and legally binding maternity, paternity and parental leaves, which thereby protect women's human capital and their contribution to economic growth and the regime of accumulation. It also delivers gender justice, which is good for economic growth. The development of this strategy is dependent upon the deepening of democracy, especially in its gendered dimension, so that the projects of those currently excluded can be included in decision-making to the benefit of all.

The theorization of these changes in the gender regime requires a more nuanced approach than that found in the traditional dualisms of de-/familialization, male/dual breadwinner or production/reproduction. This nuancing can be achieved by introducing the distinction between two forms of the public gender regime: the neoliberal and social democratic. This distinction enables recognition that women have not been pushed back into the home by cuts in public services but have maintained their attachment to the labour market (though sometimes being unemployed rather than employed). The distinction recognizes the different ways in which the public gender regime may be constituted. It helps to make visible the nature of the contested gendered changes.

8

Conclusions:
Implications for Social Theory
and Public Policy

What conclusions can be drawn for social theory and public policy from the analysis of the crisis offered in the preceding chapters? These conclusions are presented in four parts: a retelling of the narrative of the crisis; the rethinking of key concepts and theories in social science, especially sociology; analysis of the implications for public policy, especially for models of sustainable economic growth and social justice; and the presentation of alternative futures consequent on alternative policy scenarios.

Narrating the Crisis

A narrative identifies: the starting point and key events; the main actors; the nature of the process connecting events; the underpinning social value, policy or political goal; and the end point or conclusion (Ricoeur 1984). The following narrative of the crisis draws on the theory and evidence presented in this book.

Starting point of the crisis

The starting point of the crisis was the removal of democratic control over finance. Without adequate regulation, finance grew in ways that exacerbated its inherent instability while it also became several times larger than the real economy. This removal of regulation during the period from the mid-1980s onwards made financial crisis inevitable at some point. The regulations that were removed included those that had been imposed on capital in the Bretton Woods settlement in 1944 as a result of the lessons learnt from the financial crash of 1929, which had led to the 1930s depression, rise of fascism, genocide and world war (see chapter 3).

Two alternative starting points of the crisis are rejected. The narrative that starts with excessive government spending creating a fiscal crisis which was exacerbated by the EU is rejected. Even the IMF agrees that the UK budget deficit in 2010 was predominantly the result of the decline in government income from taxation due to the recession created by the financial crash (see chapter 5). The starting point of the crisis was a financial crisis that eventually cascaded into a fiscal crisis; it did not start in fiscal matters. The narrative that starts with the exhaustion of the regime of capital accumulation inevitably leading to unstable financialization is also rejected. There is scope for improvements in the organization of the economy so as to deliver economic growth (see chapters 4 and 7); financialization was contingent not on the exhaustion of the regime of accumulation, but on the removal of the regulations on finance (see chapter 3).

Competing projects

The gendered neoliberal project became victorious over the gendered social democratic project. The gendered neoliberal project grew in strength, resources and allies, and became embedded in governmental programmes from the 1980s. It promoted and achieved deregulation of the economy, including finance, as well as privatization of previously publicly provided and funded services. The gendered social democratic project became weaker during the same period, losing ground within the political party that had previously been its main host, as well as in governmental programmes. The consensus between political parties over 'light-touch' regulation of finance meant there was little political opposition to the deregulation of finance.

The relative strength of these projects draws on changes in the social systems which constituted their environment, or fitness landscape, especially the industrial and political systems, since these have implications for political organization. The rise of the neoliberal project is linked to the increased significance of finance capital, both in itself and in the way it has penetrated industrial capital and financialized many aspects of everyday life. Lobbying to protect finance from democratic regulation has been extraordinarily successful in the UK. The decline in strength of the social democratic project is linked to the decline in the traditional base for unionized male workers in mining and heavy manufacturing. The potential re-emergence of the social democratic project depends on its re-gendering and incorporation of a new constituency among women, in particular those employed in the public services. The gendered deepening of the depth of democratic institutions that facilitates the political mobilization of women and the ongoing development of the political institutions of the European Union together foster the growth of an alternative project to neoliberalism (see chapter 6).

Each competing project seeks to re-shape the social formation in line with its vision, predominantly but not exclusively, by becoming governmental programmes. The capacity to define the cascading crisis as caused by the 'other' project has been significant. Realizing this definition depends not only on the agility with which the projects construct their narrative but also on the resources in their environment that are available to draw upon. This environment includes all the multiple social systems that are coupled together in the social formation.

Process and events

The crisis cascaded from finance to the real economy to government budgets to the political and democratic institutions. The crisis, as it cascaded, caused significant damage to each of these systems.

Finance Not only was the financial system unstable as a consequence of deregulation but it had also grown in size to become several times larger than the real economy, which meant a growth in its potential effects on the real economy. The financial crash of 2007/8 was triggered by the pricking of the bubble in house prices in the US in 2007, which, in turn, was linked to the energy crisis and dramatic rise in the price of the petrol used for suburban commuting (see chapter 3).

Economy The crash in the financial system caused a recession in the real economy, reducing the supply of credit. This affected not only economic output but also employment and living standards. While output is no longer falling and the number of hours worked had recuperated by 2015, living standards at this time have not regained their pre-crash level (see chapter 4).

Fiscal The recession in the real economy led to a decline in government income from taxation, which resulted in fiscal tensions. The crisis in Greece provided the context that allowed the budget deficit in the UK to be interpreted as a fiscal crisis. The incoming 2010 government, a coalition of Conservatives and Liberal Democrats, announced a crisis. They abandoned their manifestos and implemented a series of previously unplanned cuts in public expenditure known as austerity (see chapter 5).

Political   This austerity led to a further slowdown in economic growth and to increased poverty and inequality. The hegemonic narrative of the crisis, which focuses on the fiscal crisis, has diverted attention away from the need for the major re-regulation of finance, which consequently remains unstable. There was a growth in nationalist sentiment, fuelling the growth of both UKIP, which attacked the EU for allowing migration into the UK and provoked the Conservatives into promising a referendum on EU membership, and the SNP, who seek more independence from the UK. The SNP only narrowly (45/55) lost a referendum on Scotland leaving the UK in 2014. There remains the potential for major constitutional crises, both over UK relations with the EU and over Scottish relations with the UK (see chapter 6).

End point?   In 2015 the effects of the crisis are still cascading through society with no end in sight. There remains the prospect of major constitutional crisis with regard to the political domain. There is the prospect of a further crash in finance since the reforms have been too minor to ensure stability. A further financial crash would be likely to trigger a further round of crises over economic output and fiscal deficits. The process of the cascading of the crisis from one societal domain to another is made possible by the close coupling of the systems of finance, real economy, state and politics in a 'society' (see chapter 2).

Underpinning goals

Support for sustainable economic growth and for social justice is hegemonic, though the policies through which these are to be achieved are contested. The neoliberal project assumes that deregulation of markets and privatization will invigorate the economy, and since this is seen as the best context for the delivery of well-being it is therefore deemed 'fair'. The social democratic project promotes the regulation of markets to prevent distortion by powerful interests and corruption, and holds that democracy and social investment are necessary to secure social justice.

Lessons

These alternative beliefs about the functioning of economy and society can be subjected to appraisal by social science rather than being treated as if they were fundamental values. The crisis could be treated as generating evidence to test these rival theories on strategies to promote the better functioning of markets. It could be used to test whether regulating markets makes them more or less efficient in the allocation of resources.

The belief that deregulating markets is good for economy and society has been found wanting when confronted with the social scientific evidence; reducing the regulation of markets concerning finance led to the crisis starting in finance which continues to cascade through society. However, the belief that markets are more efficient if they are unregulated rather than regulated remains hegemonic. This is at least partly because the narration of the crisis as a fiscal rather than financial crisis has become hegemonic, thereby allowing the marginalization of this test of theories about markets. Narrating the crisis as if it were primarily a fiscal rather than a financial crisis enables the construction of the most relevant political debate as one centred on the level of public expenditure rather than on the regulation of finance. It facilitates the side-stepping of the real causes of the crisis, found in the failure to regulate finance, and thus of the examination of the potential policies which would prevent it from happening again.

Theoretical Conclusions

Rethinking the concept of society

A concept and theory of society are necessary for an understanding of the way in which a crisis in one institution, finance, can cascade into crises in other institutions, including the real economy, the state and politics. It is not sufficient to analyse and theorize one set of institutions in isolation from others. The separation of analyses by the separate social sciences concerning finance, the economy, the welfare state and politics is inadequate for a crisis that has cascaded through all these sets of institutions. It is necessary to analyse the ways in which these institutions intersect and connect, which requires repairing the traditional separation of the social science disciplines relevant to the crisis. It is important to revitalize the traditional goal of sociology to study all of society in order to reach an understanding of a crisis that has cascaded through many social institutions. This understanding requires the concept of society as a social system. It demands sociological inquiry at a macro level, not only at the meso and micro levels.

The revitalization of a theory of society requires a reform of the concept of social system. The sociological canon has embedded a concept of society that drew on a specific early formulation of the concept of system. There have been severe criticisms of the traditional concept of society in sociology which was developed across a wide range of traditions from Durkheim to Marx. A system is a set of relations that reproduces itself. Traditional concepts of social system have long been criticized for several reasons: for being too rigid to cope adequately with social change and with intersecting multiple inequalities; for the mistaken assumption that systems will normally return to equilibrium after a disruption or perturbation; and for the mistaken assumption of proportionality between cause and effect. The revised concept of social system, drawing on complexity science, rejects the assumption that a system is best understood as comprising 'parts' and replaces it with the notion that a system takes all other systems as its environment. This notion enables much greater flexibility in the deployment of the concept of system at the same time as retaining its core advantages. For example, it removes the necessity of thinking that parts of a system must be nested inside the system. It makes it possible to address multiple regimes of inequality existing within the same territory without assuming that they must neatly map onto each other or be confined to the same borders.

It is time to renew the concept of system that underpins the concept of society. This is best achieved by drawing on the insights of complexity science, which has been rethinking the concept of system across a range of sciences. A refreshed concept of system enables a revision of the concept of society to avoid the criticisms rightly levelled at earlier versions. Ten revisions should be made to the traditional sociological concept of social system, using developments in complexity science, in order to make it fit for purpose in the analysis of crisis and indeed other social phenomena.

1 Systems are not always in equilibrium but can be far from equilibrium; nor do they necessarily return to equilibrium after a disturbance, so the notion of a system as self-balancing and self-equilibrating is mistaken.

2 Feedback loops within the system are not always negative but can also be positive: disturbances, or perturbations, of a system can sometimes be subject to negative feedback loops that restore the original condition, or they can be subject to positive feedback loops that move the system even further from equilibrium.

3 Positive feedback loops are important in generating change that is not gradual and linear but sudden and non-linear.
4 Change can occur as a 'punctuated equilibrium', meaning that it is made up of both gradual and sudden forms of change.
5 A system is better conceptualized as taking all other systems as its environment than as a system made up of parts, since this conceptualization allows greater flexibility in the analysis of relationships between systems.
6 Systems do not need to be conceptualized as nested, nor do they need to be congruent in the same space.
7 Systems can be coupled together so as to form larger systems; this coupling may vary in the extent to which it is tight or loose.
8 The relationship between systems can be that of mutual adaptation, in which their intersection changes both systems, rather than one system impacting on and changing the other in a one-way direction.
9 There can be multiple potential points of equilibrium for a system such that it takes not one universal form but rather diverse forms of path dependency.
10 Causes do not need to be proportionate to their effects if they are acting in a context of complex systems; a small change can create a large effect. These changes to the concept of system enable the development of a more fluid and flexible concept of society without abandoning the explanatory power of the concept of system (see chapter 2).

Rethinking the concept of crisis

A 'crisis' is a point of sudden and potentially major change in a system. The social sciences have developed a series of specialized concepts concerning crisis which have been devised to fit the contours of specific fields. The utilization of a shared conceptual vocabulary developed through engagement with complexity science would facilitate the exchange of knowledge between these sub-fields of social science and consequently promote their improvement. In political sociology, the concept of revolution is used to indicate a large crisis, often in contrast with that of revolt to indicate a smaller crisis with less far-reaching consequences. In the environmental sciences, the concept of disaster is used to indicate a crisis, often developed within a broader appreciation of the wider contexts affecting the reach of a crisis. The concept of normal accident identifies a small crisis which holds potential for large consequences depending on whether it cascades beyond its immediate context (see chapter 2).

The concept of crisis may be expressed in more technical language as a potential 'tipping point', or 'critical turning point'. The significance of the crisis, and the extent to which its effects become large, depend upon its environment and the extent to which the systems in that environment are tightly or loosely coupled.

It is necessary to develop a theory of social systems and of social change to theorize crisis adequately. It is necessary to be able to conceptualize, in order to address, the nature of the links between the various systems that co-exist in the environment. The revised concept of social change allows for disproportionality in size between cause and effect so that it becomes possible for a small change to have a large effect. If social systems are unstable then a small event may cause a large change to these systems. Social systems may be loosely or tightly coupled together to form a large social system. The more tightly coupled the systems then the greater the likelihood that change in one system will cause changes in the other systems to which it is coupled. A system that has a more modular form rather than a more integrated form is one in which the systems are more loosely coupled. A change in one system in the more modular form is less likely to cascade into changes in the other systems.

The extent to which systems are closely or loosely coupled is relevant to the understanding of the financial crisis. The speed and extent to which a change in one part of the financial system affects other parts of the financial system is dependent upon the closeness of the coupling of the systems. Hence, for example, the barrier separating retail and casino banking, introduced in 1944 and removed during the 1980s, is a form of modularization of the financial system that reduces the likelihood of financial problems cascading from one section to the other. The removal of this barrier increased the vulnerability of the financial system to failure. Macro-prudentialism addresses the financial system as a system, including the extent of its modularization. The principle of macro-prudentialism concerns the development of those aspects of the financial system that affect its functioning as a system, while that of micro-prudentialism concerns the functioning of each individual financial institution. Drawing on complexity theory makes it possible to devise ways of making financial systems more stable. Small fluctuations in finance and the economy are routine and may not cause larger effects. Such bubbles and business cycles do not cascade beyond the economy into having serious effects on the state's budgets (see chapter 3).

The concept of crisis seen through the lens of complexity science can be understood as a potential tipping point or critical turning point. Improving the theorization of crisis requires use of the reworked concept of social system discussed here. This facilitates the analysis of the wider environment, including the closeness or looseness of the coupling of systems, which is central to whether a small cause has a large effect (see chapter 2).

Rethinking the concept of market

Markets are sites of exchange between different parties. Markets are social institutions. The hegemonic concept of market abstracts a notion of market in a way that neglects the social institutions in which it is embedded. This dominant approach to markets is seriously problematic and in need of major revision. The notion that a market is more pure the more it is abstracted from the social institutions in which it is necessarily situated is deeply flawed. Markets are intrinsically shaped by the social relations in those institutions. Markets are sites of exchange and are thereby shaped by powerful forces seeking advantage during these exchanges. As recognized even by Adam Smith, without regulation by other forces, markets become sites of unequal exchange and of corruption. The concept of market is core to the discipline of economics and has become increasingly important in sociology and other social sciences. But the version of the concept that became hegemonic in economics was denied the insights of Smith and needs revision to encompass its institutional elements.

Markets need regulation to reduce corrupt and manipulative practices, unfair discrimination that favours some parties above others, and the accumulation of monopoly power that increases prices. It is important to reject the notion that markets are more efficient if they are unregulated. The project of deregulation of markets does not necessarily lead to their improvement and greater efficiency. The deregulation of markets does not result in 'pure' markets but in distorted markets, since it increases the likelihood of manipulation by powerful forces. The fairest markets are those where there are regulations to remove distortions, corruption, discrimination and monopoly power.

Markets do not necessarily tend towards equilibrium. Following the insights of complexity science, markets, like other systems, may have positive feedback loops that drive the system further from equilibrium as well as negative feedback loops that tend towards equilibrium. The crisis has shown that: markets do not always return to equilibrium;

and markets can move further away from equilibrium. Markets in finance in particular have endogenously generated instability.

Markets complexly intersect in a diverse environment. The outcome of any one market depends on its interaction with other markets. Hence, the regulation of one market depends upon the regulation of all markets. A macro perspective that takes this interaction into account is essential. It is necessary to go beyond perspectives limited to individual rational agency and the flawed assumption of perfect, self-balancing, self-regulating and equilibrating markets.

The concept of market has been idealized and purified through inappropriate forms of abstraction. When tested against evidence from the real world, such a concept is found in need of significant revision. Markets should be conceptualized as social institutions in order to analyse their operation in economy and society. Regulations are necessary to reduce their distortion by powerful or corrupt interests (see chapters 3 and 4).

Rethinking finance and the economy

Finance matters. Sociology has typically ignored finance, mistakenly assuming that employment was its central object of concern within the economy. Finance is not reducible to the economy in general but has its own specific logic and dynamics. The sociology of finance, financialization and financial crisis should be of concern to the discipline of sociology. The struggle over the control of money, of the financial system, is crucial to the form of society. Keynes and Minsky should be assimilated into the canon of sociological theory.

Finance should be conceptualized as a social relationship rather than as an object. Finance is best understood as a form of capital. It can also be understood as an industry in the sense that 'financial services' is a form of industry within industrial classifications, and as a 'market' in that financial markets are one of the mechanisms by which finance flows.

Finance is a different form of capital to industrial capital. Finance capital is centred in money and debt; industrial capital is centred in machines and buildings. Finance capital and industrial capital can potentially have different interests, in that while finance capital makes profits from economic instability, industrial capital is disrupted, may face bankruptcy and is likely to make fewer profits during economic instability.

Financialization is the process in which finance enters industry and everyday life. This mingling of finance with industrial capital and with the assets of everyday life, such as mortgages and pensions, can sometimes make it hard to separate the interests of finance from the interests of those subject to the demands of finance. Thus the conceptual separation of the interests of financial and industrial capital identified here may be far from clear in any given empirical context.

The growth of finance, the process of financialization and the financial crisis are a consequence of the deregulation of finance. This is a political process. Financialization is not the result of the exhaustion of the regime of accumulation; of the failure of capitalism to generate profits from industrial capital. It is a mistake to account for changes in finance capital by changes in industrial capital. Political projects are important for the regulation and deregulation of finance and hence for its impact on economy and society. The practical application of such regulations requires an understanding of finance as a macro system and of the available forms of legal regulation and supervision (see chapter 3).

Rethinking the concepts of state and democracy

All states in the EU are democratic. The reduction in the scope of governance by the state is a reduction in the depth of democracy. The use of the term 'bureaucracy' or 'coordinated' rather than 'democratic state', and use of the term 'red tape' to describe democratically determined forms of regulation, are best avoided, since these terms carry not only negative but incorrect assumptions.

The EU is a polity. It has many of the properties of a state except that it has very limited competence in relation to military matters.

It is important to consider variations in the depth of democracy. Elections every four or five years in the context of free association and a plurality of political parties are necessary for democracy but are insufficient by themselves to guarantee its depth. Deeper forms of democracy offer additional procedures to increase the presence of women and minorities in the parliamentary and decision-making arenas, and thus to provide access for these voices to the deliberative processes necessary for deep democracy in a plural society. The application of the principle of democratic governance to more rather than fewer institutions, such as the public services of health, education and care, broadens and deepens democracy. The removal of areas of economic life from state control should be understood as a form of de-democratization.

The crisis has exposed weaknesses in many democratic states in the translation of the will of the people into governmental action.

This should be understood as a political crisis that has teetered on the brink of cascading into a democratic crisis. There have been occasional declarations of states of emergency and descent into violence, but not yet in a systematic, routine manner (see chapter 6).

The concept of project

Projects have been important in the generation of the context for the crisis. A project is a cohesive set of ideas and practices that provide an account of the way the world works and how it can be improved. The gendered neoliberal project has become hegemonic at the expense of the gendered social democratic project. It is becoming embedded in political parties and governmental programmes and increasingly sedimented in the social formation.

A project is a collective process within civil society that develops meanings and goals for action. While the concept of project includes the ideational elements that are contained in concepts of 'discourse', 'frame' and 'narrative', it goes beyond these to include 'practices' and is also different in that it is necessarily oriented towards social change. It differs from the concept of social movement in that it goes beyond 'protest' to include practices, such as lobbying, that are less visible, and includes forms of institutionalization.

A project is not the expression of essentialized identities such as those of class, gender or ethnicity; rather it includes the reconstitution of goals, practices and subjects through joint activities and discussions. Projects thus have a complex relationship to the social systems constituting their environment. A project draws on a range of both rhetorical and material resources. While there are links between financial and economic position and political projects, there is not a simple relationship between them, since how people perceive their interests is shaped by social processes and struggles (see chapter 6).

Analysing the contradictions in neoliberalism

Neoliberalism is a project which has become embedded in governmental programmes and social formations. At the centre of its rhetorical claims is the notion that prices and markets are efficient mechanisms for the organization of the economy. The neoliberal project thus purports to seek to roll back the state, to reduce state regulations over the economy, to privatize economic activities that are run by the state, and to reduce the activities and expenditures of the state, including welfare. The neoliberal project takes a gendered form in contemporary (2015) UK and Europe in which a significant target has become the reduction in state expenditure on gendered welfare and gendered social investment.

However, the neoliberal project is subject to several contradictions. As already noted, the regulation of markets is needed in order to prevent corruption and distortion, so deregulated markets do not work well, as evidenced by the advent of the financial crisis. Capital has a tendency to seek the creation of monopolies rather than perfect markets to increase its profits through reduced competition. Finance capital could destroy industrial capital as a consequence of its instability if it is not regulated, thereby generating tensions within capital itself. A further contradiction is the rise of inequality and discontent. In practice, this leads to an increase in the size of the security state; contradicting populist claims that neoliberalism could produce a smaller state. These contradictions give practical expression to the lack of coherence in the intellectual foundations of neoliberalism, discussed in chapter 3.

Analysing the re-gendering of social democracy

Social democracy is a project which has historically been embedded in governmental programmes and social formation. At the centre of its claims is the notion that democracy is important for social justice and for the effective working of the economy to meet the needs of all rather than the few. The long-standing tension between capitalism and democracy was intended to be stabilized through compromise in this project. Since the middle of the twentieth century, the social democratic project has been a gendered project which has sought to include women as political citizens and, varying according to time and place, sometimes to socialize domestic labour to secure full employment for all as a route to economic growth.

Social democracy has faced many challenges. These challenges have included global processes which have tilted the balance of power away from labour towards capital, and the decline in the industrial base that generated its traditional male, skilled-worker constituency. However, the re-gendering of the potential constituency for the social democratic project may be opening up new possibilities.

The concept of gender regime

The contesting projects in the crisis are gendered. The analysis of these varied gender relations requires the development of the conceptualization of varieties of gender regime. Not only do these regimes take domestic and public forms but also the public form is differentiated between a neoliberal and a social democratic form.

The neoliberal project is gendered. The struggle over the fiscal aspect of the crisis that has become the centre of the neoliberal narrative of the crisis is a gendered struggle over gendered state expenditures. The analysis of the crisis requires an analysis of this specific intersection of class and gender regimes. It is necessary to separate the gender regime analytically from capitalism, so that the different changes and dynamics can be seen, before they are reintegrated in empirical analysis.

This approach involves rethinking the traditional way that gender has been conceptualized as primarily an issue of identity and culture, so that instead the concept of gender regime includes the financial, economic, fiscal and political institutions that are both constitutive of gender and constituted by gender relations. The adoption of the concept of gender regime in general, and that of varieties of gender regime in particular, is essential in capturing the changes involved in the crisis at a macro level. The crisis is a critical turning point in the trajectory of the gender regime. The trajectory of development of the gender regime is changing from a more social democratic to a more neoliberal form (see chapter 7).

Conclusions For Public Policy: Models of Sustainable Growth and Social Justice

While there are many goals for public policy, two in particular are prominent following the crisis: the achievement of the re-emergence of sustainable growth; and the achievement of social justice. Ideally, both would be achieved together. The qualification 'sustainable' in relation to economic growth is necessary since growth which destroys the planet through inattention to the production of carbon dioxide is self-defeating. The conceptualization of social justice is more varied and ranges from the ambiguously open 'fairness' to the more tightly defined 'equality' and 'reducing poverty'.

The conclusions of the book for the best way to achieve sustainable growth combined with social justice will be considered in relation to finance, the fiscal, economic growth and democracy, drawing on the relevant chapters in turn.

Finance

Financial crises wreck the real economy. The Bank of England considered the cost of the last financial crisis to be larger than astronomical and as leading to economic losses that will probably never be recuperated. The standard of living in 2015 has still not recovered to the level it had reached in 2008. Preventing further financial crises is a key step towards sustainable economic growth.

All major commissions of inquiry agreed that the financial crisis was a result of the failure to regulate finance properly. They have recommended a substantial set of reforms. The most important development has been the proposed strategy of macro-prudentialism, which pays attention to the regulation of the financial system as a whole, as an addition to that of micro-prudentialism, which attends to the detailed governance of individual financial institutions.

Drawing on these agendas for action, four types of reforms are proposed here. First is better regulation, including: better policing of the existing rules to reduce evasion, avoidance and abuse (House of Commons Public Accounts Committee 2012b; House of Commons Treasury Committee 2009); increasing transparency in financial transactions (G20 2012; OECD 2013); better and increased regulation of banking and financial markets (Independent Commission on Banking 2011; Krugman 2008; Stiglitz et al. 2010); and adoption and implementation of the principle of macro-prudentialism in the governance of the financial architecture (Crockett 2000; Haldane 2010). Second is collecting tax, including: reform of the intersection of financial and taxation regimes to reduce tax dodging (G20 2009, 2012; OECD 2013); and introducing a tax on financial transactions, sometimes called the Tobin tax (Attac 2015; European Commission 2011c). Third is de-financialization to reduce the size of the financial sector relative to the 'real' economy (Krugman 2008). Fourth is deepening democracy by increasing the democratic component of the governance of finance (Stiglitz 2010), including, for example, placing women and workers on boards and regulatory committees.

The development of macro-prudentialism, potentially the most important shift in thinking in this area, is being increasingly articulated by central bankers including those at the Basel-based Bank of International Settlements and at the Bank of England. However, although gaining ground ideationally, it has yet to be put significantly into practice. Its implementation depends on increasing democratic control over finance, which is most likely to be achieved by action at the EU level rather than by individual states. There will be another financial crisis in the UK, the EU and globally unless macro-prudentialism is implemented (see chapter 3).

Fiscal

Fiscal crisis challenges democratic states. The main cause of the fiscal crisis is the financial crisis, which led to a recession resulting in decreased government income from taxation. The most important policy reform is thus to ensure financial crisis never recurs, which requires the four main types of reform outlined previously.

Most of the effort to reduce fiscal deficits has concerned cuts in public expenditure – in other words, 'austerity'. This has slowed economic recovery and hence exacerbated fiscal tensions. Policies concerning economic growth are addressed in what follows.

A further contribution to fiscal tension has been the reduction in the capacity of states to collect taxes over recent years. Governments have faced increased difficulty in collecting taxes as a consequence of the development of finance, the fragmentation of company structures, and the movement of funds transnationally and offshore. The policy reforms to address fiscal issues therefore overlap with those proposed for finance.

Four types of reforms on fiscal matters are proposed here. First, reduce the fiscal deficit and its destabilizing effects by collecting more taxes (overlapping with financial reform). This can be achieved by reducing and eliminating secrecy jurisdictions or tax havens through building on and extending bilateral deals and minor increases in transparency, to move towards the structural elimination of all financial and economic dealings with remaining secrecy jurisdictions; by increasing the policing of and sanctions on tax evasion through using the state's capacity for surveillance to bring tax criminals to justice; by reintegrating the territorial location of firms' business activity, legal incorporation, headquarters and taxation responsibilities, to reduce legal tax avoidance through transnational movement of funds; by taxing financial transactions in order to tax income from activities that are recognized by financial oversight bodies as 'socially useless'; by raising the minimum wage to the living wage, thereby reducing state subsidy of low wages; and by introducing Eurobonds, or the equivalent, to support EU states whose treasuries are under attack through herding in financial markets (see chapter 5). Second, increase economic growth by social investment in social housing, human capital and public care. Third, deliver social justice by reducing social inequality through embedding the goals of full employment and gender equality whenever fiscal institutions are restructured, as is likely at the next crisis. Fourth, deepen democracy, including by reducing gender imbalance in fiscal decision-making; and by routinely applying gender budgeting analysis to make visible the distributive effects of changes in taxation and expenditure.

While fiscal matters have usually been considered as properly the legal competence of Member States rather than the EU level, the current intertwining of fiscal matters with finance and economic markets, which are the competence of the EU level, means that the EU level is involved. The fiscal reforms thus depend on the capacity of the EU to act, and this is considered in what follows (and in chapter 6).

Economy: output, employment and pay

The financial crisis caused a major recession in output, employment and pay. In the UK, the amount of employment has returned to pre-crisis levels, but productivity (and therefore output) and pay (and therefore living standards) have not (in 2015). How should the crisis in productivity and living standards be addressed? The current policy (2015) is to seek further deregulation and privatization. While these policies may lead to an increase in profits, they are unlikely to increase productivity and living standards. There is considerable under-utilized capacity in the economy as a consequence of the failure to encourage the completion of the transition in the gender regime from a domestic to a public form. This incomplete transition is, at least in part, because of the priority accorded to developing a neoliberal rather than social democratic form.

Six policy reforms are proposed here. First, prioritize the goal of full employment, including that of women, using all available policy levers, including central banks. Second, encourage the full employment of women by decreasing the discrimination against women which distorts the market in labour and unfairly reduces wages, thereby reducing the incentive for women to be employed. Third, encourage full employment of carers by investing in state-funded and state-provided quality childcare, to enable carers to combine employment and care-work. Fourth, encourage life-long learning by making further and higher education freely available, so that workers being made redundant in old industries can train for jobs in new industries. Fifth, invest in emerging sectors of the economy, such as the knowledge economy and low-carbon energy, rather than sectors of the economy that are or should be in decline, such as cars and roads, and sectors of the economy that are wasteful and destructive, such as the military, security and finance. Sixth, deepen democracy by developing gender balance in economic decision-making from central banks through to company boards.

This approach aligns the goals of sustainable growth and social justice. It draws on the emerging concept of the social investment state. It places a high value on the dignity of labour and on equality. This is a high-value-added route which would replace that of using ever cheaper labour as the route to economic growth. It depends upon the creation of a knowledge economy. It treats the completion of the transformation of the gender regime from a domestic regime into a social democratic public gender regime as the engine of the next regime of economic growth. The fuller utilization of women's labour, already highly educated and skilled, by judicious investment in human capital and capacity is the best way of combining a future of economic growth and social justice (see chapters 4 and 7).

Democracy

The deepening of democracy is key to the achievement of each of these sets of policy reforms. Without the deepening of democracy, it is unlikely that these reforms are feasible. There has long been a tension between democracy and capitalism. The post-1944 settlement between capital and democracy provided thirty years of unparalleled prosperity and freedom. But this has come to an end. The consequence has been the near-destruction of the real economy by unregulated finance. Markets need regulation; unregulated markets are distorted by power and corruption. A new settlement is needed.

This requires six developments: encourage the growth of new, creative political projects that envisage another world is possible; extend the range of institutions that are subject to governance through the democratic principle; develop democratic procedures that enable the equal participation of women and proportionate participation of minorities in political decision-making; develop gender balance and worker and minority presence in financial and economic decision-making from banks through to boards; strengthen the capacity of the European Union to support the fiscal capacity of Member States through the creation of Eurobonds; and strengthen the capacity of the European Union to act to implement the will of the people to regulate finance and to reduce its scale and power (see chapter 6).

The current scale of capital is such that individual states are not sufficiently powerful to achieve a new settlement between democracy and capitalism. The most likely polity to achieve this is the European Union. This may not happen. It would require rethinking the financial and fiscal architecture of the European Union. It is possible. But it may not happen.

Alternative Futures

There are many alternative futures possible, of which the two most likely are intensified neoliberalism or reformed social democracy.

The consequences of intensified neoliberalism might be: another financial crisis; recession and deflation; increased fiscal tensions; further decline in living standards and increase in inequality; the further growth of nationalist and ethno-nationalist movements; the fragmentation of the EU, which would further erode its capacity to regulate markets and justice; increase in violence by individuals, protesters and states; and a democratic crisis.

The consequences of a reformed social democracy might be: increasing the depth of democracy by deepening EU financial and fiscal architecture; the regulation of finance; the creation of a Eurobond infrastructure to stabilize fiscal tensions; the increased capture of taxes by the erosion of secrecy jurisdictions that protect tax havens and through introduction of a financial transactions tax, thus reducing fiscal tensions; the development of a social investment state that enables the transition of the gender regime to a social democratic public form in order to facilitate full employment among women/carers, which would stimulate economic growth and reduce gender inequality as well as leading to sustainable economic growth and social justice, a low-carbon and full-employment future.

The pivot between forms of society, as can be seen from these scenarios, is the deepening of democracy. To understand crisis requires the rethinking of the theory of society.

References

Abbott, Andrew (2001) *Time Matters*. Chicago: University of Chicago Press.

Abendschön, Simone and Stephanie Steinmetz (2014) 'The gender gap in voting revisited: Women's party preferences in a European context', *Social Politics*, 21(2): 315–44.

Accounting Degree (2014) *The Ten Worst Corporate Accounting Scandals of All Time*. Available at http://www.accounting-degree.org/scandals

Agamben, Giorgio (1998) *Homo Sacer: Sovereign Power and Bare Life*. Stanford: Stanford University Press.

Agamben, Giorgio (2005) *State of Exception*. Chicago: University of Chicago Press.

Aglietta, Michel (2000a) [1976] *A Theory of Capitalist Regulation: The US Experience*. London: Verso.

Aglietta, Michel (2000b) 'Shareholder value and corporate governance', *Economy and Society*, 29(1): 146–59.

Aglietta, Michel (2008) 'Into a new growth regime', *New Left Review*, 54: 61–74.

Akerlof, George and Paul Romer (1994) *Looting: The Economic Underworld of Bankruptcy for Profit*. NBER Working Paper No. R1869.

Alessandri, Piergiorgio and Andrew Haldane (2009) 'Banking on the state'. Available at http://www.bankofengland.co.uk.ezproxy.lancs.ac.uk/publi cations/Documents/speeches/2009/speech409.pdf

Aradau, Claudia and Rens van Munster (2009) 'Exceptionalism and the "war on terror": Criminology meets International Relations', *British Journal of Criminology*, 49(5): 686–701.

Arendt, Hannah (1970) *On Violence*. London: Harcourt.

Arendt, Hannah (1973) [1953] *The Origins of Totalitarianism*. San Diego: Harcourt.

Arestis, Philip and Malcolm Sawyer (2005) 'Neoliberalism and the third way', in Alfredo Saad-Filho and Deborah Johnston (eds) *Neoliberalism*, pp. 177–83. London: Pluto Press.

Armstrong, Jo and Sylvia Walby (2012) *Gender Quotas in Management Boards*. Brussels: European Parliament, FEMM Committee. Available at http://www.europarl.europa.eu/document/activities/cont/201202/201202 16ATT38420/20120216ATT38420EN.pdf

Armstrong, Jo, Sylvia Walby and Sofia Strid (2009) 'The gendered division of labour: How can we assess the quality of employment and care policy from a gender equality perspective?' *Benefits: Journal of Poverty and Social Justice*, 17(3): 263–75.

Arrighi, Giovanni (1994) *The Long Twentieth Century*. London: Verso.

Arrighi, Giovanni (2007) *Adam Smith in Beijing: Lineages of the Twenty-First Century*. London: Verso.

Arthur, W. Brian (1994) *Increasing Returns and Path Dependence in the Economy*. Michigan: University of Michigan Press.

Attac (2015) 'About Attac'. Available at http://www.atac.org.uk

Baden, Sally (1996) 'Gender issues in financial liberalisation and financial sector reform'. Paper for European Commission DG VIII. University of Sussex: IDS, Bridge. Available at http://www.bridge.ids.ac.uk/Reports/re39c.pdf

Bagguley, Paul (1991) *From Protest to Acquiescence? Political Movements of the Unemployed*. Basingstoke: Macmillan.

Bagguley, Paul and Yasmin Hussain (2008) *Riotous Citizens: Ethnic Conflict in Multicultural Britain*. Aldershot: Ashgate.

Bagguley, Paul, Jane Mark-Lawson, Dan Shapiro, John Urry, Sylvia Walby and Alan Warde (1990) *Restructuring: Place, Class and Gender*. London: Sage.

Baker, Andrew (2013) 'The new political economy of the macroprudential ideational shift', *New Political Economy*, 18(1): 112–39.

Bakker, Isabella and Stephen Gill (eds) (2003) *Power, Production and Social Reproduction*. Basingstoke: Palgrave Macmillan.

Ball, George W. (1973) [1969] 'Foreword', in Walter Hallstein *Europe in the Making*. New York: Norton.

Bank of International Settlements (2013) *Highlights of the BIS International Statistics 8 December 2013*. Available at http://www.bis.org/publ/qtrpdf/r_qt1312b.htm

Barnett, Alina, Sandra Batten, Adrian Chiu, Jeremy Franklin and Maria Sebastiá (2014) 'The UK productivity puzzle', *Bank of England Quarterly Bulletin 2014 Q2*. Available at http://www.bankofengland.co.uk/publica tions/Documents/quarterlybulletin/2014/qb14q201.pdf

Barrett, Michèle and Anne Phillips (eds) (1992) *Destabilizing Theory: Contemporary Feminist Debates*. Cambridge: Polity.

Baud, Céline and Cédric Durand (2012) 'Financialization, globalization and the making of profits by leading retailers', *Socio-Economic Review*, 10(2): 241–66.

Beck, Ulrich (1992) *Risk Society: Towards a New Modernity*. London: Sage.

Beck, Ulrich (2009) *World at Risk*. Cambridge: Polity.

Beck, Ulrich (2013) 'Why "class" is too soft a category to capture the explosiveness of social inequality at the beginning of the twenty-first century', *British Journal of Sociology*, 64(1): 63–74. Available at http://onlinelibrary.wiley.com/doi/10.1111/1468-4446.12005/pdf

Becker, Gary S. (1964) *Human Capital: A Theoretical and Empirical Analysis with Special Reference to Education.* Chicago: University of Chicago Press.

Bell, David and David Blanchflower (2009) 'What should be done about rising unemployment in the UK?' Available at http://www.bankofengland.co.uk/publications/speeches/2009/speech379paper.pdf

Berman, Sheri (2006) *The Primacy of Politics: Social Democracy and the Making of Europe's Twentieth Century.* Cambridge: Cambridge University Press.

Bertalanffy, Ludwig von (1968) *General Systems Theory.* New York: George Braziller.

Blackburn, Robin (2002) *Banking on Death Or, Investing in Life: The History and Future of Pensions.* London: Verso.

Bornschier, Volker and Christopher Chase-Dunn (eds) (1999) *The Future of Global Conflict.* London: Sage.

Boyer, Robert (2000) 'Is a finance-led growth regime a viable alternative to Fordism?', *Economy and Society*, 29(1): 111–45.

Braudel, Fernand (1966) [1949] *The Mediterranean and the Mediterranean World in the Age of Philip II. Vol. II.* 2nd edn. Berkeley: University of California Press.

Braudel, Fernand (1992) [1979] *Capitalism and Civilisation 15th–18th Century: The Wheels of Commerce.* Berkeley: University of California Press.

Braunstein, Elissa and James Heintz (2008) 'Gender bias and central bank policy: Employment and inflation reduction', *International Review of Applied Economics*, 22(2): 173–86.

Brenner, Robert (2006) *The Economics of Global Turbulence.* London: Verso.

Browne, James (2011) 'The impact of tax and benefit reforms by sex'. *IFS Briefing Note 118.* Available at http://www.ifs.org.uk/bns/bn118.pdf

Browne, James and Peter Levell (2010) 'The distributional effect of tax and benefit reforms to be introduced between June 2010 and April 2014', *IFS Briefing Note* 108.

Bruff, Ian (2014) 'The rise of authoritarian neoliberalism', *Rethinking Marxism*, 26(1): 113–29.

Brush, Lisa (2002) 'Changing the subject: Gender and welfare regime studies', *Social Politics*, 9(2): 161–86.

Bukharin, Nicolai (1972) [1915] *Imperialism and World Economy.* London: Merlin.

Burawoy, Michael (2003) 'For a sociological Marxism: The complementary convergence of Antonio Gramsci and Karl Polanyi', *Politics & Society*, 31(2): 193–261.

Burawoy, Michael (2010) 'From Polanyi to Pollyanna: The false optimism of global labor studies', *Global Labor Journal*, 1(2): 301–13.

Business Taskforce (2013) *Cut EU Red Tape: Report of the Business Taskforce*. Available at https://www.gov.uk/government/uploads/system/uploads/attachment_data/file/249969/TaskForce-report-15-October.pdf

Buvinic, Mayra (2009) 'The global financial crisis: Assessing vulnerability for women and children, identifying policy responses'. Presented to UN CSW, New York. Available at http://www.un.org/womenwatch/daw/csw/csw53/panels/financial_crisis/Buvinic.formatted.pdf

Buzan, Barry and Lene Hansen (2009) *The Evolution of International Security Studies*. Cambridge: Cambridge University Press.

Buzan, Barry, Ole Wæver and Jaap de Wilde (1998) *Security: A New Framework for Analysis*. Boulder: Lynne Rienner.

Byrne, David (1998) *Complexity Theory and the Social Sciences*. London: Routledge.

Cabinet Office (2014) *Red Tape Challenge*. Available at http://www.redtapechallenge.cabinetoffice.gov.uk/themehome/pm-speech-2

Calhoun, Craig and Georgi Derluguian (eds) (2011a) *Business as Usual: The Roots of the Global Financial Meltdown*. New York: Social Science Research Council and New York University Press.

Calhoun, Craig and Georgi Derluguian (eds) (2011b) *The Deepening Crisis: Governance Challenges after Neoliberalism*. New York: Social Science Research Council and New York University Press.

Calhoun, Craig and Georgi Derluguian (eds) (2011c) *Aftermath: A New Global Economic Order?* New York: Social Science Research Council and New York University Press.

Callinicos, Alex (2010) *Bonfire of Illusions: The Twin Crises of the Liberal World*. Cambridge: Polity.

Capra, Fritjof (1997) *The Web of Life*. London: Flamingo.

Caprio, Gerard, Ash Demirgüç-Kunt and Edward J. Kane (2008) *The 2007 Meltdown in Structured Securitization: Searching for Lessons, not Scapegoats*. World Bank. Available at http://www-wds.worldbank.org/external/default/WDSContentServer/WDSP/IB/2008/11/25/000158349_20081125132435/Rendered/PDF/WPS4756.pdf

Carroll, William (2010) *The Making of a Transnational Capitalist Class: Corporate Power in the 21st Century*. London: Zed Books.

Carter, Nancy and Harvey Wagner (2011) *The Bottom Line: Corporate Performance and Women's Representation on Boards*. Catalyst. Available at http://www.catalyst.org/knowledge/bottom-line-corporate-performance-and-womens-representation-boards

Castellani, Brian and Frederic Hafferty (2009) *Sociology and Complexity Science: A New Field of Enquiry*. Berlin: Springer.

CBI (Confederation of British Industry) (2014) 'Factsheet 2: Benefits of EU membership outweigh costs'. Available at http://www.cbi.org.uk/campaigns/our-global-future/factsheets/factsheet-2-benefits-of-eu-membership-outweigh-costs

Chakrabortty, Aditya (2014) 'In the market: Council bids to buy homes to ease crisis', *Guardian*, 2 September, pp. 1, 12–13.

Chantrill, Christopher (2014) 'UK total government debt in the twentieth century', *UK Public Spending*. Available at http://www.ukpublicspending. co.uk/uk_national_debt

Chase-Dunn, Christopher and Thomas Hall (1997) *Rise and Demise: Comparing World-Systems*. Boulder: Westview.

Chase-Dunn, Christopher, Yukio Kawano and Benjamin D. Brewer (2000) 'Trade globalization since 1795: Waves of integration in the world-system', *American Sociological Review*, 65: 77–95.

Childs, Sarah, Paul Webb and Sally Marthaler (2010) 'Constituting and substantively representing women: Applying new approaches to the UK case study', *Politics and Gender*, 6: 199–223.

Cilliers, Paul (1998) *Complexity and Postmodernism*. London: Routledge.

Clark, Ian (2009) 'Owners and managers: disconnecting managerial capitalism?', *Work, Employment and Society*, 23(4): 775–86.

Conley, Hazel (2012) 'Using equality to challenge austerity', *Work, Employment and Society*, 26(2): 349–59.

Cooper, George (2008) *The Origin of Financial Crises: Central Banks, Credit Bubbles and the Efficient Market Fallacy*. Petersfield: Harriman.

Corry, Dan (2013) 'Where is the (British) centre-left now on macro policy?', *Renewal: A Journal of Social Democracy*. Available at http://www.renewal. org.uk/articles/where-is-the-british-centre-left-now-on-macro-policy

Cortright, Joe (2008) *Driven to the Brink: How the Gas Price Spike Popped the Housing Bubble and Devalued the Suburbs*. White Paper. CEOS for Cities.

Cramme, Olaf and Patrick Diamond (eds) (2012) *After the Third Way: The Future of Social Democracy in Europe*. London: I. B. Tauris.

Crockett, Andrew (2000) 'Marrying the micro and macroprudential dimensions of financial stability: Remarks by Mr Andrew Crockett, General Manager of the Bank for International Settlements and Chairman of the Financial Stability Forum, at the Eleventh International Conference of Banking Supervisors, Basel, 20–21 September 2000'. Available at http:// www.bis.org/review/r000922b.pdf?frames=0

Crosland, Anthony (1956) *The Future of Socialism*. London: Constable.

Crouch, Colin (2011) *The Strange Non-Death of Neoliberalism*. Cambridge: Polity.

Curran, Dean (2013) 'What is a critical theory of risk society? A reply to Beck', *British Journal of Sociology*, 64(1): 75–80.

Dahl, Robert (1971) *Polyarchy*. New Haven: Yale University Press.

Dahlerup, Drude and Lenita Freidenvall (2005) 'Quotas as a "fast track" to equal representation of women', *International Feminist Journal of Politics*, 7(1): 26–48.

Daly, Mary and Katherine Rake (2003) *Gender and the Welfare State*. Cambridge: Polity.

Davies, Lord (2011) *Women on Boards*. Available at http://www.bis.gov.uk/assets/biscore/business-law/docs/w/11-745-women-on-boards.pdf

De Henau, Jerome and Cristina Santos (2011) 'Gender analysis of the changes in indirect taxes introduced by the coalition government, 2010–2011'. Women's Budget Group. Available at http://wbg.org.uk/pdfs/Indirect_tax_Budget_2011_final_report_June_20.pdf

de Larosière, Jacques (2009) *The High Level Group on Financial Supervision in the EU*. Chaired by Jacques de Larosière. Available at http://ec.europa.eu/commission_barroso/president/pdf/statement_200902 25_en.pdf

della Porta, Donatella (1995) *Social Movements, Political Violence and the State*. Cambridge: Cambridge University Press.

della Porta, Donatella (2013) *Can Democracy Be Saved? Participation, Deliberation and Social Movements*. Cambridge: Polity. https://www.gov.uk/government/uploads/system/uploads/attachment_data/file/49638/the_business_case_for_equality_and_diversity.pdf

Department for Business, Innovation and Skills (2014) *Trade Union Membership 2013: Statistical Bulletin May 2014*. Available at https://www.gov.uk/government/uploads/system/uploads/attachment_data/file/313768/bis-14-p77-trade-union-membership-statistical-bulletin-2013.pdf

Diamond, Jared (2005) *Collapse: How Societies Choose or Fail to Survive*. London: Penguin.

Dorn, Nicholas (2010) 'The governance of securities', *British Journal of Criminology*, 50(1): 23–45.

Dorn, Nicholas (2012) 'Knowing markets', *Economy and Society*, 41(3): 316–34.

Durbin, Susan (2011) 'Creating knowledge through networks: A gender perspective', *Gender, Work and Organization*, 18(1): 90–112.

Eldredge, Niles (1985) *Unfinished Synthesis: Biological Hierarchies and Modern Evolutionary Thought*. Oxford: Oxford University Press.

Elson, Diane (2002) 'International financial architecture: A view from the kitchen', *Politica Femina*, Spring. Available at http://economicsofcrisis.typepad.com/readings/elson.pdf

Elson, Diane and Çagatay, Nilüfer (2000) 'The social content of macroeconomic policies', *World Development*, 28(7): 1347–64.

Engelen, Ewald, Ismail Ertürk, Julie Froud, Sukdev Johal, Adam Leaver, Michael Moran, Adriana Nilsson and Karel Williams (2011) *After the Great Complacence*. Oxford: Oxford University Press.

Epstein, Gerald (ed.) (2005) *Financialization and the World Economy*. Cheltenham: Edward Elgar.

Erhardt, Niclas, James Werbel and Charles Shrader (2003) 'Board of director diversity and firm financial performance', *Corporate Governance: An International Review*, 11(2): 102–11.

Esping-Andersen, Gøsta (1990) *The Three Worlds of Welfare Capitalism*. Cambridge: Polity.

Esping-Andersen, Gøsta (2002) *Why We Need a New Welfare State*. Oxford: Oxford University Press.

Esping-Andersen, Gøsta (2009) *Incomplete Revolution: Adapting Welfare States to Women's New Roles*. Cambridge: Polity.

Estevez-Abe, Margarita (2005) 'Gender bias in skills and social policies: The varieties of capitalism perspective on sex segregation', *Social Politics*, 12(2): 189–215.

Estevez-Abe, Margarita (2006) 'Gendering the varieties of capitalism: A study of occupational segregation by sex in advanced industrial societies', *World Politics*, 59(1): 142–75.

EurActiv (2013) 'Council, Commission lawyers in Mexican stand-off on FTT'. Available at http://www.euractiv.com/euro-finance/council-commission-lawyers-mexic-news-532143

European Commission (2010) *Europe 2020: A Strategy for Smart, Sustainable and Inclusive Growth*. Available at http://eur-lex.europa.eu/LexUriServ/LexUriServ.do?uri=COM:2010:2020:FIN:EN:PDF

European Commission (2011a) 'EU economic governance "Six Pack" enters into force'. Available at http://europa.eu/rapid/press-release_MEMO-11-898_en.htm

European Commission (2011b) *Green Paper on the Feasibility of Introducing Stability Bonds*. Available at http://eur-lex.europa.eu/LexUriServ/LexUriServ.do?uri=COM:2011:0818:FIN:EN:PDF

European Commission (2011c) *Proposal for a Council Directive on a Common System of Financial Transaction Tax and Amending Directive 2008/7/EC*. Available at http://ec.europa.eu/taxation_customs/resources/documents/taxation/other_taxes/financial_sector/com(2011)594_en.pdf

European Commission (2011d) *Eurobarometer 74: Economic Governance in the European Union*. Available at http://ec.europa.eu/public_opinion/archives/eb/eb74/eb74_en.pdf

European Commission (2012a) *Proposal for a Directive of the European Parliament and of the Council on Improving the Gender Balance among Non-Executive Directors of Companies Listed on Stock Exchanges and Related Measures*. COM (2012) 614.

European Commission (2012b) *State Aid: Crisis-Related Aid*. Available at http://europa.eu/rapid/press-release_IP-12-1444_en.htm

European Commission (2013a) *Justice, Gender Equality: Finance and Central Banks,*. Available at http://ec.europa.eu/justice/gender-equality/gender-decision-making/database/business-finance/index_en.htm

European Commission (2013b) *Towards Social Investment for Growth and Cohesion – Including Implementing the European Social Fund 2014–2020*. Brussels, 20 February. Available at http://ec.europa.eu/social/main.jsp?langId=en&catId=1044&newsId=1807&furtherNews=yes

European Commission (2013c) *The Second Economic Adjustment Package for Greece: Third Review July 2013*. Directorate-General for Economic and Financial Affairs. Occasional Paper 159. Available at http://

ec.europa.eu/economy_finance/publications/occasional_paper/2013/pdf/o
cp159_en.pdf

European Commission (2013d) *Proposal for a Council Directive implementing Enhanced Cooperation in the Area of Financial Transaction Tax.* Available at http://ec.europa.eu/taxation_customs/resources/documents/taxation/com_2013_71_en.pdf

European Commission (2014) *Taxation of the Financial Sector.* Available at http://ec.europa.eu/taxation_customs/taxation/other_taxes/financial_sector/index_en.htm

European Commission (2015) *Transatlantic Trade and Investment Partnership.* Available at http://ec.europa.eu/trade/policy/in-focus/ttip

European Court of Justice (2014) *Judgement of the Court, 30 April 2014, UK vs. Council of the European Union: Common System of Financial Transaction Tax.* Available at http://curia.europa.eu/juris/fiche.jsf;jsessionid=9ea7d2d c30d6d19655120be046b8823b83f29038e859.e34KaxiLc3qMb40Rch0S axuOaN50?id=C%3B209%3B13%3BRD%3B1%3BP%3B1%3BC2013 %2F0209%2FJ&pro=&lgrec=en&nat=or&oqp=&dates=&lg=&language =en&jur=C%2CT%2CF&cit=none%252CC%252CCJ%252CR%252C 2008E%252C%252C%252C%252C%252C%252C%252C%252C%25 2C%252Ctrue%252Cfalse%252Cfalse&num=C-209%252F13&td=%3 BALL&pcs=Oor&avg=&mat=or&jge=&for=&cid=147778

European Parliament (2009) *Results of the 2009 European Elections.* Available at http://www.europarl.europa.eu/aboutparliament/en/00082fcd21/Resu lts-by-country-(2009).html

European Parliament (2014) *Results of the 2014 European Elections.* Available at http://www.results-elections2014.eu/en/election-results-2014.html

Eurostat (2014a) *Real GDP Growth Rate.* Available at http://ec.europa.eu/ eurostat/tgm/table.do?tab=table&init=1&language=en&pcode=tec00115 &plugin=1

Eurostat (2014b) *Unemployment Rate by Sex.* Available at http://ec.europa. eu/eurostat/tgm/table.do?tab=table&init=1&language=en&pcode=teilm0 20&plugin=1

Fagan, Colette, Maria González Menéndez and Silvia Gómez Ansón (eds) (2012) *Women on Corporate Boards and in Top Management.* London: Palgrave.

Fawcett Society (2010) 'Fawcett launches legal challenge to government budget'. Available at http://fawcettsociety.org.uk/index.asp?PageID=1165

Ferguson, Niall (2008) *The Ascent of Money: A Financial History of the World.* London: Allen Lane.

Ferree, Myra Marx (2012) *Varieties of Feminism: German Gender Politics in Global Perspective.* Stanford: Stanford University Press.

Ferree, Myra Marx and Beth B. Hess (2000) *Controversy and Coalition: The New Feminist Movement across Three Decades of Change.* 3rd edn. New York: Routledge.

FGB (Fondazione Giacomo Brodolini) and Antigone Lyberaki (2011)

Gender Aspects of the Economic Downturn and Financial Crisis. PE 453.208. Brussels: European Parliament Gender Equality Committee.

Financial Conduct Authority (2014a) 'Fines table – 2013', Available at http://www.fca.org.uk/firms/being-regulated/enforcement/fines/2013

Financial Conduct Authority (2014b) 'Fines table – 2014'. Available at http://www.fca.org.uk/firms/being-regulated/enforcement/fines

Finseraas, Henning, Niklas Jakobsson and Andreas Kotsadam (2012) 'The gender gap in political preferences: An empirical test of a political economy explanation', *Social Politics*, 19(2): 219–42.

Fishbein, Allen and Patrick Woodall (2006) 'Women are prime targets for subprime lending: Women are disproportionately represented in high-cost mortgage market'. Consumer Federation of America. Available at http://www.consumerfed.org/pdfs/WomenPrimeTargetsStudy120606.pdf

Fleckenstein, William with Frederick Sheehan (2008) *Greenspan's Bubbles.* New York: McGraw-Hill.

Foster, John Bellamy and Fred Magdoff (2009) *The Great Financial Crisis: Causes and Consequences.* New York: Monthly Review Press.

Freedom House (2014) *Freedom in the World: Methodology.* Available at https://freedomhouse.org/report/freedom-world-2014/methodology#. VTJBL_10weg

Friedman, Milton (2002) [1962] *Capitalism and Freedom.* Chicago: University of Chicago Press.

Fukuda-Parr, Sakiko (2009) 'Human impact of the global economic crisis: Gender and human rights perspectives'. Presented to UN CSW, New York. Available at http://www.un.org/womenwatch/daw/csw/csw53/panels/financial_crisis/Panel%20on%20Financial%20crisis-Fukuda%20Parr.pdf

Fung, Archon and Erik Olin Wright (eds) (2003) *Deepening Democracy: Institutional Innovations in Empowered Participatory Governance.* London: Verso.

G20 (2008) *Declaration: Summit on Financial Markets and the World Economy.* Available at http://www.g20.org/Documents/g20_summit_declaration.pdf

G20 (2009) *The Global Plan for Recovery and Reform.* 2 April. Available at http://www.cfr.org/financial-crises/g20-global-plan-recovery-reform-april-2009/p19017

G20 (2012) *G20 Leaders Declaration.* Available at http://www.consilium.europa.eu/uedocs/cms_Data/docs/pressdata/en/ec/131069.pdf

Galbraith, John Kenneth (1975) [1954] *The Great Crash of 1929.* London: Penguin.

Gallup (2012) 'Gender gap in 2012 vote is largest in Gallup's history'. Available at http://www.gallup.com/poll/158588/gender-gap-2012-vote-largest-gallup-history.aspx

Gamble, Andrew (2009) *The Spectre at the Feast.* London: Palgrave Macmillan.

Gane, Nicholas (2014a) 'The emergence of neoliberalism: Thinking through and beyond Michel Foucault's lectures on biopolitics', *Theory, Culture & Society*, 31(4): 3–27.

Gane, Nicholas (2014b) 'Sociology and neoliberalism: A missing history', *Sociology*, 48(6): 1092–106.

Genschel, Philipp and Peter Schwarz (2011) 'Tax competition', *Socio-Economic Review*, 9(2): 339–70.

George, Susan (2004) *Another World Is Possible If . . .* London: Verso.

George, Susan (2010) *Whose Crisis, Whose Future? Towards a Greener, Fairer, Richer World*. Cambridge: Polity

Giddens, Anthony (1984) *The Constitution of Society*. Cambridge: Polity.

Giddens, Anthony (1990) *The Consequences of Modernity*. Cambridge: Polity.

Giddens, Anthony (1992) *The Transformation of Intimacy: Sexuality, Love and Eroticism in Modern Societies*. Cambridge: Polity.

Giddens, Anthony (1998) *The Third Way: The Renewal of Social Democracy*. Cambridge: Polity.

Giddens, Anthony (2014) *Turbulent and Mighty Continent: What Future for Europe?* Cambridge: Polity.

Gilbert, Claude (1998) 'Studying disaster: Changes in the main conceptual tools', in E. L. Quarantelli (ed.) *What is a Disaster?*, pp. 3–12. London: Routledge.

Gladwell, Malcolm (2000) *The Tipping Point: How Little Things Can Make a Big Difference*. London: Little, Brown.

Goldstone, Jack (1991) *Revolution and Rebellion in the Early Modern World*. Los Angeles: University of California Press.

Gottfried, Heidi (2000) 'Compromising positions: Emergent neo-Fordism and embedded gender contracts', *British Journal of Sociology*, 51(2): 235–59.

Gottfried, Heidi (2013) *Gender, Work and Economy: Unpacking the Global Economy*. Cambridge: Polity.

Graeber, David (2002) 'The new anarchists', *New Left Review*, 13: 61–73.

Grahal, John and Paul Teague (2000) 'The *Régulation* School, the employment relation and financialization', *Economy and Society*, 29(1): 160–78.

Gramsci, Antonio (1971) *Selections from the Prison Notebooks of Antonio Gramsci*. London: Lawrence and Wishart.

Greenspan, Alan (2008) *The Age of Turbulence*. London: Penguin.

Greer, Scott (2014) 'Structural adjustment comes to Europe: Lessons for the Eurozone from the conditionality debates', *Global Social Policy*, 14(1): 51–71.

Gregory, Abigail, Susan Milner and Jan Windebank (2013) 'Work–life balance in times of economic crisis and austerity', *International Journal of Sociology and Social Policy*, 33(9/10): 528–41.

Guardian (2012) *Reading the Riots*. Available at http://www.theguardian.com/uk/series/reading-the-riots

Guggenheim, Michael (2014) 'Introduction: Disasters as politics – politics as disasters', *Sociological Review*, 62(S1): 1–16.

Haas, Ernst (1958) *The Uniting of Europe: Political, Social, and Economic Forces, 1950–1957*. Stanford: Stanford University Press.

Habermas, Jürgen (1996) [1992] *Between Facts and Norms: Contributions to a Discourse Theory of Law and Democracy*. Cambridge: Polity.

Habermas, Jürgen (2009) *Europe: The Faltering Project*. Cambridge: Polity.

Hacker, Jacob and Paul Pierson (2010) *Winner Take All Politics: How Washington Made the Rich Richer and Turned its Back on the Middle Class*. New York: Simon and Schuster.

Haldane, Andrew (2010) 'The $100 billion question'. Bank of England. Available at http://www.bis.org/review/r100406d.pdf

Haldane, Andrew and Robert May (2011) 'Systemic risk in banking ecosystems', *Nature*, 20 January, 469: 351–5.

Hall, Peter and David Soskice (eds) (2001) *Varieties of Capitalism: The Institutional Foundations of Comparative Advantage*. Oxford: Oxford University Press.

Hallstein, Walter (1973) [1969] *Europe in the Making*. New York: Norton.

Hanké, Bob (ed.) (2009) *Debating Varieties of Capitalism: A Reader*. Oxford: Oxford University Press.

Hanké, Bob, Martin Rhodes and Mark Thatcher (eds) (2007) *Beyond Varieties of Capitalism: Conflict, Contradictions, and Complementarities in the European Economy*. Oxford: Oxford University Press.

Hardie, Michael and Frederick Perry (2013) *Office for National Statistics Economic Review*, 5 June. Available at http://www.ons.gov.uk/ons/dcp171766_302181.pdf

Hardie, Michael, Pete Lee and Frederick Perry (2013) 'Impact of changes in the National Accounts and economic commentary for Q1 2013'. ONS, 27 June,. Available at http://www.ons.gov.uk/ons/guide-method/method-quality/specific/economy/national-accounts/articles/2011-present/index.html

Harris, Edward (2013) 'Financial secrecy index casts doubt on G-20 transparency reforms'. *Africa Progress Panel*. Available at http://www.africaprogresspanel.org/financial-secrecy-index-casts-doubt-on-g20-transparency-reforms

Harvey, David (2005) *A Brief History of Neoliberalism*. Oxford: Oxford University Press.

Harvey, David (2011) *The Enigma of Capital and the Crises of Capitalism*. London: Profile Books.

Haseler, Stephen (2008) *Meltdown*. London: Forumpress.

Hay, Colin (1996) 'Narrating crisis: The discursive construction of the "winter of discontent"', *Sociology*, 30(2): 253–77.

Hay, Colin (2013) *The British Growth Crisis: A Crisis of and for Growth*. Sheffield Political Economy Research Institute Paper No. 1. Available at http://speri.dept.shef.ac.uk/wp-content/uploads/2013/01/

SPERI-Paper-No.-1-%E2%80%93-The-British-Growth-Crisis-FINAL. pdf

Hayek, Friedrich (1945) 'The use of knowledge in society', *American Economic Review*, 35(4): 519–30.

Hayek, Friedrich (1948) *Individualism and Economic Order*. Chicago: University of Chicago Press.

Hayek, Friedrich (2001) [1944] *The Road to Serfdom*. London: Routledge.

Heckman, James (2006) 'Skill formation and the economics of investing in disadvantaged children', *Science*, 312(5782): 1900–2.

Held, David (1995) *Democracy and the Global Order*. Cambridge: Polity.

Heyes, Jason, Paul Lewis and Ian Clark (2012) 'Varieties of capitalism, neoliberalism and the economic crisis of 2008–?', *Industrial Relations Journal*, 43(3): 222–41.

Hicks, Alexander and Lane Kenworthy (2003) 'Varieties of welfare capitalism', *Socio-Economic Review*, 1: 27–61.

Hilferding, Rudolf (1981) [1910] *Finance Capital: A Study of the Latest Phase of Capitalist Development*. London: Routledge.

Himmelweit, Susan (2002) 'Making visible the hidden economy: The case for gender impact assessment of economic policy', *Feminist Economics*, 8(1): 49–70.

HM Government (2010) *A Strong Britain in an Age of Uncertainty: The National Security Strategy*. Cm 7953. Available at http://www.direct.gov. uk/prod_consum_dg/groups/dg_digitalassets/@dg/@en/documents/digital asset/dg_191639.pdf?CID=PDF&PLA=furl&CRE=nationalsecuritystrat egy

HM Government (2011) *State Pension Age Timetables*. Available at https:// www.gov.uk/government/uploads/system/uploads/attachment_data/file/18 1343/spa-timetable.pdf

HM Treasury (2010) *Overview of the Impact of Spending Review 2010 on Equalities*. Available at http://cdn.hm-treasury.gov.uk/sr2010_equalities. pdf

Hobsbawm, Eric (1978) 'The forward march of labour halted', *Marxism Today*, September: 279–86.

Hoel, Marit (2008) 'The quota story: Five years of change in Norway', in Susan Vinnicombe, Val Singh, Ronald Burke, Diana Bilimoria and Morten Huse (eds) *Women on Corporate Boards of Directors: International Research and Practice*, pp. 79–87. Cheltenham: Edward Elgar.

Hofäcker, Dirk and Stefanie König (2013) 'Flexibility and work–life conflict in times of crisis: A gender perspective', *International Journal of Sociology and Social Policy*, 33(9/10): 613–35.

House of Commons (2013) *Welfare Benefits Uprating Bill*. Research Paper 13/01. London: House of Commons.

House of Commons Library (2010) *2010 June Budget: Direct Taxes, Benefits and Tax Credits – Gender Impact*. Available at http://www.fawcettsociety. org.uk/index.asp?PageID=1164

House of Commons Public Accounts Committee (2012a) *Extracts from the Public Accounts Committee 57th Report: Oversight of User Choice and Provider Competition in Care Markets on Southern Cross/Care Markets.* Available at http://moderngov.southwark.gov.uk/documents/s30337/Appendix%20a%20Select%20Committee%20report%20on%20care%20markets.pdf

House of Commons Public Accounts Committee (2012b) *House of Commons Public Accounts Committee 87th Report of Session 2010–12, HM Revenue and Customs: Compliance and Enforcement Programme.* HC 1892. Available at http://www.parliament.uk/business/committees/committees-a-z/commons-select/public-accounts-committee/news/hmrc-compliance/

House of Commons Treasury Committee (2009) *Banking Crisis: Regulation and Supervision. Fourteenth Report of Session 2008–09.* London: TSO.

Huber, Evelyne and John D. Stephens (2000) 'Partisan governance, women's employment, and the social democratic service state', *American Sociological Review*, 65: 323–42.

Huber, Evelyne and John D. Stephens (2001) *Development and Crisis of the Welfare State: Parties and Policies in Global Markets.* Chicago: University of Chicago Press.

Huber, Joseph and James Robertson (2000) *Creating New Money: A Monetary Reform for the Information Age.* New Economics Foundation. Available at http://b.3cdn.net/nefoundation/1254f6e8b233409758_oym6iv00y.pdf

Hudson, Barbara (2009) 'Justice in a time of terror', *British Journal of Criminology*, 49(5): 702–17.

Hutton, Will (1986) *The Revolution That Never Was: An Assessment of Keynesian Economics.* London: Addison-Wesley.

Hutton, Will (2008) 'A Marshall Plan for the financial system', in Philip Collins and Peter Harrington (eds) *After the Apocalypse: Lessons from the Global Financial Crisis*, pp. 37–41. London: Demos.

ILO (International Labour Organization) (2009) *Global Employment Trends for Women 2009.* Geneva: International Labour Organization. Available at http://www.ilo.org/wcmsp5/groups/public/---dgreports/---dcomm/documents/publication/wcms_103456.pdf

IMF (International Monetary Fund) (2011) *Regional Economic Outlook: Europe Navigating Stormy Waters.* Available at http://www.imf.org/external/pubs/ft/reo/2011/eur/eng/pdf/ereo1011.pdf

Independent Commission on Banking (2011) *Final Report.* Available at http://bankingcommission.s3.amazonaws.com/wp-content/uploads/2010/07/ICB-Final-Report.pdf

Ingham, Geoffrey (2001) 'Fundamentals of a theory of money', *Economy and Society*, 30(3): 304–23.

Ingham, Geoffrey (2004) *The Nature of Money.* Cambridge: Polity.

Inglehart, Ronald (1997) *Modernization and Postmodernization: Cultural, Economic, and Political Change in 43 Societies.* Princeton: Princeton University Press.

Inglehart, Ronald and Pippa Norris (2000) 'The developmental theory of the gender gap: Women's and men's voting behaviour in global perspective', *International Political Science Review*, 21(4): 441–63.

Inter-Parliamentary Union (2014) *Women in National Parliaments*. Available at http://www.ipu.org/wmn-e/world.htm.

Iversen, Torben and Frances Rosenbluth (2006) 'The political economy of gender: Explaining cross-national variation in the gender division of labour and the gender voting gap', *American Journal of Political Science*, 50(1): 1–19.

Iversen, Torben and Anne Wren (1998) 'Equality, employment, and budgetary restraint: The trilemma of the service economy', *World Politics*, 50(4): 507–46.

Jarman, Jennifer, Robert Blackburn and Girts Racko (2012) 'The dimensions of occupational gender segregation in industrial countries', *Sociology*, 46(6): 1003–19.

Jenson, Jane (1997) 'Who cares? Gender and welfare regimes', *Social Politics*, 4(2): 182–7.

Jenson, Jane (2009) 'Lost in translation: The social investment perspective and gender equality', *Social Politics*, 16(4): 446–83.

Jessop, Bob (2013) 'Recovered imaginaries, imagined recoveries: A cultural political economy of crisis construals and crisis management in the North Atlantic financial crisis', in Mats Brenner (ed.) *Before and Beyond the Global Economic Crisis: Economics, Politics and Settlement*, pp. 234–54. Cheltenham: Edward Elgar.

Jones, Daniel Stedman (2012) *Masters of the Universe: Hayek, Friedman and the Birth of Neoliberal Politics*. Princeton: Princeton University Press.

Jones, Huw (2013) 'EU lawyers say transaction tax plan is illegal', *Reuters*. Available at http://www.reuters.com/article/2013/09/10/us-eu-transactiontax-idUSBRE9890F620130910

Kandil, Hazem (2012) *Soldiers, Spies and Statesmen: Egypt's Road to Revolt*. London: Verso.

Kantola, Johanna (2010) *Gender and the European Union*. London: Palgrave Macmillan.

Karamessini, Maria and Jill Rubery (eds) (2013) *Women and Austerity: The Economic Crisis and the Future for Gender Equality*. London: Routledge.

Kauffman, Stuart (1993) *The Origins of Order: Self-Organization and Selection in Evolution*. Oxford: Oxford University Press.

Keynes, John Maynard (1936) *The General Theory of Employment, Interest and Money*. London: Macmillan.

Klasen, Stephan (2002) 'Low schooling for girls, slower growth for all? Cross-country evidence on the effect of gender inequality in education on economic development', *World Bank Economic Review*, 16(3): 345–73.

Klein, Naomi (2007) *The Shock Doctrine: The Rise of Disaster Capitalism*. London: Allen Lane.

Knutsen, Oddbjørn (2001) 'Social class, sector employment, and gender as party cleavages in the Scandinavian countries: A comparative longitudinal study, 1970–95', *Scandinavian Political Studies*, 24(4): 311–50.

Korpi, Walter (1983) *The Democratic Class Struggle*. London: Routledge and Kegan Paul.

Korpi, Walter (2002) 'The great trough in unemployment: A long-term view of unemployment, inflation, strikes and the profit/wage ratio', *Politics & Society*, 30: 365–426.

Korpi, Walter (2003) 'Welfare-state regress in Western Europe: Politics, institutions, globalization, and Europeanization', *Annual Review of Sociology*, 29: 589–609.

Kouvelakis, Stathis (2011) 'The Greek cauldron', *New Left Review*, 72: 17–32.

Krippner, Greta R. (2005) 'The financialization of the American economy', *Socio-Economic Review*, 3: 173–208.

Krippner, Greta R. (2011) *Capitalizing on Crisis: The Political Origins of the Rise of Finance*. Cambridge: Harvard University Press.

Krugman, Paul (2008) *The Return of Depression Economics and the Crisis of 2008*. London: Penguin.

Lahey, Kathleen (2009) 'Budget 2009: Designed to leave women behind – again', *Progressive Economics Forum*. Available at http://www.progressive-economics.ca/2009/01/31/gender-analysis-of-budget-2009

Lapavitsas, Costas (2011) 'Theorizing financialization', *Work, Employment and Society*, 25(4): 611–26.

Lapavitsas, Costas, Annina Kaltenbrunner, George Labrinidis, Duncan Lindo, James Meadway. Jo Mitchell, Juan Pablo Painceira. Eugenia Peres. Jeff Powell, Alexis Stenfors, Nuno Teles and Leonidas Vatikiotis (2012) *Crisis in the Eurozone*. London: Verso.

Lawson, Neal (2009) *All Consuming*. London: Penguin.

Lazonick, William and Mary O'Sullivan (2000) 'Maximising shareholder value', *Economy and Society*, 29(1): 13–35.

Lenin, Vladimir (1934) [1917] *Imperialism*. London: Lawrence and Wishart.

Levi, Michael (2008) [1981] *The Phantom Capitalists: The Organisation and Control of Long-Firm Fraud*. Aldershot: Ashgate.

Levi, Michael (2013) [1987] *Regulating Fraud: White Collar Crime and the Criminal Process*. London: Routledge.

Lewis, Jane (1992) 'Gender and the development of welfare regimes', *Journal of European Social Policy*, 3: 159–73.

Lewis, Jane (ed.) (1997) *Lone Mothers in European Welfare Regimes*. London: Jessica Kingsley.

Liddle, Roger (2014) *The Europe Dilemma: Britain and the Drama of EU Integration*. London: I. B. Tauris.

Lim, Joseph (2000) 'The effects of the East Asian crisis on the employment of women and men: The Philippine case', *World Development*, 28(7): 1285–306.

Lipset, Seymour Martin (1959) 'Some requisites of democracy: Economic development and political legitimacy', *American Sociological Review*, 53(1): 69–105.

Lister, Ruth (1994) '"She has other duties": Women, citizenship and social security', in Sally Baldwin and Jane Falkingham (eds) *Social Security and Social Change*, pp. 31–44. Hemel Hempstead: Harvester Wheatsheaf.

Lombardo, Emanuela and Maxine Forest (eds) (2011) *The Europeanization of Gender Equality Policies: A Discursive Sociological Approach*. Basingstoke: Palgrave Macmillan.

Luhmann, Niklas (1995) *Social Systems*. Stanford: Stanford University Press.

Lyotard, Jean-François (1978) *The Postmodern Condition*. Minneapolis: University of Minnesota Press.

McBride, Dorothy and Amy Mazur (2010) *The Politics of State Feminism: Innovation in Comparative Research*. Philadelphia: Temple University Press.

McDowell, Linda (1997) *Capital Culture: Gender at Work in the City*. Oxford: Blackwell.

MacKenzie, Donald (2006) *An Engine, Not a Camera: How Financial Models Shape Markets*. Cambridge: MIT Press.

McKinsey & Co. (2007) *Women Matter: Gender Diversity, a Corporate Performance Driver*. McKinsey. Available at http://www.mckinsey.com/features/women_matter

Mahoney, James (2000) 'Path dependency in historical sociology', *Theory and Society*, 29: 507–48.

Majone, Giandomenico (1996) *Regulating Europe*. London: Routledge.

Malešević, Siniša (2010) *The Sociology of War and Violence*. Cambridge: Cambridge University Press.

Mansbridge, Jane (2005) 'Quota problems: Combating the dangers of essentialism', *Politics and Gender*, 1(4): 622–37.

Mansley, David (2014) *Collective Violence, Democracy and Protest Policing*. London: Routledge.

Manza, Jeff and Clem Brooks (1999) *Social Cleavages and Political Change: Voter Alignments and U.S. Party Coalitions*. Oxford: Oxford University Press.

Marshall, Thomas Humphrey (1950) *Citizenship and Social Class and Other Essays*. Cambridge: Cambridge University Press.

Martin, Randy (2002) *The Financialization of Everyday Life*. Philadelphia: Temple University Press.

Massey, Doreen and Richard Meegan (1982) *The Anatomy of Job Loss*. London: Routledge.

Marx, Karl (1959) [1894] *Capital. Vol. 3*. London: Lawrence and Wishart.

Marx, Karl and Frederick Engels (2012) [1848] *Communist Manifesto*. New Haven: Yale University Press

Maturana, Humberto and Francisco Varela (1980) *Autopoeisis and Cognition*. Dordrecht: Reidel.

Mellor, Mary (2010) *The Future of Money*. London: Pluto.

Milward, Alan S. (1992) *The European Rescue of the Nation-State*. New York: Routledge.

Minsky, Hyman (2008) [1986] *Stabilizing an Unstable Economy*. 2nd edn. New York: McGraw-Hill.

Mirowski, Philip (2013) *Never Let a Serious Crisis Go to Waste: How Neoliberalism Survived the Financial Meltdown*. London: Verso.

Moghadam, Valentine M. (2005) *Globalizing Women: Transnational Feminist Networks*. Baltimore: Johns Hopkins University Press.

Montgomerie, Johnna and Brigitte Young (2010) *Home Is Where the Hardship Is: Gender And Wealth (Dis)Accumulation in the Subprime Boom*. Working Paper No. 79. University of Manchester: CRESC.

Moore, Barrington, Jr (1966) *Social Origins of Dictatorship and Democracy*. Harmondsworth: Penguin.

Moravcsik, Andrew (1993) 'Preferences and power in the European Community: A liberal intergovernmentalist approach', *Journal of Common Market Studies*, 31: 473–526.

Morel, Nathalie, Bruno Palier and Joakim Palme (eds) (2012) *Towards a Social Investment State: Ideas, Policies and Challenges*. Bristol: Policy Press.

Morgan, Glenn (2010) 'Legitimacy in financial markets', *Socio-Economic Review*, 8(1): 17–45.

Morris, Charles (2008) *The Two Trillion Dollar Meltdown*. New York: Public Affairs.

Mouffe, Chantal (1993) *The Return of the Political*. London: Verso.

Mudge, Stephanie Lee (2008) 'What is neoliberalism?', *Socio-Economic Review*, 6(4): 703–31.

National Assembly of France (1789) *The Rights of Man*. Available at http://avalon.law.yale.edu/18th_century/rightsof.asp

Nolan, Brian (2013) 'What use is "social investment"?', *Journal of European Social Policy*, 23(5): 459–68.

O'Connor, James (1973) *The Fiscal Crisis of the State*. Basingstoke: Macmillan.

O'Connor, Julia, Ann Shola Orloff and Sheila Shaver (1999) *States, Markets, Families: Gender, Liberalism and Social Policy in Australia, Canada, Great Britain and the United States*. Cambridge: Cambridge University Press.

OECD (Organization for Economic Cooperation and Development) (2010) 'Mancession?', *OECD Observer* no. 278, March. Available at http://www.oecdobserver.org/news/printpage.php/aid/3240/Mancession_.html

OECD (Organization for Economic Cooperation and Development) (2013) *Global Forum on Transparency*. Available at http://www.oecd.org/tax/transparency

Ong, Aihwa (2006) *Neoliberalism as Exception: Mutations in Citizenship and Sovereignty*. Durham: Duke University Press.

ONS (Office for National Statistics) (2007) *UK Standard Industrial Classification of Economic Activities 2007*. London: ONS.

ONS (Office for National Statistics) (2009) *Labour Market Statistics*. December.

ONS (Office for National Statistics) (2012) *Labour Market Statistics*. December.

ONS (Office for National Statistics) (2013a) *GDP and the Labour Market, Q1 2013, June GDP Update*. Available at http://www.ons.gov.uk/ons/dcp171780_315996.pdf

ONS (Office for National Statistics) (2013b) *Statistical Bulletin GDP Estimates*. 25 October. Available at http://www.ons.gov.uk/ons/rel/gva/gross-domestic-product--preliminary-estimate/q3-2013/stb-gdp-prelimin ary-estimate--q3-2013.html

ONS (Office for National Statistics) (2013c) *UK Economic Accounts: GDP by Category of Income*. Last updated 23 December 2013. Available at http://www.ons.gov.uk/ons/datasets-and-tables/data-selector.html?cdid=CGBX-&cdid=CGBZ&cdid=CMVL&cdid=DTWM&cdid=YBHA&dataset=uk ea&table-id=A3

ONS (Office for National Statistics) (2013d) *Labour Productivity in the UK: 2013 Q3*. Available at http://www.ons.gov.uk/ons/rel/productivity/labour-productivity/q3-2013/info-labour-productivity.html

ONS (Office for National Statistics) (2013e) *Labour Productivity in the UK*. Available at http://www.ons.gov.uk/ons/rel/productivity/labour-productiv ity/q3-2013/info-labour-productivity.html

ONS (Office for National Statistics) (2013f) *Gross Domestic Product Preliminary Estimate 2013 Q3*. Available at http://www.ons.gov.uk/ons/dcp171778_331535.pdf

ONS (Office for National Statistics) (2013g) *Labour Market Statistics*. December. Available at http://www.ons.gov.uk/ons/rel/lms/labour-mar ket-statistics/december-2013/index.html

ONS (Office for National Statistics) (2015a) *Rate of Inflation*. Available at http://www.ons.gov.uk/ons/dcp171780_399052.pdf

ONS (Office for National Statistics) (2015b) *Labour Market Statistics*. May. Available at http://www.ons.gov.uk/ons/rel/lms/labour-market-statistics/may-2015/index.html

O'Reilly, Jacqueline and Colette Fagan (eds) (1998) *Part-Time Prospects*. London: Routledge.

Orloff, Ann Shola (1993) 'Gender and the social rights of citizenship: The comparative analysis of state policies and gender relations', *American Sociological Review*, 58(3): 308–28.

Osborne, George (2010) *Spending Review Statement*. Available at http://www.hm-treasury.gov.uk/spend_sr2010_speech.htm

Osborne, George (2013) *Chancellor of the Exchequer's Keynote Speech on the Economy*. 9 September. HM Treasury. Available at https://www.gov.uk/government/speeches/chancellor-speech-on-the-economy

Palan, Ronen, Richard Murphy and Christian Chavagneux (2010) *Tax Havens: How Globalization Really Works*. Ithaca: Cornell University Press.

Parsons, Talcott (1951) *The Social System*. New York: Free Press.

Pearson, Ruth and Caroline Sweetman (eds) (2011) *Gender and the Economic Crisis*. Rugby: Practical Action.

Peck, Jamie (2010) *Constructions of Neoliberal Reason*. Oxford: Oxford University Press.

Penna, Sue and Martin O'Brien (2006) 'What price social and health care? Commodities, competition and consumers', *Social Work and Society*, 4(2): 217–31.

Perez, Carlota (2002) *Technological Revolutions and Finance Capital*. Cheltenham: Edward Elgar.

Perez, Carlota (2009) 'The double bubble at the turn of the century: Technological roots and structural implications', *Cambridge Journal of Economics*, 33: 779–805.

Perrons, Diane (2005) 'Gender mainstreaming and gender equality in the new (market) economy: An analysis of contradictions', *Social Politics*, 12(3): 389–411.

Perrow, Charles (1999) [1984] *Normal Accidents: Living with High-Risk Technologies*. Princeton: Princeton University Press.

Perrow, Charles (2011) [2007] *The Next Catastrophe: Reducing Our Vulnerabilities to Natural, Industrial and Terrorist Disasters*. Princeton: Princeton University Press.

Phillips, Anne (1995) *The Politics of Presence*. Oxford: Clarendon.

Picone, Domenico (2002) *Collateralised Debt Obligations*. City University and Royal Bank of Scotland. Available at http://citeseerx.ist.psu.edu/viewdoc/download?doi=10.1.1.139.4676&rep=rep1&type=pdf

Pierson, Paul (1994) *Dismantling the Welfare State?* Cambridge: Cambridge University Press.

Pierson, Paul (1998) 'Irresistible forces, immovable objects: Post-industrial welfare states confront permanent austerity', *Journal of European Public Policy*, 5(4): 539–60.

Pierson, Paul (2000) 'Increasing returns, path dependence, and the study of politics', *American Political Science Review*, 94(2): 251–68.

Pierson, Paul (2001b) 'Coping with permanent austerity: Welfare state restructuring in affluent democracies', in Paul Pierson (ed.) *The New Politics of the Welfare State*, pp. 410–56. Oxford: Oxford University Press.

Piketty, Thomas (2014) *Capital in the Twenty-First Century*. Cambridge: Belknap Press of Harvard University Press.

Pitluck, Aaron (2014) 'Watching foreigners: How counterparties enable herds, crowds, and generate liquidity in financial markets', *Socio-Economic Review*, 12(1): 5–31.

Polanyi, Karl (1957) *The Great Transformation: The Political and Economic Origins of Our Time*. Boston: Beacon Press.

Potter, David, David Goldblatt, Margaret Kiloh and Paul Lewis (eds) (1997) *Democratization*. Cambridge: Polity.

Public Services Commission (2011) *Commission on the Future Delivery of*

Public Services. Scottish Government. Available at http://www.scotland. gov.uk/resource/doc/352649/0118638.pdf

Rake, Katherine (2009) *Are Women Bearing the Brunt of the Recession?* London: Fawcett Society.

Reinhart, Carmen and Kenneth Rogoff (2009) *This Time is Different*. Princeton: Princeton University Press.

Ricoeur, Paul (1984) *Time and Narrative*. Chicago: University of Chicago Press.

RMTLondonCalling (2014) 'European Trade Union Confederation gender equality survey'. Available at http://www.rmtlondoncalling.org.uk/ node/5067

Robinson, William I. (1996) *Promoting Polyarchy: Globalization, US Intervention, and Hegemony*. Cambridge: Cambridge University Press.

Robinson, William I. (2004) *A Theory of Global Capitalism: Production, Class, and State in a Transnational World*. Baltimore: Johns Hopkins University Press.

Robinson, William I. (2014) *Global Capitalism and the Crisis of Humanity*. Cambridge: Cambridge University Press.

Robinson, William and Mario Barrera (2012) 'Global capitalism and twenty-first century fascism', *Race & Class*, 53(3): 4–29.

Rousseau, Jean-Jacques (1968) [1762] *The Social Contract*. London: Penguin.

Rubery, Jill (ed.) (1988) *Women and Recession*. London: Routledge.

Rubery, Jill and Anthony Rafferty (2013) 'Women and recession revisited', *Work, Employment and Society*, 27(3): 414–32.

Rueschemeyer, Dietrich, Evelyne Huber Stephens and John Stephens (1992) *Capitalist Development and Democracy*. Cambridge: Polity.

Sainsbury, Diane (1996) *Gender, Equality and Welfare States*. Cambridge: Cambridge University Press.

Sassen, Saskia (2001) *The Global City*. 2nd edn. Princeton: Princeton University Press.

Sassen, Saskia (2009) 'Too big to save: The end of financial capitalism', *Open Democracy*, 1 April. Available at http://www.opendemocracy.net/ article/too-big-to-save-the-end-of-financial-capitalism-0

Saxonberg Steven (2013) 'From defamilialization to degenderization: Toward a new welfare typology', *Social Policy and Administration*, 47(1): 26–49.

Sayer, Andrew (2014) *Why We Can't Afford the Rich*. Bristol: Policy Press.

Schäfer, Armin and Wolfgang Streeck (2013) 'Introduction: Politics in the age of austerity', in Armin Schäfer and Wolfgang Streeck (eds) *Politics in the Age of Austerity*, pp. 1–25. Cambridge: Polity.

Schmidt, Vivien A. and Mark Thatcher (eds) (2013) *Resilient Liberalism in Europe's Political Economy*. Cambridge: Cambridge University Press.

Schuberth, Helene and Brigitte Young (2011) 'The role of gender in governance of the financial sector', in Brigitte Young, Isabella Bakker and Diane

Elson (eds) *Questioning Financial Governance from a Feminist Perspective*, pp. 132–54. London: Routledge.

Schumpeter, Joseph (1954) *A History of Economic Analysis*. New York: Allen and Unwin.

Scott, Jacqueline, Shirley Dex and Anke Plagnol (eds) (2012) *Gendered Lives: Gender Inequalities in Production and Reproduction*. Cheltenham: Edward Elgar.

Shaxson, Nicholas (2011) *Treasure Islands: Tax Havens and the Men who Stole the World*. London: Bodley Head.

Shiller, Robert (2008) *The Subprime Solution*. Princeton: Princeton University Press.

Shire, Karen (2007) 'Gender and the conceptualization of the knowledge economy in comparison', in Sylvia Walby, Heidi Gottfried, Karin Gottschall and Mari Osawa (eds) *Gendering the Knowledge Economy: Comparative Perspectives*, pp. 51–77. London: Palgrave.

Singh, Val and Susan Vinnicombe (2004) 'Why so few women directors in top UK boardrooms? Evidence and theoretical explanations', *Corporate Governance: An International Review*, 12(4): 479–88.

Skocpol, Theda (1979) *States and Social Revolutions*. Cambridge: Cambridge University Press.

Smelser, Neil (1959) *Social Change in the Industrial Revolution*. London: Routledge and Kegan Paul.

Smith, Adam (1986) [1776] *An Inquiry into the Nature and Causes of the Wealth of Nations*. Harmondsworth: Penguin.

Smith, Jackie and Dawn West (2012) *Social Movements in the World-System: The Politics of Crisis and Transformation*. New York: Russell Sage Foundation.

Soros, George (2008) *The New Paradigm for Financial Markets: The Credit Crisis of 2008 and What it Means*. London: Public Affairs.

Sparr, Pamela (ed.) (1994) *Mortgaging Women's Lives: Feminist Critiques of Structural Adjustment*. London: Zed Books.

Spourdalakis, Michalis (2014) 'The miraculous rise of the "Phenomenon SYRIZA"', *International Critical Thought*, 4(3): 354–66.

Standing, Guy (2011) *The Precariat: The New Dangerous Class*. London: Bloomsbury Academic.

Stiglitz, Joseph (2002) *Globalization and its Discontents*. London: Allen Lane.

Stiglitz, Joseph (2006) *Making Globalization Work*. London: Penguin.

Stiglitz, Joseph (2009) 'Principles for a new financial architecture'. The Commission of Experts of the President of the UN General Assembly on Reforms of the International Monetary and Financial System. Available at http://www.un.org/ga/president/63/commission/newfinancialarchitecture. pdf

Stiglitz, Joseph (2010) *Freefall: Free Markets and the Sinking of the Global Economy*. London: Penguin.

Stiglitz, Joseph and Members of UN Commission of Financial Experts (2010) *The Stiglitz Report: Reforming the International Monetary and Financial Systems in the Wake of the Global Crisis.* New York: New Press.

Storvik, A. and Teigen, M. (2010) *Women on Board: The Norwegian Experience.* Berlin: Friedrich Ebert Stiftung, International Policy Analysis. Available at http://library.fes.de/pdf-files/id/ipa/07309.pdf

Streeck, Wolfgang (2009) *Re-Forming Capitalism: Institutional Change in the German Political Economy.* Oxford: Oxford University Press.

Stumbling and Mumbling (2013) 'The wage problem'. 2 November. Available at http://stumblingandmumbling.typepad.com/stumbling_and_mumbling (See linked chart at http://stumblingandmumbling.typepad.com/.a/6a00d83451cbef69e2019b0093eb6d970d-pi)

Tavakoli, Janet (2003) *Collateralized Debt Obligations and Structured Finance: New Developments in Cash and Synthetic Securitization.* Indianapolis: John Wiley.

Tax Justice Network (2007) *Tax Havens Cause Poverty.* Available at http://www.taxjustice.net/cms/front_content.php?idcat=2

Taylor-Gooby, Peter (2012) 'Resisting welfare state restructuring in the UK', *Journal of Poverty and Social Justice,* 20(2): 119–13.

Taylor-Gooby, Peter (2013a) *The Double Crisis of the Welfare State and What We Can Do About It.* London: Palgrave.

Taylor-Gooby, Peter (2013b) 'Riots, demonstrations, strikes and the Coalition programme', *Social Policy and Society,* 12(1): 1–15.

Terjesen, Siri, Ruth Sealy and Val Singh (2009) 'Women directors on corporate boards: A review and research agenda', *Corporate Governance: An International Review,* 17(3): 320–37.

Tett, Gillian (2009) *Fool's Gold.* London: Little, Brown.

Thévenon, Olivier, Nabil Ali, Willem Adema and Angelica Salvi del Pero (2012) *Effects of Reducing Gender Gaps in Education and Labour Force Participation on Economic Growth in the OECD.* OECD Social, Employment and Migration Working Papers No. 138. Available at http://www.ined.fr/fichier/t_telechargement/56059/telechargement_fichier_fr_th.venon.et.al._2012.pdf

Thomson, Peninah with Tom Lloyd (2011) *Women and the New Business Leadership.* Basingstoke: Palgrave Macmillan.

Tilly, Charles (1978) *From Mobilization to Revolution.* Reading: Addison-Wesley.

Tilly, Charles (1990) *Coercion, Capital and European States, A.D. 990–1992.* Oxford: Blackwell.

Towers, Jude and Sylvia Walby (2012) *Measuring the Impact of Cuts in Public Expenditure on the Provision of Services to prevent Violence Against Women.* Trust for London/Northern Rock Foundation. Available at http://www.trustforlondon.org.uk/VAWG%20Full%20report.pdf

Treanor, Jill (2008) 'Toxic shock: How the banking industry created a global

crisis', *Guardian*, 8 April. Available at http://www.theguardian.com/busi
ness/2008/apr/08/creditcrunch.banking

TUC (Trades Union Congress) (2014) *At What Price Justice? The Impact
of Employment Tribunal Fees*. London: TUC Equality and Employment
Rights Department.

Tucker, Paul (2011) 'Discussion of Lord Turner's lecture "Reforming
finance: Are we being radical enough?"' University of Cambridge.
Available at http://www.bankofengland.co.uk/publications/Documents/
speeches/2011/speech477.pdf

Turner, Adair (2009) *The Turner Review*. London: Financial Services
Authority. Available at http://www.fsa.gov.uk/pubs/other/turner_review.
pdf

Turner, Adair (2010) 'What do banks do, what should they do and what
public policies are needed to ensure best results for the real economy?'
Cass Business School. Available at http://www.fsa.gov.uk/pubs/speeches/
at_17mar10.pdf

Urry, John (2003) *Global Complexity*. Cambridge: Polity.

Urry, John (ed.) (2005) 'Special Issue on Complexity', *Theory, Culture &
Society*, 22(5).

Urry, John (2011) *Climate Change and Society*. Cambridge: Polity.

Urry, John (2013) *Societies Beyond Oil: Oil Dregs and Social Futures*. London:
Zed Books.

Urry, John (2014) *Offshoring*. Cambridge: Polity.

van Staveren, Irene (2002) 'Global finance and gender', in Albrecht Schnabel
and Jan Aart Scholte (eds) *Civil Society and Global Finance*, pp. 228–46.
London: Routledge.

Vargas, Virginia and Saskia Wieringa (1998) 'The triangles of empower-
ment: Processes and actors in the making of public policy', in Geertje
Lycklama à Nijeholt, Virginia Vargas and Saskia Wieringa (eds) *Women's
Movements and Public Policy in Europe, Latin America and the Caribbean*,
pp. 3–23. New York: Garland.

Verloo, Mieke (2006) 'Multiple inequalities, intersectionality and the
European Union', *European Journal of Women's Studies*, 13(3): 211–28.

Villa, Paola and Mark Smith (2010) *Gender Equality, Employment Policies
and the Crisis in EU Member States*. Brussels: European Commission DG
Employment.

Visser, Jelle (2006) 'Union membership statistics in 24 countries', *Monthly
Labor Review*, January: 38–49.

Visser, Jelle (2013) *ICTWSS: Database on Institutional Characteristics of Trade
Unions, Wage Setting, State Intervention and Social Pacts in 34 Countries
between 1960 and 2012*. Available at http://www.uva-aias.net/207

Walby, Sylvia (1990) *Theorizing Patriarchy*. Oxford: Blackwell.

Walby, Sylvia (1997) *Gender Transformations*. London: Routledge.

Walby, Sylvia (1999) 'The new regulatory state: The social powers of the
European Union', *British Journal of Sociology*, 50(1): 118–40.

Walby, Sylvia (2003) 'The myth of the nation-state: Theorizing society and polities in a global era', *Sociology*, 37(1): 531–48.

Walby, Sylvia (2005) 'Gender mainstreaming: Productive tensions in theory and practice', *Social Politics*, 12(3): 1–25.

Walby, Sylvia (2007a) 'Complexity theory, systems theory and multiple intersecting social inequalities', *Philosophy of the Social Sciences*, 37(4): 449–70.

Walby, Sylvia (2007b) *Gender (In)equality and the Future of Work*. Manchester: Equal Opportunities Commission.

Walby, Sylvia (2009) *Globalization and Inequalities: Complexity and Contested Modernities*. London: Sage.

Walby, Sylvia (2011a) *The Future of Feminism*. Cambridge: Polity.

Walby, Sylvia (2011b) 'Is the knowledge society gendered?', *Gender, Work & Organization*, 18(1): 1–29.

Walby, Sylvia (2013a) 'Finance versus democracy: Theorising finance in society', *Work, Employment and Society*, 27(3): 489–507.

Walby, Sylvia (2013b) 'Violence and society: Introduction to an emerging field of sociology', *Current Sociology*, 61(2): 95–111.

Walby, Sylvia and Wendy Olsen (2002) *The Impact of Women's Position in the Labour Market on Pay and Implications for Productivity*. London: Department of Trade and Industry Women and Equality Unit.

Walby, Sylvia, Heidi Gottfried, Karin Gottschall and Mari Osawa (eds) (2007) *Gendering the Knowledge Economy: Comparative Perspectives*. London: Palgrave.

Walby, Sylvia, Jo Armstrong and Sofia Strid (2012a) 'Intersectionality: Multiple inequalities in social theory', *Sociology*, 46(2): 224–40.

Walby, Sylvia, Jo Armstrong and Sofia Strid (2012b) 'Intersectionality and the quality of the gender equality architecture', *Social Politics*, 19(4): 446–81.

Waldrop, Mitchell (1992) *Complexity: The Emerging Science at the Edge of Order and Chaos*. London: Penguin.

Wall Street Journal (2013a) 'Where J.P. Morgan's settlement sits in history of corporate fines'. Available at http://blogs.wsj.com/moneybeat/2013/10/19/where-j-p-morgans-settlement-sits-in-history-of-corporate-fines

Wall Street Journal (2013b) '5 of the biggest corporate fines ever'. Available at http://www.marketwatch.com/story/5-of-the-biggest-corporate-penalties-ever-2013-09-27

Wallerstein, Immanuel (2000) *The Essential Wallerstein*. New York: New Press.

Wallerstein, Immanuel (2011a) [1974] *The Modern World-System I: Capitalist Agriculture and the Origins of the European World-Economy in the Sixteenth Century*. 2nd edn. Berkeley: University of California Press.

Wallerstein, Immanuel (2011b) 'Dilemmas of (unresolved) global crisis', in Craig Calhoun and Gergi Derlugian (eds) *Business as Usual: The Roots of the Global Financial Meltdown*, pp. 69–88. New York: SSRC.

Warth, Lisa (2009) *Gender Equality and the Corporate Sector*. Geneva: UNECE. Available at http://www.unece.org/fileadmin/DAM/oes/disc_papers/ECE_DP_2009-4.pdf

Waylen, Georgina (2007) *Engendering Transitions: Women's Mobilization, Institutions, and Gender Outcomes*. Oxford: Oxford University Press.

Weber, Max (1968) [1922] *Economy and Society*. Ed. Guenther Roth and Claus Wittich. New York: Bedminster Press.

Wolf, Martin (2009) *Fixing Global Finance*. New Haven: Yale University Press.

Wolf, Martin (2014) *The Shifts and the Shocks: What we've Learned – And Have Still to Learn – From the Financial Crisis*. London: Allen Lane.

Women's Budget Group (2010) *A Gender Impact Assessment of the Coalition Government Budget, June 2010*. Available at http://www.fawcettsociety.org.uk/documents/Women's%20Budget%20Group%20Emergency%20Budget%20Response%20(June%202010).pdf

Women's Budget Group (2013) *The Impact of the Autumn Financial Statement 2012 and Welfare Benefits Up-Rating Bill 2013*. London: Women's Budget Group.

Women's Budget Group (2014) *The Impact on Women of Budget 2014: No Recovery for Women*. Available at http://www.wbg.org.uk/wp-content/uploads/2014/03/FINAL-WBG-2014-budget-response.pdf

Woodward, Alison (2004) 'Building velvet triangles: Gender and informal governance', in Thomas Christiansen and Simona Piattoni (eds) *Informal Governance in the European Union*, pp. 76–93. Cheltenham: Edward Elgar.

World Bank (2014) 'Table 4.2', in *World Development Indicators*. Available at http://wdi.worldbank.org/table/4.2

Wright, Erik Olin (2010) *Envisioning Real Utopias*. London: Verso.

Yodmani, Suvit (2001) 'Disaster risk management and vulnerability reduction: Protecting the poor'. Presented at the Asia and Pacific Forum on Poverty organised by the Asian Development Bank. Available at http://drr.upeace.org/english/documents/References/Topic%205-Risk%20Management%20and%20Adaptation%20to%20Climate%20Change/Yodmani%202000%20Disaster%20Risk%20Management.pdf

YouGov (2014) *The Gender Gap*. Available at https://yougov.co.uk/news/2014/02/11/gender-gap

Young, Brigitte, Isabella Bakker and Diane Elson (eds) (2011) *Questioning Financial Governance from a Feminist Perspective*. London: Routledge.

Index

United States (US)
  banks 37
  'subprime' housing finance 37–8,
    57–8
  Transatlantic Trade and
    Investment Partnership
    (TTIP) 135

violence and democracy 119–21
voting 129

wages, decline in 75
Walby, S. 9, 26, 28, 47, 77, 96,
    102, 115–16, 120, 123, 148

Armstrong, J. and 4, 60, 64
  et al. 30, 100, 129
  and Olsen, W. 102
  Towers, J. and 98, 101, 152
Weber, M. 120
welfare state(s) 91–2, 96–7,
    147–8
women *see* employment/
    unemployment; gender;
    gender regime
Women's Budget Group 98
working time 84, 156
World Trade Organization (WTO)
    102, 103